GARLAND
PUBLICATIONS
IN
COMPARATIVE
LITERATURE

General Editor
JAMES J. WILHELM
Rutgers University

Associate Editors
DANIEL JAVITCH, New York University
STUART Y. MCDOUGAL, University of Michigan
RICHARD SÁEZ, The College of Staten Island/CUNY
RICHARD SIEBURTH, New York University

A GARLAND SERIES

CAROL LOUISE HALL

BLAKE
AND
FUSELI

A Study in the
Transmission of Ideas

GARLAND PUBLISHING, INC.
NEW YORK & LONDON
1985

Library of Congress Cataloging in Publication Data

Hall, Carol Louise, 1939–
Blake and Fuseli.

(Garland publications in comparative literature)
Bibliography: p.
1. Blake, William, 1757–1827—Aesthetics.
2. Blake, William, 1757–1827—Friends and associates.
3. Fuseli, Henry, 1741–1825—Influences—Blake.
4. Europe—Intellectual life— 18th century.
I. Title. II. Series.
PR4148.A35H35   1985   821'.7   84-48365
ISBN 0-8240-6710-X (alk. paper)

The volumes in this series are printed on
acid-free, 250-year-life paper.

Printed in the United States of America

For Frances Ellen Swanson Hill
Mother of my *Mortal Part*

Acknowledgments

I wish to express my appreciation to the Andrew W. Mellon Foundation for its generous grant in 1978 in support of this study. To Robert L. Owens, III, Dean of the College of Liberal Arts, Howard University, Washington, D.C., and to the Department of German and Russian, Howard University, I owe special thanks for releasing me from teaching responsibilities for the calendar year 1978, that I might devote full time to my research and writing.

The staff and research facilities of the following libraries have been invaluable to me: The Folger Shakespeare Library, Washington, D.C.; The Rare Book Room of the Library of Congress, as well as the personnel of its Stack and Reader Division; The Rare Book Collection of the Milton S. Eisenhower Library, The Johns Hopkins University, Baltimore, Maryland; the Mullen Library of The Catholic University of America, Washington, D.C.; The McKeldin Library of the University of Maryland, College Park, Maryland; and Founder's Library of Howard University, Washington, D.C.

For the generous loan of materials available in their collections I express my thanks to: Alderman Library, University of Virginia, Charlottesville; Library of the University of Colorado, Boulder; Duke University Library, Durham, North Carolina; Enoch Pratt Library, Library of the Peabody Institute, Baltimore, Maryland; The University of Illinois, Urbana; and Princeton University Library, Princeton, New Jersey. To Mrs. Kay Blair of the Interlibrary Loan Division of the Library of Congress, I am grateful for kind, efficient, and persistent aid in obtaining materials from these libraries throughout the country.

I wish to acknowledge the following institutions for permission to publish the illustrations included in this volume: The Folger Shakespeare Library for Blake's engraving of Lavater and for the title page of Fuseli's Winckelmann translation; The British Library for the frontispiece of Fuseli's Rousseau pamphlet; The Huntington Library for the frontispiece and title page of Blake's copy of Lavater's *Aphorisms on Man*; The Special Collections Division of the Milton S. Eisenhower Library; The Johns Hopkins University for the title pages of Lavater's *Regeln*, 1787 and 1788; the Zentralbibliothek Zürich for the portrait of Lavater by Markus Dinkel; the Staatsgalerie Stuttgart for von Mechel's engraving of Fuseli's group portrait of his friends in Barth; The Library of Congress for the frontispiece of Kendrick's translation of *Emile*. To Oxford University Press, I express thanks for permission to quote widely from Blake, *Complete Writings with Variant Readings*, edited by Geoffrey Keynes (1966); reprinted with corrections, 1972.

Finally, I would like to express my debt to Professor John Fuegi and Professor Christoph Herin of the University of Maryland, College Park, without whose enthusiastic, consistent, and patient support this work could not have been accomplished. The amazingly informed and intelligent typing and proofreading skills of Inge Engel got me over the last hurdle.

Contents

x

Illustrations

Introduction

In 1764, William Blake had his second recorded vision. As Gilchrist reports: "Sauntering along, the boy looks up and sees a tree filled with angels, bright angelic wings bespangling every bough like stars." His biographer adds that only his mother's intercession prevented James Blake, "his honest father," from giving the boy a thrashing.[1] But, while the eight-year-old English boy was seeking out the green pleasures of St. George's Fields, passing his time in dream and imaginative reveries,[2] a young Swiss émigré, newly arrived in London from Zurich via Berlin, was undergoing an equally formative, if less divine transformation: Johann Heinrich Füssli became John Henry Fuseli. Fuseli's biographer describes what confronted the young man on one of his first walks through the streets of London:

> No sooner was he fixed than he wrote to his father,...his feelings roused...and in a gloomy state of mind, he sallied forth looking for the post office. At this time there was much greater brutality of demeanour exercised by the lower orders of the English towards foreigners than there is at present. Meeting with a vulgar fellow, Fuseli inquired his way to the post office, in a broad German pronunciation: This produced only a horse-laugh from the man. The forlorn situation in which he was placed burst on his mind; he stamped his foot, while tears trickled down his cheeks. A gentleman who saw the transaction, and felt for Fuseli, apologised for the rudeness which he had received, explained its cause, and told him that, as a foreigner, he must expect to be treated so by the lower orders of the people. Finding his name was difficult of pronunciation to the Englishman, he shortly after altered the arrangement of the letters, and signed Fusseli.[3]

Fuseli must have told the tale often; for, in another account, Allan Cunningham notes that Fuseli told him: "I stood cursing him in Shakespearean English."[4]

Approximately twenty-three years later, the brilliant and imaginative young Englishman was to become a friend of the *Zürcher*, who, despite his change of name and language, never lost the offending accent. The common influences and mutual borrowings of graphic designs in the works of Fuseli and Blake have been studied in recent years and have revealed a closer artistic sympathy between them than had formerly been recognized. Gilchrist's famous and partisan statement that Fuseli was in the habit of declaring that "Blake was d----d good to steal from" is seen in a different perspective by scholars who now see the more mature artist as the teacher of the younger.[5] In his recent assessment of Blake's art, Morton D. Paley goes so far as to say: "Indeed, Blake so assimilated certain aspects of Fuseli's style that at times it is hard to tell conscious from unconscious imitation."[6] Less attention has been paid to the shared philosophical and literary interests of the two artists. Just as the bold, expressionistic line favored by Fuseli can be seen in Blake's designs after they became acquainted, the mark of Fuseli's presence can be detected in Blake's awareness of Winckelmann, Rousseau, and Lavater: three men whose works occupied Fuseli's mind and pen from early youth until his middle years.

Examination of Fuseli's educational background and his literary efforts in Switzerland, Germany, and England shows that the elder, erudite Fuseli was well versed in, in fact, was a product of, the major intellectual developments in Switzerland, Germany, France, and England in the latter half of the eighteenth century. Werner Paul Friedrich, who has contributed much to the comparative studies of European thought, has said: "Students of comparative literature turn their attention not only to emitters and receivers but also transmitters. They may be translators (A.W. Schlegel), brilliant essayists (Mme. de Staël), or entire countries may serve as a medium for transmitting new ideas from one country to another."[7] Fuseli was just such a transmitter.

What happened to Blake from childhood to his thirtieth year has been related by Alexander Gilchrist and the Blake biographers who have followed him. In recent years, the scant factual details of Blake's early life have been documented with a thoroughness and precision unexcelled in literary scholarship.[8] While all chronicles of Blake's career take note of his admiration for Fuseli, few studies in English have explored the specific experiences, interests, and writings that formed the intellect and wit that so arrested Blake's attention and affection. Blake held Fuseli in higher esteem than any other contemporary artist. In defending Fuseli against harsh critical judgment in 1804, Blake called him an "invulnerable" artist and added that he would "not be ashamed to set my hand and shoulder, and whole strength, against those wretches who under the pretense of criticism use the dagger and poison" (K864).[9] To know the unorthodox mind and personality which engendered such loyalty from Blake, one must look back to Switzerland of the *Sturm und Drang* epoch, where the seeds of Fuseli's original perspectives of art and literature were first planted. Only against that background can Fuseli's English writings be seen as more than the merely eccentric effusions most of his English critics took them to be.

Born Johann Heinrich Füssli in Zurich, Fuseli was sent to London in 1764 as the protégé of J.G. Sulzer and J.J. Bodmer. His mission was to be an emissary between the German and English intellectual worlds: an ambassador in London for the foremost intellectuals in Zurich and Berlin. In addition to reporting on the state of literature in London, he sent his mentors regular shipments of the latest British books and journals. He earned his living through translating and essay writing and sought in his publications to promulgate the critical perspectives of his teachers through the medium of his own intense rhetorical style. That William Blake should prove the most eager and, in modern judgment, most famous beneficiary of Fuseli's mission to England is an irony of history. The fact is that most of Fuseli's literary efforts were greeted with disdain or scorn in England. It was as a painter that Fuseli was welcomed into the British establishment, and later as an erudite, if eccentric, art historian. When he finally gained recognition as a painter of some importance and was accepted into the Royal Academy in 1790, most of his associates and colleagues, while they admired and even feared his erudition, were wary of his "wild" theories. It was the "mad" Blake, struggling as an engraver and totally ignored as a poet, who saw true genius where others saw eccentricity and perverse fantasy.

Fuseli's literary career has been rediscovered and appreciated only in the last twenty-five years. Most major studies of his written work have appeared in the German language. The authoritative and exhaustive study of Fuseli's literary and artistic opus produced by Gert Schiff in 1973, *Johann Heinrich Füssli 1741-1825: Text und Oeuvrekatalog*, supersedes all other documentary studies of the life and work of the artist.[10] The first attempt to publish the life and works of Fuseli was made by his childhood friend, Felix Nüscheler: *Heinrich Füssli sämtliche Werke nebst einem Versuche seiner Biographie* (Zurich, 1807).[11] The book is extremely rare and Fuseli disavowed this unauthorized biography which was published anonymously. John Knowles, who was a close friend of Fuseli's later years, published the first comprehensive life of his friend in 1831, six years after his death. This three-volume work, *The Life and Writing of Henry Fuseli* (London),[12] contains the English *Aphorisms* and the *Lectures on Painting*, along with selections from letters and critical articles written in English. Knowles's work is still the standard life, and much of the biographical information was given orally to him by Fuseli. In 1982 a reprint of Knowles's edition was published with a brief introduction by David Weinglass, thus making more accessible writings that had been found only in the older, rather rare three-volume edition of 1831.[13] A facsimile edition of Fuseli's *Lectures*, excerpted from a 1848 collection of lectures by Barry, Opie, and Fuseli appeared in 1979.[14] David E. Weinglass's 1982 edition of *The Collected English Letters of Henry Fuseli* is an invaluable source, containing all the known letters written in English from 1759 to 1831.[15]

The first treatment of Fuseli as a literary figure is found in Ernst Wirz's unpublished dissertation, *Die literarische Tätigkeit des Malers Johann Heinrich Füssli: ein Beitrag zu den englisch-schweizerischen Beziehungen und zu der Ästhetik des 18. Jahrhunderts* (1922).[16] This study broke new ground, as Wirz was working from original documents such as the unpublished German letters and poems. Wirz also wrote about Fuseli's relation to English literature and men of letters. This work is still respected by Fuseli scholars and is frequently cited. Another dissertation, which was subsequently published in a large, attractive monograph with numerous illustrations, is Arnold Federmann's *Johann Heinrich Füssli: Dichter und Maler 1741-1825* (1927).[17] Because this was the first book published which contained selections from the German letters and poetry, Federmann is often credited as having "discovered" Fuseli. Most of the biographical information in Federmann derives from Knowles, although he does repeat some of the inaccuracies of Nüscheler. Interest in Zurich in Fuseli as a patriot and famous son of the city assured that he was never completely "forgotten" there, but the occasion of the centennial of his birth and the first retrospective exhibit of his work there inspired a number of articles in various journals and

Festschriften during the decade that followed. In 1942 Walter Muschg edited and published the German letters in *Heinrich Füssli: Briefe,*[18] which still represents the major source of his letters back to his friends in Germany and Switzerland. The "Fuseli Revival" in England was signaled by the publication of Ruthven Todd's "The Reputation and Prejudices of Henry Fuseli" in *Tracks in the Snow* (1946).[19] Todd's appraisal is of significance, for he is also a student of Blake, the poet and the artist, and is himself a Canadian poet of some note. In 1947 Paul Ganz published an extensive collection of Fuseli's drawings: *Die Zeichnungen Hans Heinrich Füsslis,*[20] which was translated and published in London in 1949. The first work in English to deal with Fuseli's philosophical positions was Eudo C. Mason's *The Mind of Henry Fuseli* (1951),[21] which contained translations from some of the German letters and poems. This remains the best English source for Blake scholars dealing with the Blake-Fuseli relationship. Frederick Antal's *Fuseli Studies* (London, 1956)[22] was written mostly from the point of view of art history, but contains several excellent essays dealing with his *Sturm und Drang* background and his relation to European intellectual trends of his time. Marcia Allentuck's 1964 dissertation, "Henry Fuseli: The Artist as a Man of Letters and Critic," was the first dissertation in English to assess Fuseli's career as an art historian and critic.[23] In 1972 Peter Tomory published *The Life and Art of Henry Fuseli* (London),[24] the text of which provided for the first time an informative and accessible book for the nonspecialist. With the publication in 1973 of Fuseli's *Sämtliche Gedichte* (Zurich),[25] edited by Martin Bircher and Karl S. Guthke, the poems which had been available only in Federmann's selections and in Mason's translations were made available in one volume. Recently valuable articles by Mason, Guthke, and others, which will be referred to later in this study, have contributed much to understanding Fuseli's literary career.

The wealth of new and more accessible information about Fuseli's life and works lends support to Antal's statement of 1954 that he was "the most important art historian of his day."[26] In 1969, Garold Davis, in his study of German thought and influence in England, names Fuseli as "the most important artist to come to England from Germany in the eighteenth century."[27] Jean Hagstrum recognized Fuseli's importance in literature and the arts in 1958 in a footnote inviting further investigation: "Fuseli's entire life, including his relations to Cowper, Alderman Boydell, and the Milton Gallery is itself an example of the relations of the arts...."[28] From the evidence in Fuseli's letters back to his Swiss friends, and from revisions and variant states of his own poems, it is clear that Fuseli, like Blake, was truly a *Malerdichter* and not just an illustrator of other men's poems. In view of this mutual love of poetry, it is curious that there is no reliable evidence about what Fuseli thought of Blake as a poet or that Blake even knew of the existence of Fuseli's poems.

Each man's defense of the other was limited to praises of their respective genius as graphic artists. But Fuseli and Blake were in complete agreement in their beliefs that the creative urge, whether to paint or to write, came from the same divine source. Clearly what matters to each artist is the conception, inspiration, the genius, with which things are combined. The stubborn refusal of either man to submit to systems and the fervent belief of each man in his own superiority to the taste and fashion of his own time is balanced by a profound grasp of the major intellectual and aesthetic trends of the day. On Fuseli's part, this knowledge was the result of a rigorous education under the direction of the Swiss fathers of preromanticism. On Blake's part, it was the result of a brilliant and insatiable intellect, self-directed, and enhanced by his relationship with the fiery Swiss *Genie* who resolved at the age of twenty-nine to become the greatest painter in England. However different the content and success of their creative production might be, the starting point of each artist was based on a similar aesthetic, formed not in isolation, but in response to and reaction against the thoughts of others. It is this response and reaction in Blake's works which Fuseli helped guide. Fuseli brought Winckelmann, Rousseau, and Lavater to Blake as rebels and innovative thinkers who sought to explore truth, each in his own individuated manner: Winckelmann, delineator of the sublime; Rousseau, enemy of authority and hypocrisy; Lavater, mild Christian and reader of the human form and soul.

Fuseli had a close personal interest in the three figures whose work he promoted in England. Winckelmann, whose cause had been championed early in his career by Fuseli's father, was to occupy his thoughts for the first several years after he came to England in 1764. Fuseli had brought to London with him as a farewell gift a priceless packet of letters written to the elder Füssli by Winckelmann from Rome. Fuseli intended to translate Winckelmann's *Geschichte der Kunst des Altertums*; but chance and circumstances only allowed him the opportunity to publish a brief translation, *Reflections on the Painting and Sculpture of the Greeks*, based on several of Winckelmann's shorter articles. The translation was completed in 1765. Somehow William Blake obtained a copy a decade or so later. His signature in the copy indicates he had the book in the 1770s. In this slender volume Blake, the young apprentice, was to find a romanticized neoclassicism which strongly influenced his vision of art and the artist, and an apotheosis of the Sublime Raphael that he was to endorse throughout his career.

Rousseau had been a hero for Fuseli since his student days in Zurich, when he placed the work of the Genevan rebel in the same worshipful light with Christ and Socrates. He had read everything written by Rousseau up to the time he left for England and finally had the opportunity to meet him personally in Paris in 1767. A few months later, he published his analysis of Rousseau's thought and behavior in a small anonymous pamphlet, *Remarks on the Writing and Conduct of J.J. Rousseau*. In this first critical attempt in English to assess the entire opus of Rousseau to 1767, Fuseli was particularly interested in the most controversial aspect of Rousseau's thought at that time, which was religious in nature. A trained theologian, Fuseli embraced Rousseau's nonconformist rejection of conventional piety. It is most probably Fuseli's version of Rousseau as a truth-bringing devil that added fuel to Blake's own rejection of puritan self-righteousness in *The Marriage of Heaven and Hell*.

Johann Caspar Lavater, whom Fuseli had known since his first year in seminary in Zurich, was Fuseli's most intimate friend. It was with Lavater that Fuseli launched into his only direct involvement with revolution and politics, and with Lavater that he fled into voluntary exile from his native city as a result of his love of truth and freedom. Their friendship survived the geographical separation, and Fuseli became instrumental in disseminating the ideas of the gentle pastor and *Menschenkenner* to the English-speaking world. He adapted Lavater's homey rules for life and published them as *Aphorisms on Man* in 1788. Blake's annotations to Fuseli's Lavater adaptation are now considered to be among the most interesting and revealing of his nonpoetic works and are included in both standard editions of the poetry and prose.[29] Fuseli's role in the impact of this book on Blake has not been sufficiently studied. Blake's contribution to the engraved frontispiece is evidence of an interest in the *Aphorisms* from the beginning of the project. The genuine affection that he displayed for Lavater, the man, and his thought, must also be seen as the result of Fuseli's influence.

Critics who have been perplexed by the intimacy between Blake and Fuseli often place too much emphasis on the fact that Fuseli's art seems to be almost exlcusively secular, whereas Blake's entire artistic production is set in a religious context. One needs only to look at the problematic relationship between Fuseli and Lavater to see that neither Lavater's outspoken mysticism, nor his search for spirits and religious *Schwärmerei* prevented a lifelong friendship which can only be termed passionate in the days of their youth. It is true that Fuseli often quarreled with Lavater's hymning and religious hypotheses, but this did not damage their loyalty to one another or affect their promotion of each other's work. As in the case of Fuseli and Blake, the difference between a secular and a metaphysical cast of mind is not as strong a factor in artistic kinship as is aesthetic agreement and a shared vision of the nature of poetic and artistic activity. To a certain extent, the cult of reverence that surrounds the "prophetic" Blake and the modern emphasis on the erotic and macabre in Fuseli's art have obscured rather than illuminated their association. The statement made by Nicholas Powell is characteristic: "It is important to emphasize again, that while Blake's approach to his work was spiritual and inspired, that of Fuseli was intellectual and neurotic."[30] Bernard Fehr, another student of Fuseli's art, has called the friendship of Fuseli and Blake *"ein Wunder und ein Rätsel zugleich."*[31] Although this study is limited to the examination of Fuseli's role in transmitting specific concepts and attitudes to Blake, it is hoped that it is only a beginning of a clearer definition of the "miracle" and a partial answer to the "riddle" of their relationship.

Part One
Fuseli's European Background
and his Literary Activities
1749-1787

Dearest Heart:

...I call upon you to judge for yourself whether your heart pulses towards me as, God is my witness, mine pulses toward you. But that is my fate, and my tears are not intended to coax tears from your eyes. I lay aside my pen for a moment, to embrace your picture and to cover it with kisses....

But now my brain is afire. I am becoming too agitated. I must cease—Oh, you who are now lying alone—dream of me—Oh, that my soul could meet with yours, as the hand of Sulamith, reaching through the trellis, met her dew-drenched lover!

Mein allerliebstes Herz!

...Ich rufe dich selber zum Richter auf, ob dein Herz gegen mich ebenso walle wie, Gott ist mein Zeuge, das meinige gegen dich—aber das ist mein Schicksal, und meine Tränen sind nicht gemacht, die deinigen aus deinem Auge zu locken. Ich lege die Feder für einen Augenblick nieder, dein Bild zu umarmen und durch und durch zu küssen.... Doch mein Gehirn gerät in Feuer, ich werde zu lebhaft, ich muss hier abbrechen—o du, der itzt alleine liegt—träume von mir—o dass meine Seele der deinigen begegnete wie die Hand der Sulamith durchs Gegitter ihrem vom Taue triefenden Geliebten!

> Henry Fuseli to Johann Caspar Lavater
> from Berlin to Zurich, November 13, 1763
> (*Briefe*, pp. 73, 80).

Henry Fuseli, Self-Portrait ca. 1777-1779. Black chalk heightened with white. (By permission, National Portrait Gallery, London)

Fuseli and Lavater in Switzerland
1741-1764

Beginnings

Henry Fuseli was born Johann Heinrich Füssli in Zurich on February 6, 1741. Nine months later Johann Caspar Lavater was born in the same city. The two boys shared a common background, growing up as they did in the comfortable circumstances of old and relatively prosperous families of the Zurich middle-class establishment. Johann Heinrich's family can be traced back to a line of weapons makers and bell casters who had already made the name Füssli famous in the city by 1386.[1] Fuseli's father, Johann Casper Füssli, had spent sixteen years wandering about Germany and Austria studying art and serving as portrait painter for various German princes before settling down in Zurich in 1740. There he became a drawing master, portrait painter, publisher, art historian, writer, and general patron of art and artists.[2] In his *Wanderjahre* he had met many artists of reputation, and he was instrumental in championing the talents and fame of Mengs and Winckelmann among members of Zurich's intellectual circle.[3] In 1756 he was elected *Ratschreiber* of the city government. Johann Caspar Lavater's father, Johann Heinrich Lavater, was a doctor of medicine and a member of the senate of Zurich.[4] Although he was, in Lavater's own words, *"weder Genie, noch ein philosophischer Kopf,"* he was the model of an upright citizen who derived his greatest joy from his profession, his family, and his Bible.[5]

The ruling class of Zurich society which produced Fuseli and Lavater was not founded around a military aristocracy, but around a rich and lettered bourgeois elite which looked to the greater powers of Germany and England as its intellectual and cultural mentors. Although the great neighboring country of France exerted considerable cultural influence upon this Swiss city, Zurich had never been "frenchified" in the manner that her rival city of Berne had been. It remained, "toujours la ville de Suisse ou l'on parlait et ou l'on écrivait le mieux,—ou le moins mal—l'allemand."[6]

From Lavater's memoirs we learn that he was sent to public school at an early age. There his pale countenance and awkward and timid ways caused him to be the object of derision from both teachers and classmates. He was not particularly coddled at home—*"kein vorzüglicher Liebling weder meines Vaters noch meiner Mutter"*—and he was teased at school. His sense of alienation and his natural sensitivity caused him to "concentrate his ideas within himself."[7] Lavater remembered those days:

Ich fühlte einen immerregen Trieb, gewisse Dinge zu sagen, gewisse Empfindungen und Gemüthszustände auszudrücken und mitzutheilen—und ich fand weder Worte, noch Menschen; bey Hause gedrückt, gedrückt in der Schule—lustig zwar in der Freyheit und auf der Gassen—aber, in jedem stillen einsamen Momente wieder voll Eckel an diesen leeren Lustigkeiten, voll Bedürfnisses eines höhern Objecktes, wenigstens eines Freundes—von meiner Mutter und Wärterinn wegen meines flüchtigen Bethens oft gewarnt—was blieb mir übrig, als Zufluct zu Gott?[8]

Lavater's early God-seeking and his subsequent revelations and visions were eventually to free him from his youthful tongue-tied reticence, as the prolific writings and famous sermons of his maturity bear witness. At the age of ten he announced to his parents that he would become a "minister of the Gospel." Although at first they evidently had other plans for his future and were somewhat frightened by the intensity of his religious inclinations,[9] Lavater's parents later supported this early decision from which he never faltered.

Fuseli's early education and equally precocious choice of vocation did not follow such a smooth course. As fluent of speech as the young Lavater was awkward in his, Johann Heinrich semed to his father to be amazingly gifted in manner of expression and in choice of words. It was decided very early that Johann Caspar Füssli's second son was destined for the ministry. Although the boy was passionately fond of drawing from the time he could hold a pencil, Fuseli was never encouraged to study art or drawing in any formal way. In fact, it seems he was prohibited from doing so. Knowles tells us that Fuseli often spoke of hiding candles and drawing supplies in his bed when he was a boy, so that he could make copies from his father's prints and execute his own designs after everyone had gone to bed and the house was dark.[10] It seems puzzling now that Johann Caspar should have encouraged Fuseli's elder brother, Rudolf, to become a painter while denying the much more talented Heinrich the same choice.[11] But perhaps it was because Fuseli showed such brilliance and promise as a child that the rather uncertain and not always respectable life of the artist was not considered good enough. His father had seen the life of an artist *"von seinen guten und schlechten Seiten."*[12] Knowles, in his attempt to dignify every aspect of his friend's life and character, explains that his father checked young Henry's attempts to follow in his footsteps, "knowing from his own pursuits the difficulty of arriving at any eminence in the fine arts, except a man's whole mind and attention be given to them...."[13] At any rate, letters written by Fuseli when he was just beginning his career in art at the age of twenty-six show that the conflict between father and son on this matter was never resolved and that his father never approved or even supported Fuseli's training as a painter.

To the end of creating a successful clergyman out of his son, Johann Caspar, who "seldom ever attended public worship," but "who was not ignorant of the principles of religion," employed a private tutor in the person of a young minister who was to "initiate him in these [doctrines] as well as the classics."[14] Fuseli's childhood education took place in his home, both in Zurich and in the country, where he went with his family for a period of several years and where his teachers were his parents and his tutors. To acquaint his son with the most eloquent and enlightened manner of preaching, Johann Caspar often read aloud to the young boy from collections of current sermons from England and France. These efforts on the part of the elder Füssli had a rather amusing and unexpected effect, if we are to trust Knowles's assertion, presumably related to him by Fuseli himself, that while "the father was reading the paraphrases of Doddridge, or the sermons of Götz or Saurin, the son was not infrequently employed in making drawings; and the better to escape observation, he used his left hand for that purpose. This practice made him ambidextrous during his life."[15] We know, however, that Fuseli was never successfully thwarted from drawing, for one-sixth of the drawings that have survived and have been catalogued by Schiff were executed by Fuseli before the age of twenty.[16]

In his later years Fuseli gave contradictory versions of what his early childhood had been like. Joseph Farington recorded in his diary that Fuseli had said he "passed those early days in crying & drawing: every day floods of tears at being forced to read, which were relieved by stolen hours for his favorite amusement." It was not until he got to Italy that he *applied to literature with inclination*, and lost too much time in it— The basis on which his after acquisitions in this way were raised had been flogged into him."[17] Cunningham, on the other hand, reported that "he loved when he grew old to talk of those days of his youth" and of "the enthusiasm with which he surveyed the works of his favourite masters, and the secret pleasure which he took in acquiring forbidden knowledge."[18] Cunningham also tells us that he secretly sold his clandestine drawings to his schoolfellows and "presently found more money in his pocket than he knew what to do with."[19] The truth must lie somewhere in between; for, whether or not it is true that his early lessons were "flogged into him," he was certainly very proud of his learning and was admirably prepared for the university when he entered it, being able "to do in minutes what would have cost his fellows hours; for the rest of the day he had other occupations."[20]

It was when Lavater and Fuseli entered the *Collegium Carolinum* in 1758 or 1759 that they became intimate friends. In that famous school, which, according to legend, was founded by Charlemagne himself, they became students of Johann Jakob Bodmer and Johann Jakob Breitinger, the two most famous leaders of Swiss preromanticism. At the time of the admission of the two youths, Bodmer was professor of *"Vaterländische Geschichte"* and Breitinger was professor of Hebrew.[21] But the relationship between the illustrious professors and their students was neither remote nor purely academic. Bodmer, especially, became mentor, philosopher-teacher, father-confessor, and protector of Fuseli and Lavater. Bodmer's benevolent patronage of his students was remembered in the eulogy delivered at his funeral:
"Den Schülern war er nicht bloss Lehrer, er war ihr Freund. Er hatte sie gern um sich auf dem Spaziergang; er sparte keine Mühe, wenn er aus irgendeinem Menschen etwas Edlers bilden oder eine schöne Anlag entwicklen zu können glaubte."[22] Both Bodmer and Breitinger were close friends of Fuseli's father, who painted portraits of each of them at the height of their

fame when Fuseli was yet a boy at home with his tutors. In early letters to his classmates, Fuseli speaks of regular informal meetings with his teachers and Bodmer's peripatetic lectures through the streets of Zurich. One such note was written to Jakob Hess,[23] a close friend, and a major figure in Lavater's later life: *"Du kannst nicht—gut, höre. Ich hole um ½ 2 Uhr Bodmer auf seinen mir diesen Augenblick gegebenen Befehl zu Nüscheler ab. Er will uns lesen. Dich erwartet er. Gott befohlen, Fuessli."*[24]

In spite of the bitterness with which Fuseli was later to complain of his father's *"unverantwortliche Vorurteile"* which prevented him from following his natural inclination toward painting—*"mein unerwürgbarer Trieb"*[25]—the letters of Fuseli's student days do not indicate that he felt his courses boring, nor that he was being forced into the theological college of the *Carolinum*. At this period in his life he regarded poetry as his true vocation. At nineteen he was writing odes in the manner of Klopstock, the young poet whose *Messias* had been inspired by Bodmer's Milton translation, and who was seen by the Swiss scholar as the new genius capable of instilling the spirit of greatness in German poetry. One of Fuseli's earliest odes, *"Ode an Meta,"* which Bodmer had published in his *Freymüthigen Nachrichten* in 1760, was written "in the person" of Klopstock himself. The poem was unsigned, and the style so like that of Klopstock that many took it for one of his own poems.[26] In the same year he completed a translation of Shakespeare's *Macbeth* and another original drama, both of which are lost.[27] Fuseli's calling as *Dichter* was not at odds with his theological studies. As Eudo Mason has noted: "It was possible for him to interpret his preaching office as in some way appertaining to his poetic vocation, since a liberalised pietistic theology still formed an integral part of the new literary movement's [Bodmer's and Breitinger's] programme."[28] After all, in subject matter, tone, and feeling, Klopstock's poetry was religious poetry, even if the poet himself was to fall short of Bodmer's expectations because of his impious behavior. Lavater's attitude toward poetry at this time represents a similar synthesis of aesthetics and religion and went beyond the pious attitude of Bodmer and Breitinger. *"Poesie,"* Lavater wrote in 1759, *"ist mir nichts als Empfindung über Gott.... Er soll mein Gegenstand in Betrachtung der Natur, Er meine Dichtkunst sein."* He was never to alter this view and was to apply it to all forms of artistic expression in his later works.[29]

A glance at the reading list that emerges from Fuseli's early letters shows how great an emphasis was placed upon poetry in his theological training. In addition to the holy scriptures, which he knew well enough to be considered *"bibelkundig"* during his entire lifetime, Fuseli and his classmates were reading Homer, Dante, Petrarch, Milton, Young and, above all, Shakespeare—all in the original languages in which these poets wrote. Among foreign contemporary thinkers admired by the Zurich circle, the British were the most influential. In addition to his adaptation of Addison's *Spectator—Discourse der Mahlern* (1721-1723)—Bodmer had translated Milton in six editions by 1780, Pope's *Dunciad* (1728-1742), Samuel Butler's *Hudibras* (1663-1678), as well as some of the songs of Percy, which he attempted to render in the manner of Wolfram von Eschenbach (!) (1765).[30] The progressive thinkers in England were viewed by Bodmer and his followers as their "natural prototypes and allies" in their program of political activism and cultural and moral reform.[31]

The intellectual stimulation and almost wild enthusiasm with which the young seminarian, Fuseli, was even then immersing himself in the works of the Bard and all things English, is seen in a letter to Jakob Hess written in 1759:

> ...Sonst sprachen wir gern
> of graves, of worms and epitaphs,
> did make dust our paper, and with rainy eyes
> write sorrow on the bosom of the earth.
> Willh. Sh.

> Doch arbeite ich as an ass—ich bin bei Breitinger etlichemal gewesen und bin itzt ein Narr, ich weiss nicht, was ich schreibe. Wenn du dieses Narrengeschwätz, dies after supper page bekömmst, liesest und das bei deinem Pulte, wo du deine Netz und Gruben, "jenes Ding" zu fangen, ausgestellt hast oder darüber bist, Thompson in neue Moden zu kleiden, ihm einen Tresenhut und eine galonierte Weste gibest, denn mag es mir gehn
> as in a theatre the eyes of men
> after a wellgraced actor leaves the stage
> are idly bent on him that enters next
> thinking his prattle to be tedious—
> Even so, or with much more contempt, their eyes
> will scowl on me; will never cry, God save him!...[32]

He signs the same letter:

> Dein everlasting, Fyssli.

The curious sprinkling of English phrases throughout such early letters and the arbitrarily misquoted and edited lines from Shakespeare indicate that Fuseli was actively using English at this time—even if only to show off—and that he was quoting Shakespeare from memory. His ability in languages and the prodigious memory that was to startle and "terrify" his English colleagues in later years was already in evidence.[33] By the time he was in his mid-twenties he was reasonably fluent not only in ancient Greek, German, French, and English, but also Italian and Hebrew. When one considers that his formal university education was limited to the two years between the time he was received into theological college and his ordination in 1761, one can appreciate how intense his reading in classics and world literature must have been under his tutors, and with Bodmer and Breitinger. It was Bodmer, too, who had introduced him to the works of a very contemporary genius, Jean Jacques Rousseau. In August 1760, Fuseli writes of Rousseau:

> Ich kenne ihn dank meinem bessern Dämon, schon mehr als ein Jahr und opfre ihm wirklich Tag vor Tag und Nachtstunden meine denkendsten Augenblicke. Zum zweiten Male lese ich nun seinen Discours sur l'inégalité und finde da, wo ich zuerst nur einen Stein sah, die Gestalt eines Gottes.[34]

The influence of Rousseau on Fuseli's thought remains of great importance, at least until the 1800s, and will be of significance, too, for his later relationship with William Blake. For the nineteen-year-old Swiss in 1760, as for other young incipient *Stürmer und Dränger* in Germany, Rousseau was more than a writer; he was a symbol of new ideas, a prophet of rebellion against the old ways. It was he who had vexed officials and exposed the repressive tendencies of the reactionary-oligarchical forms of governments which controlled the "republican" cities of Geneva and Zurich.[35] Surely Fuseli exceeded the intentions of his teachers' respect for the controversial thinker when he called Rousseau a god. But Bodmer and Breitinger were to be shocked and dismayed to no small degree by the emotional cultism that grew out of ideas that they fostered in an entirely different spirit. Fuseli was to refine and widen his knowledge of literature in his years of independent study in Italy and England. The initial impetus to explore these great master-pieces of world literature and his tendency to view Homer, Shakespeare, Dante, Petrarch, Milton, and later, Michelangelo, as isolated and heroic *Urkünstler* came from his early teachers, the leaders of the "Swiss School."

Lehrjahre: The Influence of Bodmer and Breitinger

Although a thorough discussion of the contributions of Bodmer and Breitinger to European literature, philology, and aesthetics would be outside the scope of this study, it is important here to consider the aims and motiva-tions of the two men in teaching and forming the literary consciousness of the young theological students entrusted to them. Neither Fuseli nor Lavater was ever to break completely with the attitudes they learned at the *Carolinum.* The two professors, in their fervent desire to reform and enliven the linguistic and stylistic state of German language and literature, con-sidered themselves also as patriot-reformers of the political decadence of their city and country. They chose as their "weapons" in both battles the great imaginative works of world literature. They were among the first "rediscoverers" of Dante, Milton, Petrarch, and Shakespeare in the eight-eenth century. They found in the works of those authors, set against the background of Christian civilization, the great epic struggle, historical and symbolic, of individual man against tyranny, ignorance, and evil. Dante's *Divine Comedy,* for example, became for Bodmer not only an expression of poetry, the greatness of which depended upon feeling and imagination and which defied the proscriptions of French Classicism; it represented in sub-ject matter an epic survey of the evils of political and moral decline and the clash of great individuals. This ideological and anachronistic interpretation, however unsatisfactory it might seem in the light of modern critical at-titudes, was nonetheless the principal motivation which prompted Bodmer and Breitinger to reveal the glories of the great medieval poet to the German-speaking world. Bodmer's interest in Homer, which lasted a lifetime, must also be seen in this light; for it represented more than a literary and aesthetic enthusiasm. Influenced by Blackwell's *Inquiry into the Life and Writings of Homer,* which he translated as early as 1735, he saw Homer as the great ar-chetypal poet of the dawn of history. It was this interpretation of Homer and Bodmer's search for *Urpoesie* that was responsible for his interest in the German Middle Ages and for his rediscovery of the *Nibelungenlied.*[36]

Zurich had not been without its share of worthy men of letters before the time of Bodmer and Breitinger. The Reformer Zwingli was to prove the pro-totype of a series of thinkers who combined and sometimes confounded the study of theology with philology, history, antiquity, and the fine arts.[37]

Fuseli's mentors belong to this tradition, but the order and sense of critical method which they brought to their scholarly activities was without precedent in this fiercely protestant city.

As young men, Bodmer and Breitinger were to become leaders of a group who had ushered the ideas of the Enlightenment into their city. In old age, their influence was to penetrate to the north, where they provided a program for the poetics of a new, romantic sensibility in German poetry. In every project in which they participated, in every society which they founded, and in every journal they published, *literature* was the central point of departure.[38] To define it, to describe it, to translate it, and above all, to understand the source of its inspiration constituted the life's work of each man.

The literary reform efforts of Bodmer and Breitinger were in a sense part of a continuing tradition which had not begun in Switzerland, but in Germany with Martin Opitz (1597-1639),[39] and had reached its apex with the efforts of Gottsched, the "German Boileau."[40] The goal of Gottsched, who was eventually to become the target of polemic attack from the Swiss School, was actually not much different from their own. He had performed an essential service for the development of German literature in his struggle against dialects and foreign corruption of the language and in his call for the establishment of linguistic unity and regularized literary forms. But the aspect of his theories and "rules" that offended the Swiss thinkers was his cold and rational approach to literature and his dependence upon the models of French Classicism. They accused him of denying the imaginative and fantastic side of the creative process. He had a rationalist's secular orientation and did not see the use of mythology, Christian or pagan, in art.[41] Above all, he saw the imitation of empirical nature as the true task of the artist. In contrast, the outlook of the Swiss thinkers was at base metaphysical. The importance that their sincere religious faith played in the formulation of their aesthetics and in the choices of the works that they promulgated, emulated, and translated cannot be overemphasized. The "truth" that they demanded from a work of art was the same truth that they sought as theologians of a fervent and liberated pietism.

This is perhaps best exemplified in the attitude of Bodmer toward John Milton and *Paradise Lost*. Under the influence of Addison's defense of Milton's poem, Bodmer had translated *Paradise Lost* into German as early as 1724. Because the conservative censors of Zurich regarded the poem as a too frivolous treatment of a sacred subject, Bodmer was not able to publish the translation until 1732. The controversy that grew up in the 1740s between Leipzig and Zurich centered around the requirement for verisimilitude in poetry. For Gottsched this meant the correspondence between what is depicted by the artist and that which can be perceived in accordance with the laws of nature. The northern German critic agreed with Voltaire's point of view concerning the battle of the good and bad angels. Such fantastical representations constituted *"den Gipfel der Unwahrscheinlichkeit und damit der Geschmacklosigkeit."*[42] For Bodmer it was no less important for the poet to represent reality—it became a matter of definition. Imaginative literature such as Milton's did not violate nature, but was instead a reflection of a much wider view of what constituted nature and the universe. *Natur* must be the *Urbild* of the artist, but Bodmer was interested in depictions of the invisible as well as the visible world.

As Wolfgang Bender has shown, when Bodmer and Breitinger spoke of *"möglichen Welten,"* they had in mind a system of the sort of Leibnitz's *"infinité des Univers possibles dans les idées de Dieu."*[43] Again it was the metaphysical acceptance of the absolute reality of the hereafter that matters. The imagination, *Einbildungskraft,* of the poet of genius which allows him to perceive the possible universe that transcends the limited everyday world of empirical nature and leads to the marvelous, *dem Wunderbaren.*[44] In much the same manner, Lavater's life-long search for actual manifestations of the miraculous from the other side of eternity and Fuseli's depictions of marvelous and fantastic images were not based on anti-Enlightenment, reactionary flights into irrationalism, but were explorations into the "possible" world of dream and imagination—psychology, in modern terminology—undertaken with the same seriousness with which natural scientists were measuring the limits of perceptible nature. The physiognomist Lavater searched for traces of the eternal, moral, other universe in the physical formations of the more limited now. The artist/genius was seen as one who is given the special charism of divining such signs and of recreating the possible world—hidden from most—through art. The chapter headings of Bodmer's *Critische Abhandlung von dem Wunderbaren in der Poesie und dessen Verbindung mit dem Wahrscheinlichen in einer Vertheidigung des Gedichts John. Miltons von dem verlohrnen Paradiese,* written in 1740, a year before the birth of Fuseli and Lavater, demonstrate the matter-of-factness in which the author accepts the existence of a world beyond:

Der erste Abschnitt: Von der Wahl der Materie aus der unsichtbaren Welt.

Der zweyte Abschnitt: Von der Vorstellung der Engel in sichtbarer Gestalt.

Der dritte Abschnitt: Von der Wahrscheinlichkeit des Characters und der Handlung der Engel.

Der vierte Abschnitt. Von dem Zusammenhang in Miltons Vorstellungen der Engel.

Der fünfte Abschnitt: Von dem Character und den Handlungen des Todes, der Sünde, der Geister in dem Chaos.

Der sechste Abschnitt: Von der Wahrscheinlichkeit des Characters und der Handlung der ersten Menschen.

Der siebende Abschnitt: Von Miltons Anbringung der mythologischen Geschichte und Theologie in seinem Gedichte.[45]

Bodmer interpreted Milton and the other great poets who were to become Fuseli's principal themes in painting in an "exceptionally intense way," as Antal tells us, "as harbingers of passion and original geniuses. He not only believed that the good and agreeable should be themes of poetry and painting but also the sad and the terrible."[46] Milton's poem was the greatest "modern" example of Bodmer's ideal. The central position of Milton in the work of Bodmer and Breitinger was to leave lasting influence upon Fuseli, who considered his ambitious "Milton Gallery" (1790-1800) as the most important work in his career as an artist. The high value that Fuseli placed upon *Paradise Lost* and the character of its author represents a common interest of great significance for William Blake's admiration of Fuseli and his work.

At the time that Fuseli and Lavater entered the *Carolinum,* the literary and scholarly activities of Bodmer had entered a new phase. After three decades of amazingly industrious and fruitful collaboration with Breitinger in the areas of criticism, aesthetics, and searching for medieval German texts, literary-historical research gave way more and more to Bodmer's own pedagogical and patriotic poetry. This gradual change from scholar to poet cannot be explained away by Bodmer's lack of success with his academic works, nor, as Max Wehrli has said, with the effects of approaching senility.[47] Considering the esteem in which he was held by his disciples, senility can hardly have entered the picture. The fact remains that, despite his great standing in the annals of literary history, Bodmer's own poetry and drama have always been an embarrassment, even to partisan scholars. The Bodmer scholar Wolfgang Bender admits that any attempt to salvage the *Dichter* in Bodmer can hardly be justified.[48] His numerous poems and tragedies in emulation of the ancient Greeks and Romans and his attempts at biblical epic poetry in the manner of Milton are unreadable today. But when Lavater and Fuseli came under his influence, his reputation alone was enough to engender respect and awe. In addition to his standing as academician and statesman, he had an almost obsessive desire to launch new poets, to find new "Miltons" from among the ranks of his attentive students. Klopstock and Wieland were eventually to prove a disappointment to him, perhaps because they were too much of their own minds as poets and refused to be his creations.[49] Lavater and Fuseli were the next generation to which he looked for a savior of German letters and a moral standard in the manner of his great English protestant idol. It was in this spirit that he encouraged their talents and sensibilities.

Bodmer had also by this time developed a peculiar critical perspective that might be best described as ahistorical. The past became interesting to him only insofar as it provided a "better" example of the present.[50] Even in serious historical studies of the city of Zurich he wanted to edit out the bad and leave only the exemplary. This is a curious turn of affairs for one who was fostering at the same time the terrible and the sublime in poetry. But the point was that the older Bodmer began to see his literary heroes—Aeneas, Parzival, and the giants of the *Nibelungenlied*—apart from the perspective of the times and culture which they represented, and to present them "*dass sie zum gesellschaftlichen Umgang mit unseren Voreltern führen; indem wir sie lesen, setzen wir den Zeitraum unseres Lebens etliche Jahrhunderte zurück; wir leben so viel früher und mit ihnen.*"[51] The great writers became united in a common spirit, so that *Parzival* appears in Bodmer's words "*Eschilbachs [sic] homerische Poesie.*"[52] Homer and the other great *Urdichter* were to embody for him a brotherhood from a realm on the other side of history. And, finally, he styled himself a sort of patriarch. Wehrli states:

> *Er stilisiert sich selber zum Patriarchen, er lässt sich von Wieland den Ältervater aller Dichter in Europa nennen, er ist selber Homer, selber der Noah, der in seiner Arche die Werke naiver Zeiten herübergerettet hat und der einzige Statthalter verlorener Zeit auf Erden ist.*[53]

In 1761 Lavater and Fuseli, the fledglings of this patriarch, were ordained as Zwinglian ministers. The respective choices of Fuseli and Lavater for their inaugural sermons after ordination tell much about the attitude with which each launched his ministerial career. Fuseli, perhaps seeing himself as a latter-day "Paul" in Athens, chose to speak on curiosity. His text was from Acts 16:18: "Some also of the Epicurean and Stoic philosophers met him. And some said, 'What would this babbler say?'" His passionate delivery, in which he attempted to employ the new "*Gefühlssprache*," and his "nervous style" were not well received by the citizens of Zurich. Lavater's text, which may be said to be equally revealing, was Ecclesiastes 7:2: "It is better to go to the house of mourning than to go to the house of feasting; for this is the end of all men, and the living will lay it to heart." Lavater's fame as a controversial "man of God," as a preacher, and a healer of souls extended almost uninterruptedly from the time of this first sermon. Fuseli's early biographer, Nüscheler, tells us somewhat archly that even if circumstances had not interrupted his ecclesiastical pursuits in 1762, Heinrich would have had to look somewhere other than the pulpit to further his career in the church.[54]

In that same year Rousseau's *Emile* and the *Contrat Social* were burned by order of the government of Geneva and the author was sentenced to prison. Muschg suggests that Rousseau's flight, his subsequent banishment, and the controversy stirred by these events were the immediate occasion that fired the young ministers to undertake the bold political act that was to determine their future lives and to make them famous patriots in the history of the city of Zurich.[55]

In 1762 Fuseli and Lavater became charter members of the *Helvetisch-Vaterländische Gesellschaft zu Schumachern*, founded by Bodmer with the purpose of instilling in its young members the brave and manly virtues of their forefathers, and, in so doing, to rejuvenate and renew the Fatherland. Their leader was their good friend Johann Jakob Hess. They, along with Leonhard Usteri and Hans Heinrich Thomann, were each and every one *Theologen*; and Hess, like Fuseli and Lavater, was an ordained minister.[56] The existence and founding of such a group was a logical extension of their discipleship to Bodmer. In the fall of 1762 Fuseli and Lavater circulated an anonymously written attack against the corrupt official, Grebel. In so doing they were acting in a manner which they thought both patriotic and in accordance with the best "heroic" tradition in which they had been steeped.

Fuseli, Lavater, and the "Grebel Affair"

Had Fuseli not taken the ideals of his liberal teachers so much to heart, and had he not formed a passionate friendship with Lavater, he probably would not have become a famous "English" painter, but would most probably have pursued a literary career in the German language. As irony would have it, his patriotism for his native city forced him to leave Zurich and eventually determined his emigration to England. The direction of Lavater's life was also set when, on August 27, 1762, a letter written by Fuseli and his friend and signed with the initials "J.C.L." was sent to the notoriously corrupt Zurich official, Felix Grebel, Landvogt von Grüningen.[57] In this epistle, in which the Landvogt was addressed as "Tyrann, Bösewicht, Heuchler, Ungerechtester aller Richter, verabscheuungswürdigster Greuel, dessen Tod ich wünsche, Meineidiger,"[58] Grebel was given two months to make good some of the specific misdeeds with which the young reformers charged him. If he did not do so, he was promised a full and public exposé of his crimes, with documentation and witnesses. Not surprisingly, Grebel, who was the son-in-law of the highly respected mayor of the city, chose to ignore the impertinent document that was delivered to his doorstep in the dark of night. Fuseli and Lavater kept to the terms of their challenge, and on that October 21 they had a pamphlet secretly printed in which the damaging evidence against Grebel was enumerated. This unsigned document was then secretly delivered at night to the doorsteps of the leading citizens of Zurich. Entitled *Der ungerechte Landvogt oder Klagen eines Patrioten*, the polemic eventually had the desired effect of causing the senate of Zurich to initiate an investigation into Grebel's affairs. But the city was shocked at the illegal and anonymous manner in which such an unprecedented attack had been launched against a leading personage. The senate issued a *Rathsdecret* of December 4, 1762, describing *"eine gedruckte Schrift...ohne Unterschrift und Namen, in welcher sehr bedenkliche und starke Klägden enthalten, auf eine illegale und ohnordentliche Weise ausgestreuet worden."*[59] The accusers were called upon to reveal themselves and to give further evidence. At first Fuseli and Lavater did not come forward, but sent more copies of the original document to Grebel's legal representative and delivered more anonymous evidence to the senate. On the 11th and 13th of December more anonymous accusations began to appear from other quarters. In the middle of the month an investigation was begun. Fuseli and Lavater had planned from the beginning to step forward, but, quite understandably, they did not rush to do so. In his biography of his father-in-law, Lavater, Georg Gessner tells the story of how the young Johann Caspar went first to the mayor of the city to confess, and then to the *Vorsteher* of the church of Zurich whom he asked to break the news to his father.[60] We have no account of how Fuseli told his father of the matter; but, considering the great plans that the elder Fuseli had for his son, he cannot have been too pleased.

Fuseli and Lavater revealed themselves at the first meeting of the special commission called on the 20th of December. In most heroic rhetoric they stated that they had done the deed because God would not allow their consciences to do otherwise—they could not die a peaceful death knowing that innocence was being trampled upon in the face of the general silence. The motto under which they had sent their original document was *"Du, Brutus! und du schläfst? ach, wann du lebtest!—Plutarch's Leben des Brutus."*[61] When asked why they had not followed due process in the matter, Lavater, who must be regarded as the leader of the two in this endeavor, pulled from his pocket a long speech, which he had obviously prepared in answer to that very question. Stating that they were not ashamed of what they had done, Lavater nonetheless admitted that it was a crime of sorts for which they were willing to pay the price. If they had announced their intentions through proper legal channels, they knew that they would have been prevented from acting in as direct a manner as they had done because of their youth and insignificant standing in the city. They expressed delight that Zurich was now acting:

Ja—allergnädigste Herren und Väter! Ihr seyd (entfernt jeden Verdacht der Schmeicheley von dem, dessen Freymüthigkeit fast bis zur Strafwürdigkeit steigt), Ihr seyd die Edlen, die Grossmüthigen, die Väter des Vaterlandes, die wir uns gedacht haben.[62]

Although they were hailed as heroes by the liberal intellectuals of the city, they did not get off without an official reprimand deploring the manner in which they had proceeded, and an admonition not to act again in the same manner. All honors were taken from Grebel, his coat of arms was abolished, and he was banned for life from participating in the *Eidgenossenschaft*. All foreign holdings were taken from him, and he was made to pay reparations to injured parties. Bodmer was, of course, not among those dismayed or shocked at the behavior of his young friends. Around this time he wrote of the episode to a young *Zürcher* in Geneva:

Wenn Sie diese Tage bei uns gewesen wären, durch was für ein hinreissendes exempel des Patriotisme wären Sie in volle Flammen gesetzt worden!; wie hätten Sie die Unschuld, die Redlichkeit, die Unerschrockenheit, die Gegenwart des Geistes in ihrer schönsten Gestalt unüberwindlich würken gesehen! Jünglinge haben alte Männer aus dem politischen Schlafe geweckt![63]

There seems to have been little doubt that justice had been served, but this did not alter the fact that a very famous family had been disgraced in the public forum. It seemed best that the two young men absent themselves from the city for a time. Thus it was decided that they would travel to Berlin with Johann Sulzer (1720-1779), the famous mathematician and philosopher who was visiting Zurich at the time these events occurred. Sulzer, a native Swiss, was a professor of mathematics at the *Joachimsthalsches Gymnasium* in Berlin and was a close friend and former student of Bodmer's. Together with Jakob and Felix Hess, Lavater and Fuseli set out with Sulzer for the trip to Berlin. They made a leisurely trip and stopped at places of interest on the way in Saint Gall, Lindau, Augsburg, Nürnberg, Leipzig and Magdeburg. On the 27th of March 1763, they arrived in Berlin. Their reputations had preceded them, and they were enthusiastically welcomed by the intellectual circle of Berlin, by "all enemies of oppression."[64] Sulzer saw to it that they were introduced to the important men of letters in and around the area. They were to visit with Gellert in Leipzig and Johann Ludwig Gleim (1719-1803), the author of the Prussian *"Kriegslieder"* in Magdeburg, and Moses Mendelssohn (1729-1786) in Berlin.[65] Sulzer was even able to get them an audience with the crown prince, Friedrich Wilhelm. After their short tour in glory around Berlin, Sulzer sent the young men to Barth in Swedish Pomerania to study with the famous theologian, Johann Joachim Spalding (1714-1804).

The trip was seen by Bodmer as a means of rounding out the theological education of the young men, and there can be no doubt that he thought that these young ambassadors would benefit by contact with the literary world of Berlin, which was, principally through Sulzer, in close contact with the intelligentsia of Zurich. Sulzer was even at that time in the process of preparing his *Allgemeine Theorie der schönen Künste*, a four-volume encyclopedia of aesthetics which was the first of its kind in German, and which "anticipated many details of romantic expressive theories."[66] Five months later, Fuseli was to work with Sulzer on this project.

It was during this first trip away from home that the paths of Fuseli and Lavater would separate, that Fuseli would embark with the encouragement, indeed, with the urging, of Bodmer upon a literary career in "exile." Lavater's dedication to the spiritual life was reinforced in Barth, where Spalding, an early exponent of emotional theology and one of the first translators of Shaftesbury, was engaged in the mission of infusing the ideas of the English Enlightenment into Lutheranism.[67] There, in the moral liberal atmosphere that characterized the Berlin theologians, Lavater thought he had found an admirable mentor to foster his unorthodox conceptions of Christ and personal religion. The "mild" and "gentle" Spalding made a very strong impression on both young men, to be sure. Although Lavater was to go his own way when he returned to Zurich to write *Aussichten in die Ewigkeit* (1768-1773), Spalding's sincere and Rousseauistic attempt to justify religion by an "appeal to its social utility" gave a theoretical base to Lavater's pragmatic sort of mysticism.

There can be little doubt that Lavater was the dominant personality during this phase of his friendship with Fuseli. Twenty-four years after their visit with him, Spalding was to recall his impressions of Lavater in relation to Fuseli and Jakob Hess:

> *Dieser so merkwürdige Lavater war damals gewissermassen das Orakel und der Führer der beyden andern, den sie mit einer beynah kindlichen Art Wertschätzung achteten, ohne dass er sich davon im geringsten einiges Ansehn gab, indem immer die innigste brüderliche Vertraulichkeit unter ihnen in der ganzen Art ihres Umgangs herrschte.*[68]

Spalding adds that Lavater had earned the respect of his friends because of his sensitive and noble religious sentiment, but adds disapprovingly that at that time the young man had shown no signs of the *Schwärmerei* that was to later characterize his behavior and writings. At twenty-one, the good Provost assures his readers, Lavater's emotions were yet ruled by an enlightened and calm reason.[69] It seems that in his memoirs Spalding was trying to look back for signs of the rather frightening *Genies* that his young visitors were to become. By 1787, Lavater had become a very controversial character. Fuseli was by then in London, a *"mächtiges, aber fast alles bis zur Carricatur treibendes Genie, theils in GemähldEn und Zeichnungen theils in litterarischen Arbeiten...."*[70] And Spalding recalls that, even when he was a guest at Barth, this talented character was possessed of a fieriness of imagination and determination that exceeded the bounds of convention with a sort of "offensive originality."[71]

While Lavater's religious sensibilities were being nurtured by the attention of Spalding, the five-month stay in Barth marks the last period in Fuseli's life in which he was to deal seriously with theological study. Schiff suggests that the greatest influence that Spalding had on Fuseli had to do with the Pastor's great admiration for Rousseau.[72] Fuseli was preoccupied during this time with poetry and with his idol, Klopstock. Even before leaving Berlin for Barth, Fuseli was not speaking of the church when he wrote Bodmer that he was yearning as a "bridegroom for his bride." The object of his longing was a meeting with the author of the *Messias*. In his letter he addresses Klopstock figuratively:

> ...ich will dich noch küssen, ich will dir sagen, mit welcher Liebe dich Bodmer liebet und wie ich dich liebe—ich will dir beweisen, wenn es ein redliches Herz und eine Zunge, die dessen Empfindungen redet, können, dass diese nicht deine besten, die deiner würdigsten Freunde sind, die du bisher gekannt hast, und dass, dir unbekannt, Herzen für dich schlugen, die mehr wie jene alle wert sind.[73]

Although the young travelers had passed four miles from the place where Klopstock was staying on their trip to Berlin, Fuseli was not to come face to face with his idol until almost a year later.

The Parting of Ways

Fuseli remained in Barth with Lavater and Hess for over five months. A copy of a painting that he executed on the wall of Spalding's garden house there documents the mood of the young friends and the congenial Spalding. While there, Fuseli made his first attempt to earn a living by his pen. He translated the Turkish travel letters of Lady Montague: *Briefe der Lady Marie Wortley Montague*. This first effort was published in Leipzig in 1763. In October of 1763, Sulzer recalled Fuseli to Berlin. He desired the assistance of the youthful scholar in the writing of his *Allgemeine Theorie der schönen Künste*. Seven of the articles in that lexicon were written by Fuseli or were a result of his collaboration with Sulzer. These entries were entitled: *Allegorie, Ausarbeitung, Anordnung, Gruppen, Anatomie des Homers, das Erhabene*, and *Schoenheit*.[74]. It is upon his return to Berlin that Fuseli mentions for the first time Bodmer's plan to send him to England as a literary emissary between the English and German intellectual worlds. Schiff believes that the plan might well have been worked out by Sulzer and Bodmer in Zurich or before Fuseli left for Barth, for Fuseli had met Sir Andrew Mitchell, the British Ambassador to Berlin almost immediately upon arriving there. It was with Mitchell that Fuseli was to cross the Channel for the first time.[75] At any rate, it seems that the actual decision to send Fuseli on such a mission was not made until the end of November.

When Fuseli left Hess and Lavater in Barth and traveled by himself back to Sulzer in Berlin, he sensed for the first time his isolation from friends and fatherland. During that trip he wrote his wildest testimony to the *Sturm und Drang* tradition—a long, free verse lament entitled "*Klagen*." In this work he bemoans his exile from home, his alienation from all that had once been familiar, and, most of all, his acute distress at being parted from his beloved soul mate, Lavater. The poem borrows heavily from Young's *Night Thoughts*. After some revisions upon arriving in Berlin he sent the poem to Lavater, who was both amazed and delighted with it and who in turn sent a copy of it on to Herder. It is from Herder's *Nachlass* that the work has come down to us.[76] As literature, "*Klagen*" is an unparalleled document of the fervent sentimentalism and passionate linguistic excesses of Storm and Stress rhetoric. In his pioneering study on Fuseli's literary work, Arnold Federmann went so far as to compare "*Klagen*" with *Werther*; and, in truth, some passages of Goethe's early work do sound exactly like Fuseli's intimate testimony of love and despair.[77] From the evidence of letters which Fuseli wrote to Lavater from Berlin, it would appear that he had written Lavater about the poem and Lavater had replied, asking for a copy of it. Fuseli hesitated at first, offended by what he perceived to be a coolness in Lavater's responses to his own passionate letters:

> Du verlangst meine "Klagen"—ich darf dieselben nicht schicken, denn sie sind nur für den Lavater, bei dem ich schlief, und ich fürchte, sie möchten dem Schreiber der zween Briefe, die ich beantworte, in die Hände fallen.[78]

Other letters written by Fuseli to Lavater at this time are full of declarations of love, outbursts of jealousy, and depictions of proud, yet self-pitying loneliness:

> Die unaussprechliche Angst meiner Seele, welche die zween Tage, die mich von dir getrennet haben, zu den schrecklichsten meines Lebens voll fühlloser Tränenlosigkeit machete, bin ich zu schwach und zu furchtsam dir zu beschreiben.[79]

When, in January 1764, Fuseli finally sent a copy of his "Klagen" to Lavater, he sent an accompanying letter in which he imagines Lavater's reaction upon receiving the parcel and opening it for the first time:

> ...der Brief ist da, oder vielmehr der Nichtbrief—wird aufgemacht—niedlich Papier: "KLAGEN"—kein Brief; was sollen wir tun, wird geflüstert—man kann die nicht gleich hier lesen, wer weiss, was verbotnes drin stehet.... —wär ich nur dabei, so wollte ich versichern, dass man sie lesen darf—vielleicht geschiet es auch—ja—"O Vaterland" etc.... "Ein Schleier von Gefühlen!" wird Hess sagen, indem er sein Kinn in die Tiefe der Hand zwischen Daumen und Zeigefinger stösst und zusieht, ob dasselbe noch festhalte; "ich fürchte—auch gar keine Logik, keine Moral gelesen—ach Gott! wie wird es noch mit dem armen Füssli werden!" Das weiss ich auch nicht, lieber Hess, vielleicht wunderlich genug.[80]

Fuseli might be said to have "outgrown" some of the feelings and attitudes which he held during this period of his life, but love for Lavater was not one of them. He was to remain faithful to his friend even after Lavater had become the object of controversy and derision, and even when Fuseli himself grew impatient with Lavater's frenzied excursions into the world of the supernatural. His stubborn loyalty to his old friend is analogous to his loyalty to William Blake in later years. Blake and Lavater were the only contemporary "geniuses" whom Fuseli consistently supported in his years of fame and success. That both of those men were considered eccentric by all and mad by not a few is not without significance in an evaluation of Fuseli's own conceptions of genius and talent.

The mission of Fuseli to England was both idealistic and practical. He was receiving very little help from Zurich, other than a small sum raised for him by Bodmer. He made some money from the Montague translation, most of which he spent on travel expenses or sent to Spalding to reimburse him for the hospitality he had enjoyed there. In short, he needed somehow to make a living.[81] Evidently his mentors did not see much chance of his making a successful career in establishment circles in Zurich. That Bodmer was clearly urging him to take the assignment in London is evident from Fuseli's statement in a letter to Bodmer on the 24th of November 1763: "Mir deucht jedoch, dieses Ausstrecken Ihrer Arme etc. sagt so viel als: Gehe, eile nach

England. Wenn es Ihr Wille ist, so will ich ihm auch auf der Stelle gehorchen. Sie dürfen es nur an Sulzer schreiben.''[82] A month later the decision had been made. He was writing to Hess that his requests for books would be easier to fulfill *"Wenn ich in England bin...."*[83] Before Fuseli was to cross the Channel, there was to be one last meeting with his friends who were returning from Barth on their way back to Switzerland. Together they passed the month of February with Sulzer. At last, at the end of that month, they were able to travel to Quedlinburg, where they spent three days visiting Klopstock. From there, the three young men traveled to Göttingen, where Fuseli would leave them. At parting, Lavater presented Fuseli with a gift. It was a framed motto: *"Thue den siebenden theil von dem, was du thun kannst,"* which Lavater admonished Fuseli to hang in his room where he could see it every day.[84] It is not known whether or not Fuseli did hang it up, or what became of the motto, but a poem written thirty-eight or thirty-nine years later proves that Fuseli never forgot the gesture nor its intent.

Zweite Ode an Lavater (1802/1803)

Tue den siebten Teil von dem, was du tun kannst, so sagte,
*   Als seinem Arm ich entfloh, mein nun unsterblicher*
*   Freund.*
Tat ich den siebenten Teil von dem, was ich tun konnte?
*   Schwebst du itzt um mein Haupt, sag es, unsterblicher*
*   Freund?*
Sechzig Jahre entfloh'n, mein Haupt ist silber, der Zunge
*   Elfenbeinerne Mauer fällt in Fragmente zerknirscht.*
Zwar noch schlummern die Wächter des Haupts nicht, die
*   Fittig-Flügel*
Decken lenzlich und blond ihr immer blitzendes Licht.
Runzeln kennet die Stirne noch nicht, hat sie nicht die
*   Arbeit*
Rastlos pflügende Hand auf ihre Fläche gedrückt.
Weich empfängt und behält des Gehirns untadliche Zelle,
*   Was der entflohene Tag gab, der fliehende gibt.*
Mündel Mnemosynes noch, noch hoher Erfindungen Säugling
*   Streu' ich Ideen um mich und fühle reicher der Gab'.*
Auf dem erhabenen Pfad Homerus und Sh(akespeare) und Milton
*   Wandl' ich mit strauchelndem Fuss, zwar dennoch wandl'*
*   ich allein,*
Achtlos der Kriecher im Tal, aber wünsche durch Willen
*   erhöhet.*
Blick' ich getrost und kühn über mein Zeitalter weg,
Wenn kein Neid die Waage mehr hält, das Jahrhundert
*   gerecht wird*
*   Und der Meister nicht mehr stehet im Licht seines Werks.*
Lavater, wärest du hier...hier bin ich, bewundernd der
*   Welt Strom,*
Den dein bescheidener Mund über dich selber ergoss!

Second Ode to Lavater (1802/1803)

Do only a seventh part of what you can, so said
    As I fled from his arms, my now immortal friend.
Did I do a seventh part of that which I could?
    If you hover now above my head, tell me, immortal friend
Sixty years have passed, my hair is silver, the ivoried
        walls of the tongue
    Fall, crushed to fragments.
Still the watchmen of my head do not yet slumber, pinions
    vernal and blond still bedeck their ever-flashing light.
The forehead knows no wrinkles, but those impressed
    by the restlessly ploughing hand of labor.
Gently, the faultless cell of my brain receives and retains
    what the day gone by has given and what the passing
        day gives.
Still the ward of Mnemosyne, still the babe of high invention,
    I scatter ideas about me and feel more richly the gift.
On the sublime path of Homer and Shakespeare and Milton
    I wander with stumbling foot, yet I wander alone.
Mindless of the crawlers in the valley; wishing to be raised
    by will.
    Reconciled and dauntless, I look beyond my times,
To when jealousy no longer holds the scales, when the century
        shall become
    just, and the master no longer obscures the light of his
    work.
Lavater, were you only here...I stand here alone, in awe
    of the mighty tempest,
    which poured out of your own modest mouth to rise higher
    than you yourself!

Lavater, Felix Hess, and Heinrich Füssli (Fuseli) at the home of Spalding in Swedish Pomerania. An engraving by Christian von Mechel after Fuseli's design. Executed in 1763. (By permission, Staatsgalerie, Stuttgart)

The History and Fortune of the Winckelmann Translation

Fuseli's first English publication appeared in January 1765, a year after his arrival in London. Although Mason states that "Fuseli had probably begun...journalistic work in London in the years 1764-1765," he is not able to find an article, signed or unsigned, which is dated 1764.[1] Knowles also suggests that Fuseli was employed right away by his new publisher acquaintances: "...he laboured hard, and fortunately got ample employment from the booksellers in translating works from the French, Italian, and German languages into English."[2] But Knowles gives as an example, in the next sentence, the translation of the letters of Lady Montague, a project that was begun and completed when Fuseli was still in Berlin.[3] It is likely that most of that first year was spent in getting settled, acclimating himself to this new country and refining his ability in its language. He took rooms at the "house of a Mrs. Green." Knowles tells us that he "lived there because of economy, but also because it was close to Mr. Coutts on St. Martin's Lane." Fuseli's desire to be in the same neighborhood with the banker Coutts is understandable, for at the time, he was one of the richest men in London.

Fuseli was accepted and patronized by the upper-class intelligentsia immediately upon his arrival because of the sponsorship of the two companions with whom he crossed the Channel: Sir Andrew Mitchell (1708-1771), English Envoy to the court of Frederick the Great in Berlin; and the poet and physician, John Armstrong (1709-1779). Mitchell, for a time an intimate friend of Frederick, was said to have been better acquainted with the German literature of the day than the king himself. One of his early teachers of German had been Gottsched, "whose attack on Shakespeare he argued with considerable wit."[4] He was greatly interested in cementing close cultural and political ties between the courts of England and Prussia. Fuseli was introduced to the distinguished diplomat by Sulzer, a close friend of Mitchell's, shortly after his arrival in Berlin. Sir Andrew looked upon the young Swiss as his protégé and introduced him to men "distinguished either for rank, property, or talents," among these, the fabulously wealthy Coutts. Mitchell's sphere of influence was not limited to the titled, however, for in Knowles's words: "Sir Andrew, knowing that booksellers of respectability and probity are the best patrons of literary characters, strongly recommended him to Mr. Andrew Millar (1707-1768) and Joseph Johnson (1738-1809)."[5]

John Armstrong, who had gained some fame as the author of a long didactic poem in blank verse entitled "The Art of Preserving Health" (1744), was quite a different character. A physician, who had been assigned to the British troops in Germany in 1760, his poetry and essays covered a wide range of interests: from *A Synopsis of the History and Cure of Venereal Disease* (1768) to a verse essay "Taste: An Epistle to a Young Critick" (1753). Writing poems in imitation of Shakespeare at an early age, he also sought the patronage of established poets and sent his manuscripts to Thompson, Mallet, Aaron Hill, and Young, who received "copies of these verses from the youthful writer, and expressed to him their congratulations."[6] His first published poem was "The Oeconomy of Love" (1735), which Armstrong published anonymously, and quite wisely so, according to Leslie Stephen, who in 1887 called the pseudodidactic poem "a production which not many young men would care to claim. A more nauseous piece of work could not easily be found."[7] Under the guise of advice to young persons concerning the dangers and snares of passion, the poem is actually a titillating bit of pornography in blank verse, a form of which he was a master. In a sense, it was a satire of the practical "how-to" genre of the more serious "Art of Preserving Health." Despite Stephen's outraged opinion, "The Oeconomy of Love" enjoyed many editions, including several American ones.[8] Fuseli took Armstrong quite seriously as a poet, and he wrote to Lavater on December 10, 1765: *"England hat den Mangel an Köpfen, den das übrige Europa fühlet. Sein einziger Poet ist mein Freund Armstrong."*[9] It was with Armstrong that Fuseli was to set out for Italy in 1777 to study painting. In spite of a falling-out on that voyage, they were reconciled shortly before Armstrong's death in 1779. Fuseli wrote an anonymous character study of his friend in 1768 which appeared in the *Universal Museum* (6 May 1768): "...a man on whom Nature seemed to have poured parts and virtues without a design; a penetrating head without application; a spirit of enterprise without execution; a heart boiling with passions, wrapt up in phlegm, made to captivate and yet to live neglected; to mark the tide of fortune, and to let it pass by."[10] In 1788, Fuseli's brother Kaspar translated and published "The Art of Preserving Health" (*"Die Kunst die Gesundheit zu erhalten"*).[11] Most of Armstrong's works were published by Andrew Millar, who was his great friend and who would be Fuseli's first publisher also.

In addition to the support given him by these two men of influence, Fuseli had brought with him a gift from his father which was intended to aid him in launching his literary career. The gift was a bundle of letters which Johann Joachim Winckelmann had written to his Swiss friends and sponsors between 1758 and 1764. Even before Fuseli left Zurich in the company of Sulzer, Lavater, and the brothers Hess, he had in mind the worthy undertaking of translating into English the work of the classical scholar whom his father so ardently admired and supported. The elder Füssli recalled the circumstances of giving the letters to his son in a small monograph that he published, perhaps with the collaboration of Fuseli in Zurich in 1778, entitled *Geschichte von Winckelmanns Briefe an seine Freunde in der Schweiz*: *"Ich konnte meinem Sohn, bei seiner Abreise nach England, seine Bitte nicht ver-*

sagen, diese Briefe, als sein schätzbarstes Reisegerät mit sich zu nehmen."[12] Fuseli's father, perhaps in his last major attempt to set his son on the path of becoming a learned scholar-clergyman in the manner of his friends, Breitinger and Sulzer, wrote to Winckelmann, asking permission for his son to correspond with him, to translate his works into English, and to promulgate his theories in England. Füssli's letter is lost, but Winckelmann's reply, dated April 9, 1763, bespeaks the father's efforts on behalf of his son:

Sie versprechen sich zu viel, mein Freund, von mir in Engeland für Ihren Herren Sohn; Ich bin wenigen bekant [sic], und vermeide diese inhospitale Nation, wo ich kan [sic]. Ich werde aber allezeit grosses Vergnügen haben, wenn der Sohn meines würdigsten Freundes sich mit mir unterhalten will. Vielleicht findet er in Engeland einen Freund von uns beyden, welcher ihm statt aller seyn würde. Es ist sehr glaublich, dass Herr Mengs nach Engeland gehen wird, wohin ihm [sic] vier von den reichsten Herren rufen.[13]

Winckelmann's letters to the elder Füssli and other Zurich friends concerned, as Caspar Füssli remarked in his commentary to them, *"die Kunst und seine [Winckelmann's] eigene Werke"*[14] and were to be used by his son as a sort of commentary to his translations. It is fortunate that Caspar Füssli published most of the letters in his small monograph before he entrusted them to his son for future use, for the original copies were all destroyed along with other irreplaceable documents in the fire in Johnson's apartments in 1770. The disastrous impact of this fire on Fuseli's literary career will be discussed more fully in a later chapter.

In a long article, Eudo C. Mason traces the vicissitudes of Fuseli's efforts to translate Winckelmann's major work, *Geschichte der Kunst des Altertums*, a project that was later abandoned.[15] Fuseli's association with the Winckelmann material and the problematic relationship, or lack of relationship, between the young Swiss and the German classical scholar weave a puzzling tale. In spite of Winckelmann's friendly response to the requests of Fuseli's father, Fuseli did not write to the famous man right away. Four months after Caspar wrote to Winckelmann on his son's behalf, Winckelmann wrote again to his friend and patron in Zurich: *"Von Ihrem Herrn Sohn habe ich keine Nachricht. Ich wünsche, dass er nach der weiten Reise das Glück habe, Rom zu sehen, und ich ihn, um ihm den Freund seines würdigen Vaters zu zeigen."*[16] No letters survive between Fuseli and Winckelmann, but the evidence in Winckelmann's letters to others shows that more than two-and-one-half years passed between the time Fuseli's father first wrote to Winckelmann concerning Heinrich and the time that Fuseli wrote to him. They were never to meet; and, in the end, as Mason says, Fuseli *"interessierte Winckelmann fast ausschliesslich als Übersetzer seiner Werke ins Englische."*[17]

Fuseli's first English translation of Winckelmann appeared in the January 1765 issue of the *Universal Museum* under the name of "John Fussle": "A Description of a Marble Trunk of Hercules, commonly called the Torso of Belvedere; wrought by Apollonius, the Son of Nestor, and universally allowed to have been made for a statue of Hercules Spinning. Translated from the German of the abbe Winckleman [sic], librarian of the Vatican, and antiquary to the Pope &c." Fuseli never sent Winckelmann a copy of this translation, which was taken from the fifth volume of the *Bibliothek der schönen Wissenschaften und der freyen Künste* (1759).[18] Winckelmann's knowledge about Fuseli's translating of his works remained sketchy and confused until the time of his death. His letters show that he relied upon hearsay and sometimes inflated reports of the progress that Fuseli was making in his translation of *Geschichte der Kunst...*, and that Winckelmann was never to lay eyes on the only translation published in book form by Millar in April 1765: *Reflections on the Painting and Sculpture of the Greeks: With Instructions for the Connoisseur, And an Essay on Grace in Works of Art.* "Translated from the German Original of the Abbe Winkelmann [sic] Librarian to the Vatican, F.R.S. etc. etc. by Henry Fuseli, A.M." (*Gedanken über die Nachahmung der griechischen Werke in der Malerei und Bildhauerkunst*, 1755; *Erinnerung über die Betrachtung der alten Kunst*, 1759; *Von der Gratie in Werken der Kunst*, 1759.)

Evidence available about the fortune of this small book leads one to the conclusion that some recent suggestions that Fuseli was a major figure in introducing the ideas of Winckelmann to the British intellectual world have been exaggerated. Mason has given a convincing argument that what was advertised as a "second edition" in April 1766 was in fact the unsold remainder of the 1765 edition, with a new title page to which the word "corrected" had been added, with the name of Millar's successor, Thomas Cadell, joined to the publishing credits. There is no extant copy, only a newspaper notice that announced this "second edition." The conjecture that Millar, who was retiring at that time, was "cleaning house" of unsold liabilities for Cadell is reinforced by the fact that this edition was being offered for a shilling less than the first edition.[19] The book was clearly not a success in terms of sales, and Fuseli found it necessary to take a job as tutor and companion to Viscount Chewton, son of Lord Walgrave, a wealthy nobleman and friend of Mitchell's, a month after the book appeared, in spite of the generosity of his publisher. Millar insisted upon giving Fuseli the entire proceeds from the sale of the book and had enlisted subscribers prior to its publication. When Fuseli sent a copy of his translations to Sulzer in April 1765, he explained the circumstances in an accompanying letter:

Hier ist die Übersetzung von W[inckelmanns] Gedanken; ich habe ihr eine ausserordentliche freye von denjenigen Aufsäzen [sic] desselben Verfassers beygefüget die in dem Vten Bande der Bibliothek etc begraben wurden. Hr Millar welcher die Kosten des Drukes [sic] aus dem Verkaufe der Schrift bestreitet, und den Profit der erwachsen [sic] mag, nicht mit mir theilen will, thut darinn etwas welches ausser den Buchhändlern der Kinder Gottes ehe sie sich mit den Cainitinen vermischeten schwerlich ein andrer diese 5000 Jahre ab, wird gethan haben, er verdient ein Monument....[20]

Millar published the work as a favor to the young friend of Mitchell and Armstrong. It seems clear that Fuseli himself suggested the project to Millar. His bringing of the letters from Switzerland, and his father's correspondence with Winckelmann on the matter would confirm that the project was envisaged before he got to England. In his last letter to Bodmer from Berlin, he was recommending Winckelmann's *Geschichte der Kunst...*to his old teachers with enthusiasm: "*Haben Sie oder Herr Chorherr [Breitinger], dem ich durch Sie die letzte Umarmung vom festen Lande zuschicke,*

Winckelmanns vortreffliche Geschichte der Kunst schon gesehen?"²¹ There can be no question that at this time Fuseli was an admirer of Winckelmann and that his desire to translate his works was not merely for his own advancement, but because he agreed with Winckelmann's theory to a certain extent.

Mason has traced a series of incidents and coincidences that worked against the success of Fuseli's Winckelmann enterprises and perhaps had as much to do with the meager sales of the book as did subject matter, authorship, or translation. Winckelmann was not unknown in England at the time, and interest in archeology was high. French editions of his *Geschichte* (1755-1756) and other writings were available in London and were often mentioned in the newspapers and critical journals. Winckelmann was a controversial figure in the British press because of some of his more extreme views. Respected for his archeology, his cultural theories were never considered legitimate, largely because of the offense the English felt at his frequently expressed antipathy for England. Most unfortunately for Fuseli, another translation of the *Gedanken* appeared in the *London Chronicle* two weeks before his little book was published. The *Chronicle's* translation was published in seven installments in letter-form—a pure invention on the part of the anonymous translator. It was based upon the French edition edited, ironically enough, by Fuseli's mentor, Sulzer, and not on the German original. Although far less accurate than Fuseli's translation, the newspaper version of the *Gedanken*, which did not include the shorter articles which Fuseli appended to his, was written in a much more conventional style and in better English. Winckelmann's *Gräkomanie* was expressed by the translator in much milder terms. The seven-part translation was later published in book form in Glasgow in 1766. Although the identity of the author of this translation is still not known, his work was widely circulated and was the basis of several printed editions. It was even retranslated from the English into French and appeared in a Paris journal a few months after it appeared in London.²² Fuseli's faithfulness to the spirit of the translation was a disadvantage on the English market, where reviewers took exception to invidious comparisons of the genius of the Greeks and the lack thereof among northern peoples.

The tone and purpose of Winckelmann's essay must be kept in mind also. The ideas which Winckelmann expressed in the *Gedanken* were not entirely original and owed much to his avid study of history and aesthetics. What was new, and what one can still sense reading the essay today, is evangelical enthusiasm and forthright sense of mission with which Winckelmann expressed his ideas. This mood—it is more than "style"—was understood by Fuseli. He tried to convey this feeling in his translation, which is not literal, but which is almost always accurate. In Mason's brief comparison of the translation with the original, which he entitles *"Übersetzung als Steigerung"* ("Translation as Intensification"), he maintains that this tendency to intensify expression, which characterizes most of Fuseli's writing and art, leads sometimes to the point of mannered grotesque.²³ But this term, while it might be amply descriptive, should not suggest a pejorative meaning, as if through intensification Fuseli had somehow, perhaps unknowingly, gone too far or distorted meaning. This disapproving attitude often characterized contemporary assessments of all of Fuseli's work. In 1780, Walpole called Fuseli's productions "Extravagant and ridiculous; Shockingly mad, madder than ever." Cunningham wrote in 1829: "...sometimes disturbed by a demon...a desire to stretch and strain...wild and unsober." Hazlitt's assessment in 1826 was "Capable of the most wild and grotesque combinations of Fancy...distortions and vagaries are German, and not English: they lie like a nightmare on the breast of our native art." In 1883 Sidney Colvin continued the suggestion of Hazlitt that Fuseli's nationality was in part responsible for his style: "The Hobgoblinry of the Teutonic genius...is in reality a stronger point in Fuseli than either the terrible or the graceful."[24] Being a "Genius" and a "German" were sins of which both Fuseli and Winckelmann were guilty and were attributes alternately tolerated and deplored by the British press. Fuseli always knew what he was about, however, and he saw his self-confessed tendency to intensify as idealization, and not distortion: *"Es ist immer mein Schicksal gewesen, mein Subjekt in einem idealischen Lichte zu sehen, Jupiter hat mir zu oft im Zorne die Backen mit Wind gefüllt."*[25] That which Mason designates as grotesquely mannered is exactly that same quality which necessitates the invention of such adjectives as "Blakean" or "Fuseliesque" when confronted with the style of the two artists.

Alan Cunningham went so far as to say "it took some nerve" for Fuseli to acknowledge authorship of the translation, "for the book...advocates the doctrine that British genius is unequal to the task of making noble works of art—a notion, which, however absurd, seems to have sometimes possessed Fuseli himself."[26] The not always reliable Cunningham's snide suggestion that Fuseli, a great anglophile and lover of Shakespeare and Milton, shared Winckelmann's prejudices toward northern genius reflects the chauvinistic sensitivity of English criticism of the day to some of Winckelmann's theories. There are two extant reviews of Fuseli's translation, one appearing in *The Monthly Review* of May 1765 and the other in *The Critical Review* in June of the same year.

That Fuseli was not the harbinger of the Greek revival in London is made clear by the reviewer in the *Monthly*, who asserted that it "may be thought difficult, at this time of day, to advance any thing new or important, on subjects so frequently and variously treated of, as the arts of antiquity. It is true, that scarce an anecdote of the ancient artists remains, that hath not been often repeated, and hardly any comparison of their works is to be made with those of the moderns, that hath not suggested itself to one or other of the numerous writers on these curious topics."[27] While lauding Winckelmann's archeological endeavors at Herculaneum, he called the work under discussion "a tract of no great extent," in which "prepossession and opinion prevail" to such a degree that the author was forced to defend himself against the numerous objections made to his treatise.[28] Here the reviewer was alluding to Fuseli's translation of Winckelmann's "*Sendschreiben über die Gedanken....*" which Winckelmann wrote himself, using the ploy of anonymous objections to elucidate his original theories in a point-counterpoint fashion. Fuseli translated the "Sendschreiben" as "Objections to the Foregoing Reflections...." The reviewer perceived Winckelmann's device, and deplored the tactic. The remainder of the review consists of long quotations from the translation. No comment is made on the merit of the other ideas presented, nor on the quality of the translation.

The notice in the *Critical Review* also expressed admiration for the accomplishments of Winckelmann, "whose name is well-known to all connoisseurs in the fine arts, especially those of painting and sculpture." *The Reviewer* called Winckelmann's more extreme statements "digressions,...that are not uncommon to men of genius," especially referring to Winckelmann's contention that "Taste...was not only original among the Greeks, but also...peculiar to their country."[29] Calling this sort of critical perspective "illiberal and unjust," the reviewer cited numerous selections from the text and then went on to offer his own objections, not being content to repeat the objections of the "Sendschreiben," which he also correctly guessed to be from Winckelmann himself. Defending the Romans against the charge of being copiers of the greater Greek culture, he stated: "We believe Virgil understood poetry as well as Mr. Winckelmann does painting." The reviewer took exception to the fact that the German scholar "makes personal gracefulness and beauty local, and in fact, confines it to Greece." Of the most interesting aspect of Winckelmann's essay as far as Fuseli and Blake are concerned, the section on "Allegory," the reviewer took little notice:

> Allegory fills the last chapter: and here we cannot help thinking that Mr. Winckelmann's idea of a painter is somewhat like Don Quixote's of a knight errant, as he requires he should be the very pink of perfection in all arts and sciences. In this, however, he goes farther than Cicero, who, in his pleadings for Archias, admits only of a secret relation between one liberal art and another.[30]

In ending his notice, the reviewer recognized that the translator was a foreigner, but called him "a master of his original." On the whole, the review ends favorably, seeing the treatise as but one more in the argument between the ancients and the moderns, which it is not, and rather missing the point:

> The controversy between Mr. Winkelmann and his antagonist is of a very old standing and though many writers, both English and French, have explained the theory of his principles with perhaps equal justness and precision, yet the work before us certainly tends, more than any other, hitherto published, towards a reconciliation between the two manners.[31]

Fuseli must have been disappointed and angered, as Mason suggests, by the appearance of the newspaper translation, whose author claimed to be "a friend of approved taste and literature, now resident in Rome."[32] The possibility that this "anonymous" was acquainted with Winckelmann and might have produced the translation with Winckelmann's blessing, thereby undermining his own efforts, might have been responsible for Fuseli's hesitation to correspond with Winckelmann before 1765. He nonetheless continued on the ambitious task of translating the *Geschichte* after he had accepted the job as tutor and had retired to the estate of Lord Walgrave in Essex. There, in the comparative tranquility and security of a titled household, he was working on the translation and had written Winckelmann about it, exaggerating the progress he had made. His work was interrupted, however, by a "grand tour" upon which he was to conduct the young Viscount Chewton, and which was to lead him to Paris and Lyon. The intellectual stimulation he received from finally meeting Jean-Jacques Rousseau in Paris, and the impending controversy concerning his hero's feud with David Hume was to divert Fuseli from his activities as a translator and to awaken the polemicist in him.

REFLECTIONS

ON THE

PAINTING and SCULPTURE

OF

THE GREEKS:

WITH

INSTRUCTIONS for the CONNOISSEUR,

AND

An ESSAY on GRACE in Works of Art.

Tranflated from

The *German* Original of the Abbé WINCKELMANN,
Librarian of the VATICAN, F. R. S. &c. &c.

By HENRY FUSSELI, A. M.

LONDON:
Printed for the TRANSLATOR, and Sold by A. MILLAR,
in the Strand. 1765.

Title page of Fuseli's 1765 translation of Winckelmann's *Gedanken über die Nachahmung der griechischen Werke in der Malerei und Bildhauerkunst* (1756). (From the Rare Book Collection of the Folger Shakespeare Library, Washington, D.C.)

Fuseli's Continuing Literary Activities
and the Meeting with Rousseau

In November 1765, Fuseli wrote a long letter to Salomon Dälliker, a close friend of his university days, Bodmer's former pupil, and a passionate follower of Jean-Jacques Rousseau.[1] It had been one year and eleven months since Fuseli arrived in England, and in this letter he gave a somewhat boastful report back to his Zurich friends about the progress he had made in establishing himself in the world of the titled, the famous, and the rich of London. He was employed as a tutor, the inglorious calling of many an impoverished *Stürmer und Dränger*, and he seemed anxious to forestall any rebukes on the part of his freedom-loving Swiss compatriots about his having accepted the position of *Hofmeister* to a wealthy young lord:

> *Ich bin so glücklich, von der Familie, mit der ich lebe, auf einen hohen Grad geliebt zu sein. Ich bin weder sklavisch noch anmassend, weder schnell und schimmernd noch langsam und rostig, ich habe mit Persius gelernt, den auszulachen, der sein Wissen verloren denkt, wenn er es nicht einem andern unter die Nase reiben kann. Es ist nichts, als was es ist, wenn ich sage, dass ich mit allem, was in England gross ist, an der Tafel gesessen und mehr als gelitten worden bin und werde, und ich sage, was mich nicht stolz macht, um meinen Freunden mit Umständlichkeit zu gefallen.*[2]

For six months Fuseli had been in the service of Lord Waldegrave under the terms of a cordial agreement in which the young Swiss was to receive room and board and fifteen Guineas in return for acting as the intellectual mentor for Lord Chewton. Fuseli's charge, not yet fourteen years old, was a youth to whom God had given, in Fuseli's words, *"alle Äusserlichkeiten des Lebens und ein paar Passionen...eine Seele, die aus Indolenz und Ungeduld zusammengeblasen ist...."*[3] Both parties, Fuseli assured Dälliker, were free to cancel the contract at any time—a stipulation of which Fuseli ws to make use in less than a year's time.

The Dälliker letter, written over a period of four days and surviving only in a copy made by another hand, is as important a document for the understanding of Fuseli's intellectual development as is his passionate *Klagen*. Like the earlier prose poem to Lavater, this letter of 1764 is a confession, a philosophical treatise, and an argumentative dialogue with those Fuseli had left behind. He chose Dälliker as an intermediary of messages to all whom he owed correspondence and explanations: his father, his brother, his sisters, and, of course, Lavater. Although we have no correspondence from Zurich to Fuseli for this period, it is clear from the "Dälliker Pamphlet," as Fuseli was later to call this epistle, that he felt the need to defend himself against real or imagined admonitions from home, to which he had not directly responded. His stubborn silence over the last months was based, he claimed, on the fact that he was content: *"Ich bin glücklich, so glücklich als ich in dem Mittage meines Lebens zu sein wünschete...."* Had he been depressed, he would have written elegies, he assured his correspondent, with conscious reference to the *Klagen*. He admitted that his lack of financial independence left his heart in a state of uncertainty—a remark surely intended for his father, from whom he received little support, despite Lavater's intercession on his behalf.[4] In spite of this uncertainty, he stated proudly:

> *Fluktuation ist die Essenz des Lebens, und ob ich gleich von meinen andern Freunden hier gescholten und ausgelacht werde, jenes, weil ich nicht schreibe, dieses, weil ich meine Situation für ungewiss halte, ob ich gleich verschiedne Male daran gearbeitet habe, meinen Freunden Freude zu machen, so finde ich doch, dass mein Herz zum Zweifeln geboren ist und von den Affairen dieses Lebens, denen wenigstens, die zum Teile unter den Zepter der Opinion, der Mode, des Interesses gehören, hier niemals so positive sprechen wird, als es tun mag, wenn die Urne gefüllt ist und die Wirklichkeit anhebt.[5]*

His months of trial in a foreign land had given him a better opinion of himself. He had the opportunity to test his mettle. *"Niedrigkeit, Gleichgültigkeit, und wo nicht Polararmut, doch auch nicht Überfluss"* are circumstances which had the effect of strengthening his pride and independence. His determination not to bend to *"Reichtums mästende Hand"* was more instructive to him than his having memorized the whole system of Wolffian morality *"in Folio und Latein."* In the middle of this defensive treatise, Fuseli interrupted himself with an exclamation evoking the author of Tristram Shandy, whose style he imitated throughout the letter: *"Bei der Feder Sternes! Hier beginnt mein zwölftes Blatt, und noch kein Wort von Klopstock, Rousseau, Winckelmann!"*[6]

Klopstock, Rousseau, Winckelmann were the three figures foremost on Fuseli's mind at this time: Klopstock, because he was corresponding with Fuseli and had recently sent him the new verses of his continuing Miltonic epic, *Der Messias*, with the request that Fuseli furnish the illustrations for the poem; Winckelmann, because of Fuseli's ongoing project of translating the *Geschichte der Kunst*; and Rousseau, because at this time his hero was at the center of growing controversy. In October 1765, a month before the Dälliker letter, Rousseau had been once again banned from the city of Geneva for his criticisms of political conditions there and his questioning of traditional Christian dogma in his *Lettres de la Montagne*. Fuseli wrote indignantly of the shredding and burning of Rousseau's books by the citizens of Geneva:

> *Von Rousseau seit seiner Affaire mit der Genfer Canaille und den Lettres de la montagne höre ich gleichfalls nichts als zuweilen, dass er hieher zu kommen gedenkt, dass er auf einer Insel in Bielersee lebt und sich einem Hunde vergleicht. In mein entzücktes Auge strahlt er ohne Flecken; wenn die Güte einer Handlung oder die Bekanntmachung einer Wahrheit von dem Erfolge zu beurteilen ist, so bin ich mit dir einig, dass Rousseau besser getan hätte, einige seiner Sätze, obgleich demonstriert, für sich zu behalten.[7]*

The cynical attitude about the fate of truth-bringers, which Fuseli expressed in the last sentence of this excerpt foreshadows the polemical irony with which he would view the vicissitudes of the hounded Rousseau after his ill-fated sojourn in England. The more the establishment turned against his hero, the more fervently Fuseli was to defend him.

It is clear from the evidence of this letter that Fuseli, despite his successes in London, still longed for Switzerland and that he had not completely severed his emotional ties with Zurich. He begged for news of home and friends and assured Dälliker, with a characteristically earthy metaphor, that relaying such reports might do both parties a service: *"Nachrichten von diesem allem zu geben dir eine Purganz und mir ein Klistier ersparen mag."*[8] Referring to the trip he was to take to Paris with his young charge within a few months, Fuseli wrote that he planned to stay in Paris *"für wenigstens ein paar Jahre,...diesen Weg, verschiednen Menschen und vielleicht meinem Vaterlande wieder nützlich zu sein...."*[9] Fuseli still spoke of Switzerland as his home, and he still considered himself obligated to carry out the mission entrusted to him by Bodmer and Sulzer, whom he continued to supply with news of English literary activities and shipments of books. It is therefore surprising that in this same letter he stated that since he had been in England, German literature had ceased to exist for him: *"Seitdem ich in England bin, ist die deutsche Literatur für mich gestorben."*[10] This statement must not be taken out of context of what Fuseli was reading and writing at the time. It does not mean that he had given up any pretensions of a literary career in the German language. It does mean that he had been disappointed by the latest writings of the poet upon whom Bodmer and his circle had placed the hope of a great German literature: Klopstock.

Fuseli's enthusiasm for Klopstock had begun to be tempered by what he had read of the new verses of *Der Messias*. As a poet, Klopstock remained for him the "giant of the century" surpassing in his odes all poets ancient and modern.[11] Yet Fuseli had sent the drawings which Klopstock requested to Germany without so much as an accompanying note of praise or criticism. It was the religious tone of the epic that now repelled him. Klopstock had set out in his epic in the manner of Homer, Fuseli wrote, but now his verses were characterized by:

> eine Religion—die absurdeste aller Religionen, ein quintessenziertes Schulgeschwätz, die Hofsprache des Pietistenhimmels, das Galimathias eines in apokalyptischen Weinen besoffenen Gehirns, Blasenkläpfe [sic], die mehr nicht meinen als Platzen, haben die marmorne Pyramide mit Pappe, Zuckerpapier und dem Farbengemische der Garderobe ausgelegt.[12]

Fuseli's argument with Klopstock's religion heralds his lifelong objection to piety and moralism in art, and would be repeated in disagreements with his beloved Lavater about matters of the spirit. Only the strong admiration for Klopstock's mastery of the ode prevented Fuseli from rejecting him as an artist. In March 1768 he would write to Lavater: *"Um Klopstock kümmere ich mich wenig, wär er ein Heide, ich würde."*[13] Although that statement might have been calculated as much to shock Lavater as to describe his attitude toward Klopstock, Fuseli's notion of *"Religionen"* in the organized sense was consistently negative and any apology for religious moralism conflicted with the task of the artist. Fuseli was no more an atheist than was Rousseau, whose good Savoyard priest professed a faith not at all at odds with the sentimental protestant theology that Fuseli had learned in Zurich and Berlin. Spalding, Sulzer, and Bodmer, in their efforts to reform society saw themselves as a sort of advance party which could wander far from the official communion without ever having left Christianity. Klopstock's sin in Fuseli's eyes was not that he was religious, but that he had reduced God, nature, and the sublime to Sunday school piety:

> Dass Homer seinen Zeus zum Könige, Milton Jehova zum Schulmeister, Klopstock den Vater zum Kläger, Inquisitor und Richter erniedrigt, ärgert mich nicht. Die Imagination unterliegt [erliegt] der Unendlichkeit, und was immer ein Sünder wie Warburton schnufeln mag, es ist weder in Homer, Virgil, noch Milton, wo wir die Moral, Politik und Religion zu lernen haben. Vergnüge die Imagination, male die Menschen, wie sie sind, und die Götter wie du kannst, scheint das allgemeinste epische Gesetz zu sein. Aber die Religion zu fassen, um die Natur zu lähmen und, wenn man Engelszungen, jeden Flug der Einbildung, jedes männliche oder zärtliche Gefühl, jedes erhabne Bild, die Donner des Griechen, die Überredung des Römers, die Farben der Natur hat, sie mit dem mystischen Sistrum der Schelle Cramers, dem Lippengelecke eines Pariser Abts, einem mahometischen Houris-Gejucke der Terra Australis-Sprache— ἑκατόμβοι ἐννεα—vertauschen, macht mich den Dichter, wär er nicht Klopstock, verachten.[14]

Fuseli's indignation about the treatment of Rousseau in Geneva reinforced his already fervent anticlerical bent. The officials who condemned Rousseau were, in Fuseli's words, "*Despoten*" who should have read what he had written before they attacked him. He spoke sarcastically of the pious rationalists like Gilbert West[15] who would prove that the resurrection and biblical miracles are demonstrable through science, and, taking the pose of Dälliker, or one responding to his letter, Fuseli interrupted himself: "*Aber welche ist denn _deine_ Religion wirst du zuletzt fragen—*" Fuseli responded to this question with two excerpts from his own poem, "*Ode an die Geduld*," which was to be published in 1766 in Switzerland: "*Wähn nicht, Roms Furie, der von der Höll umleckt das blutbespritzte Haupt himmelanschwillt; nicht die Luthern zanken lehrte, Calvins hektische Theosophistin, wähn nicht—*" "*Ich bin ein Christ*" he interrupted his ode to say, and "*dich, mein Dälliker, denk ich einen, ob du gleich*":

> der blinden Schule wurmzernagten Quark
> Theologie verstehst und Sack und Clemme,
> die nach der Pfeife riechen; ob du gleich
> die Raserei hast, wider Rousseau auch
> Sophismen auszuhenken; ob dein Beil
> gleich blinkt, dir Glaub aus Eichenholz zu haun.[16]

Such long passages from his own poetry lace the correspondence of this period. Far from having deserted the German language, Fuseli continued to write poetry in his native tongue until his very old age. He had four odes in the manner of Klopstock published before he left Zurich in 1760. In 1764 he sent Lavater his "*Ode an Herrn-Professor Bodmer.*" It was published the same year in a periodical entitled *Vollständige und kritische Nachrichten von den besten Schriften unsrer Zeit*. The "*Ode an die Geduld*," included in part in the Dälliker letter, was published through Lavater's efforts in the same periodical in 1766. Two other poems written between 1765 and 1770 were published through Lavater in *Schweizerische Blumenlese*.[17]

Recent studies of unpublished manuscripts have revealed editing and rewriting of poems and variant versions that indicate Fuseli was preparing poems for publication as late as 1813.[18] In 1765 and again in 1766 he mentioned to friends in Switzerland that he was considering publishing his odes in monograph form in Leipzig. It was not until 1973, however, that Martin Bircher and Karl S. Guthke published the complete extant poetry of Henry Fuseli.[19] These poems represent a life's work and not the random jottings of a dilettante. Fuseli's poetry is evidence that he never gave up literary ambitions and that German remained the medium in which he expressed his deepest feelings. This poetic activity was unknown to his English friend and biographer Knowles, who mentioned no poetry in German, although he quoted Fuseli as having said: "I always think in the language in which I write, and it is a matter of indifference to me whether it be English, French, or Italian; I know each equally well; but if I wish to express myself with power it must be in German."[20] Fuseli's reputation in Germany, largely fostered by Lavater whose practice it was to circulate his more interesting letters, was that of *"Poet und Maler," "Dichtermaler," and "Dichter und Maler zugleich."*[21]

It is the Dälliker letter which gives the fullest picture of Fuseli's interests and intentions on the eve of his departure for France. It is a letter, as he himself boasted, which was worth a half a dozen ordinary letters. Dälliker's reply, Fuseli wrote, should be sent to Lord Waldegrave's address in London, from whence it could be forwarded to Fuseli's French address. For the first time, he revealed his new, Anglicised name to his Swiss friends:

> *Wenn du mir schreibest, da ich dir meine französische*
> *Adresse noch nicht geben kann, so muss dein äussers*
> *Couvert sein*
> > To the right honourable
> > John, Earl of Waldegrave
> > Saville-row
> > London
> *In dieses musst du ein anderes schliessen*
> > To Mr. Fusseli

> *Dieses wird zu Handen kommen deinem ewig treuen*
> > *Füsseli*[22]

As chance would have it, "Mr. Fusseli" and Jean-Jacques Rousseau arrived in Paris about the same time in November 1765. After some hesitation, Rousseau had come to Paris to join David Hume, who was just finishing a diplomatic assignment there. Rousseau was to accompany Hume on the trip back to England.[23] Sometime between December 1765 and January 1766 the meeting between Rousseau and his young countryman was to take place, in the company of David Hume. The only record of the meeting is found in Fuseli's letter to Bodmer, written from Lyon about six months later. Fuseli's assessment of the probable outcome of Rousseau's London trip was gloomy, it would be his ruin, Fuseli wrote in his letter to his mentor:

Der Philosoph wie der Theolog, der Kaufmann, der Magistrat müssen ihn par principe hassen...ich war für ein Paar Stunden so selig mit ihm, als man sein kann, ich sah ihn in Paris mit Hume, den er nach England begleitete. In England wird er der Ruhe geniessen können, der er zulechzt. Denn er kann da nicht tätig sein, welches sein Verderben sein würde, denn England ist keiner Verbesserung fähig, wenn es nicht durch eine Revolution geschehen soll, die nach Rousseaus eigener Meinung wenigstens so sehr zu fürchten als zu wünschen ist.[24]

Fuseli was to remain eight more months in Lyon, where he finally gave his young lord a box in the ear and sent him home. He himself wrestled during this time with a severe illness which left him with white hair and a permanent trembling of the hands. The real controversy between Hume and Rousseau, the public airing of polemic letters, the mischief of Voltaire and Walpole, the eccentric and paranoid behavior of Rousseau toward his English hosts, was thus being played out while Fuseli was ill in Lyon. By the time he returned to England the affair had climaxed and ebbed.

History and Fortune of Fuseli's
Remarks on the Conduct and Writings of J.J. Rousseau

In 1962, the *Schweizerisches Institut für Kunstwissenschaft* in Zurich published a reprint of Fuseli's very rare, anonymous pamphlet, *Remarks on the Writings and Conduct of J.J. Rousseau* (1767), under the editorship of Eudo C. Mason.[1] In addition to annotating the *Remarks,* Mason performed the amazing linguistic feat of rendering Fuseli's original, "not quite English" style back into the artist's native German: *Bemerkungen über J.J. Rousseaus Schriften und Verhalten.*[2] In his long introduction to the original text and his translated version, Mason gives an exhaustive history of the work and its fortune in England and Germany. He has corrected several misconceptions concerning the work, including the story reported by Cunningham (1829) that the project was undertaken at the suggestion of a fellow member of the Johnson circle: John Bonnycastle, the mathematician.[3] In fact, Mason's conclusion is that there is no documented evidence concerning the immediate occasion for the pamphlet, except that which may be deduced from Fuseli's letters and his associations during the period in which he wrote it.

The very nature and tone of the *Remarks* militate against its having been commissioned by any group or faction. Very similar in style and expression to the Dälliker letter, Fuseli's *Remarks* is his own personal apologia and analysis of Rousseau's thought and behavior. He did not attack Hume as the evil party responsible for Rousseau's unhappy stay in England, which he had seen doomed at the outset. If there is a villain in the piece, it is Voltaire: "that threadworn withered bastard of Fancy, that proud lesson of humility...."[4] Voltaire's enmity towards Rousseau, which dated back to the publication of the second *Discourse* (1755), was seen by Fuseli as having its origins in the jealousy of the elder philosopher of the young Genevan's genius and Rousseau's refusal to play the lackey to Voltaire: "From such an impertinent refusal of vassalage, Rousseau, 'tis most likely forfeited his favour."[5] Fuseli attributed the troubles between Hume and Rousseau to differences in temperament and misunderstanding, and correctly sensed the hand of the vitriolic old *philosophe* in the most "smashing vilification" of Rousseau that appeared in the *St. James' Chronicle* in April 1766: "*Lettre de M. de Voltaire au docteur Jean-Jacques Pansophe.*"[6] This juxtaposition of Voltaire and Rousseau reflects feelings that Fuseli had carried with him since his Zurich days: the conflict between the spirit of the Enlightenment and the new sensibility, which, as Mason says, would find its highest manifestation in *Wer-*

ther and *Urfaust* in less than ten years' time.[7] This is Rousseau in Swiss-German, *Sturm und Drang* perspective, and therefore it seems most likely that Fuseli's pamphlet was entirely his own idea and that it was he who approached Johnson, Cadell and Payne with the project.[8]

It is in keeping with the reputation of the liberal publisher Johnson that he would have undertaken the publication of Fuseli's first original English publication. He was most generous in aiding fledgling authors of republican persuasion and was to perform a similar "favor" for William Blake twenty-four years later, when—perhaps with support from Fuseli—he published the proofs of Blake's *The French Revolution.*[9] Johnson was, in the words of one of his biographers, "a very sympathetic and generous man, often purchasing manuscripts of persons in distress, which he had no intention of publishing."[10] Fuseli had other friends to support his cause, especially in Armstrong, the didactic poet whom he had described to Bodmer in 1766 as England's *"einziger Poet."*[11] Fuseli includes passages from two of Armstrong's poems in the *Remarks,* and Armstrong is the author of one of the three extant favorable reviews of the pamphlet (*Monthly Review,* 1767).[12] Of the other two, one is by Fuseli himself (*Critical Review,* May 1767), and the other is by John Payne, who as Johnson's partner was joint publisher of the *Remarks* and who wrote the review in the journal of which he was the editor, *The Universal Museum,* in April 1767.[13] It is also of significance in this connection that Armstrong was a trusted friend of David Hume and, as such, would have had access to all details of the Rousseau-Hume affair. Millar, who had published Fuseli's Winckelmann translation, had been Hume's publisher up until 1767, when he gave his business over to Thomas Cadell. Fuseli was close to Millar, who had given him "constant employment" as a reader and ghost editor since his arrival in England.[14] Mason is convinced that Fuseli's knowledge of Hume's controversial *Essay on Suicide,* which he alludes to in the *Remarks,* was the result of indiscretion on the part of Millar. Hume himself suppressed the work; and it was not published in England until 1777, a year after the philosopher's death.[15]

What we do know of Fuseli's feelings and circumstances in 1767 tells us that his own intellectual perspective, his meeting with Rousseau, his friendship with Armstrong, and his association with Johnson, Millar, and Payne provided him with the motivation, the information, and the means to join the ranks of defenders of Rousseau in the English press. But the *Remarks* is more than a defense. It is the first attempt in the English language to write a comprehensive overview of Rousseau's philosophy up to 1767. Despite its lack of success in England, the pamphlet demonstrates a remarkable critical ability as well as a keen insight into the psychology of the problematic Rousseau, which makes it valuable to modern scholarship.[16]

Here, it is useful to list the works of Rousseau which Fuseli specifically quoted, paraphrased, or analyzed in his *Remarks:*

Le Premier Discours: Si le rétalissement des sciences et des arts a contribué a épurer le moeurs, Geneva, 1750

Lettre sur la Musique Française, 1753

Le Devin du Village, 1755

Economie politique, 1755

Le Second Discours: Sur l'origine et les fondements de l'inégalité parmi les hommes,
1755
Lettre à M. D'Alembert, 1758
Extrait du Projet de Paix Perpetuelle de l'abbé de Saint-Pierre, 1761
Emile, 1761
La Nouvelle Héloise, 1761
Du Contrat Social, 1762
Lettre à M. de Beaumont, 1763
Lettres de la Montagne, 1764

In addition to these major works, Fuseli showed himself to be familiar with most of the letters that were published by both sides of the Rousseau-Hume affair in the English and French presses. He had in his possession a mysterious "M.S. on Rousseau," from which he quoted eight times in the *Remarks.* No such manuscript is extant, and its origin and nature are uncertain. Mason hypothesizes on the basis of the inaccuracy of the French in the "manuscript," that it might have been a transcription of Fuseli's own conversations with Rousseau or those of some other non-French-speaking admirer.[17]

The pamphlet is divided into ten chapters with a preface:

Chapter	I	On the INFLUENCE of the SCIENCES and ARTS on MANNERS
Chapter	II	On the origin of INEQUALITY among MANKIND, and if the law of NATURE authorises it
Chapter	III	EMILE, or on EDUCATION
Chapter	IV	HELOISE
Chapter	V	ON THE ESTABLISHMENT OF A THEATRE AT GENEVA: TO MR. D'ALEMBERT
Chapter	VI	POLITICKS
Chapter	VII	ON FRENCH MUSICK
Chapter	VIII	(The last three chapters are untitled
Chapter	IX	and deal with Rousseau's personality
Chapter	X	and his quarrel with Hume.)

The edition of Rousseau's works from which Fuseli quotes is a sixteen-volume octavo edition of 1764, published in Neuchatel.[18]

As far as Voltaire's role in Rousseau's career is concerned, Fuseli demonstrates that he is acquainted not only with the notorious "Pansophe" attack, but with almost everything that had been published by or about either party concerning their feud. Among the major works of Voltaire to which Fuseli alludes in the *Remarks* are:

Zaïre, 1732
Essai sur le Moeurs, 1737
Mahomet, 1742
Semiramis, 1748
La Pucelle, 1755
Candide, 1758
Observations sur le Jules César de Shakespeare, 176?
Poème sur le Désastre de Lisbonne, 1755/56

Quatre Lettres sur la Nouvelle Héloïse a M. Voltaire, 1761
Dictionaire Philosophique, 1764
Questions sur les Miracles, 1765
Lettre de M. Voltaire au Docteur Pansophe, 1766

Indeed, the very extent of Fuseli's erudition and his eagerness to display it add to the difficulty of reading his treatise. The hundred footnotes which accompany the text, which are as original and diverting as the body of the work itself, often are long and rambling digressions that, however interesting and clever they may be, are only tangentially related to the matter at hand. In the *Remarks* Fuseli's mind ranged from the poetry of Horace to the inequity of the Stamp Act levied against the American colonies. It is clear that by this virtuoso performance he was hoping to catch the attention of the intelligentsia of London and to establish his reputation as a satirist and wit.

Fuseli did have reason to assume a rather wide knowledge of the works of Rousseau in London intellectual circles. The works of the Swiss author were available in London in French editions almost immediately upon their publication in Amsterdam or Geneva.[19] English translations became available immediately or within a few years of the French originals. Fuseli cannot have been unaware of the publication of William Kendrick's *Miscellaneous Works of Rousseau,* which was published in 1767 by Thomas Becket. A publisher with connections to the Amsterdam book trade, Becket was a friend and former apprentice of Andrew Millar.[20] Kendrick, an eccentric follower of Sterne and Young, had been translating Rousseau's works since 1762, when he made his reputation as the translator of *Eloisa.*[21] The *Miscellaneous Works of Rousseau* contained all the major works to which Fuseli makes reference in his *Remarks.*[22] The controversy created by Rousseau's quarrel with Hume had created great interest in the works and personality of Rousseau, and was no doubt responsible for Becket's decision to bring together all of the writings translated by Kendrick in the ambitious five-volume edition.

With this favorable climate for matters concerning Rousseau, the almost legendary failure of Fuseli's pamphlet in his day is all the more striking. For, like the Winckelmann translation written two years previously, the *Remarks* was roundly rejected by hostile reviewers. Aside from the critiques written by Fuseli and his friends to promote the work, no one seems to have had any good word for the pamphlet. *The Gentleman's Magazine* of June 1767 carried a review signed "X," which opened with the following assessment: "This is one of the dullest and yet the most extravagant rhapsodies that ever appeared: It is neither praise nor censure, narrative nor argument, and answering the definition of nonsense, it is neither true nor false."[23] The reviewer had no further critical comment, but offered as proof of his condemnation eight random paragraphs, quoted out of context. *The Scotts Magazine* of Edinburgh gave a similar assessment in April 1767 and May of the same year. *The Political Register and Impartial Review of New Books* failed to find any saving grace in the little pamphlet:[24]

...the style is extremely vulgar in many parts, devoid of every drop of humour which might give it relish; and sometimes libertine without one spark of wit to give it lustre; in fact, the

subject which this production pretends to treat, is not understood; it is one of those productions which speak of the decline of literature in this age; it deserves not to be read in
the present, and will never be read in the future.[25]

If, as Knowles and Cunningham both reported, Fuseli was loath to
acknowledge authorship of the *Remarks* in later life, it was because of such
resounding critical rejection of a work into which he had poured so much of
his heart. Knowles based Fuseli's later denial of the work on two explanations, neither of which is quite convincing: the intemperate language of the
Remarks and Fuseli's disillusionment with Rousseau. Knowles wrote: "there
are in several instances a coarseness in language and indelicacies of expression which disfigure the pages of the book," suggesting that Fuseli was
ashamed of his verbal indiscretions.[26] This simply does not correspond to
what we know from the witness of several contemporaries who describe
Fuseli as a prodigious swearer, even as an old man. One of the most
humorous of these accounts also concerns William Blake and tells of a conversation that took place between Flaxman and Blake sometime after 1794:

> Flaxman had complained of Fuseli's foul language and asked what Blake did when Fuseli
> swore. "What do I do?" asked Blake. "Why I swear again!" and he says, astonished, 'Vy,
> Blake, you are svaring!' but he leaves off himself."[27]

Cunningham, writing four years after Fuseli's death, spoke not only of
Fuseli's love for obscenity and his boast that he could vent his rage in nine
languages, but also of his wild literary style:

> Fuseli seldom thought with sober feelings upon either art or literature, and he delighted
> to invest the objects of his love with the brightness of heaven—those of his hate with the
> hues of utter darkness. He poured his admiration in words which he wished to thunder
> and lighten; his irony stung like an adder, and his sarcasm cut like a two-edged sword.[28]

As for his disappointment in his former hero, one might logically expect
the attitude of a fifty-four-year-old man to have altered from views that he
held when he was twenty-six. Knowles did not meet Fuseli until 1805. By that
time Fuseli's attitude toward Rousseau and revolution would have been
tempered, like Blake's attitude in the same period, by the horrors of the post-
revolutionary events. But Fuseli was still an ardent republican and
Rousseauist as late as 1792, when he, Mary Wollstonecraft, and Joseph
Johnson planned a trip to France, to see for themselves the excitement of
the events with which they sympathized at that time.[29] It is much more in
keeping with what is known of Fuseli's character that he found reference to
the Rousseau pamphlet painful because it was a blow to his considerable
ego that it had been so poorly received, and exactly because his friends and
publishers were in on the "secret" of the authorship. The secret was, in fact,
no secret at all, for mention of it occurs in almost every contemporary account of Fuseli's life and activities. Knowles possessed a copy of it which he
read sometime between 1805 and the 1830s, and it must be assumed that
reports that the whole impression of the work went up in flames when fire
destroyed Johnson's apartment were exaggerated.

Both Cunningham and Knowles gave the impression that the fire, in which
Fuseli lost so much, took place immediately after the publication of the

Remarks. Cunningham's account was satirical, lending further credence to the theory that the work was widely read among members of Fuseli's circle:

> The enthusiasm of his hatred or love enabled him to compose his Essay with uncommon rapidity, and he printed it forthwith, with the hope that it would fly abroad to exalt Rousseau, and confound Voltaire. "It had," said one of his friends, "a short life and a bright ending." The whole impression caught fire, and either angry philosopher lived and died in ignorance whether the future professor of painting in England was his friend or his enemy.[30]

Knowles's account is brief:

> This work seems rarely to be met with, as the greater part of the impression was destroyed shortly after it was printed, by an accidental fire which took place in Mr. Johnson's house, who then resided in Paternoster Row.[31]

We know that the fire did not occur, in fact, until three years later in 1770. The pamphlet is invaluable in determining Fuseli's philosophical, political, and theological attitudes, which he became less and less willing to divulge publicly, but which, in some respects, he never altered.

There is no way of knowing whether it was Fuseli or his publishers who took the precaution of publishing the *Remarks* anonymously. In any case, anonymous pamphlets were the order of the day. Fuseli confided his authorship of the work to Bodmer as early as June 1767, when he proudly sent his former teacher the engraving from the title page and several chapters of the *Remarks*:

> To Mr. Bodmer, professor of national history & grand council of Zurich
> London 10 June 1767
> *Ich sende Ihnen hier ein paar Capiteln und das Titelblatt meiner* Remarks on the Writings and Conduct of J.J. Rousseau. *Dass sie meine sind, sage ich izo nur noch Ihnen. Hier waren sie Sternes, Smollets,Armstrongs.*[32]

Curiously, there is no mention of the *Remarks* in Fuseli's extant correspondence with Lavater, but it is certain that the work was known by Lavater and his circle. Four years after the publication of the work, Herder quoted four pages of the *Remarks* in a letter to Merck, and in 1773 he wrote to Lavater: *"Und ebenso bitt ich mir doch angelegentlichst Nachrichten von dem Füssli aus...(der* Essay on Rousseau *soll, glaub ich, auch von ihm sein)...."* Herder assured Lavater that he would be most grateful for any other of Fuseli's writings. Herder had received a copy of the *Remarks* in a package of books from England in 1771—another proof that not all copies went up in flames the year before. As early as the year of publication, Hamann had obtained a copy of the *Remarks* and had reviewed the work in three consecutive numbers of the *Königsberger Gelehrten und Politischen Zeitung auf das Jahr 1767.* He mistook Sterne for the author also.[33] Recent German scholarship has assigned an important place to Fuseli's *Remarks* in the history of the reception and reputation of Rousseau in Germany, where it was more favorably received than in England. How much of Herder's and Hamann's interest in the work rested upon the impression that it was the work of Sterne is hard to assess. As Mason and Antal have shown, there is really not much resemblance between Fuseli's style and that of Sterne. It is Fuseli himself who first suggested the analogy of his own review of the work, by denying that there is such a resemblance: "The Remarker [sic] has been said to be a copy, in great measure, of the inimitable Tristam [sic]; tho' we must own, that in one or two places excepted, we cannot find out the resemblance...."[34] Armstrong continued the suggestion in his review a month later: "His manner is somewhat of the SHANDYAN stamp, which is not remarkable for delicacy; but there are many strokes of genius and humour in his remarks, which may atone, in some measure, for any want of judgment and propriety in the writer."[35] It is interesting to note that none of the negative reviewers noted any resemblance between Fuseli's style and that of Sterne. It is probable that Fuseli and Armstrong planted the rumor of Sterne's authorship to enhance the sale of the book and to attract more attention to it.[36] Four days after the publication of the *Remarks*, Hume wrote to Davenport, who had been Rousseau's host in England:

Have you seen a little book, published within these few days, being an account of Rousseau's writings and conduct? It is a high panegyric on him; but without attempting to throw blame on me: on the contrary, it owns he is in the wrong in his quarrel with me. It is said to be the work of Dr. Sterne; but it exceeds even the usual extravagance of that gentleman's productions.[37]

Hume, with his close ties to Millar and Cadell, was soon able to identify the author, at least approximately. A few weeks later he wrote to Blair: "The Pamphlet you mention was wrote by one as mad as himself [Rousseau], and it was believed at first to be Tristram Shandy, but proves to be one Fuseli, an Engraver."[38] So it was that Fuseli's ambitious publication was dismissed even by the English half of the Hume-Rousseau debacle as the panegyric of a "mad engraver." Despite all the efforts of Fuseli and his friends, it was neither as a satirist nor as a journalist that he would achieve the acclaim he was seeking in London.

The Remarks on the Conduct and Writings of J.J. Rousseau remains Fuseli's most sincere, if also most caustic, philosophical statement. Never again will he be so honest in print, will he give full vent to his own personal loves, hatreds, and prejudices in the printed word. The expression of immediate, bold and spontaneous strokes of genius will henceforth be confined to his sketchbooks and canvasses or conversations calculated to outrage his listener. His later lectures and writings on art were to be written with an increasing awareness of the dignity expected of a professor of painting and Keeper of the Royal Academy. When he adapted Lavater's *Unphysiognomische Regeln* and wrote his own *Aphorisms on Art* in the late 1780s, he hid his own thoughts behind the name of the gentle Lavater, or couched them in the relatively objective form of the aphorism. But the Fuseli of the *Remarks* is the Fuseli known and cherished by Blake:

The only Man that I e'er knew
Who did not make me almost spew
Was Fuseli: he was both Turk & Jew—
And so, [sweet del.] dear Christian Friends, how
    do you do? (K551)

Fuseli showed himself to be both "Turk" and "Jew" in contrast to the "dear Christian Friends," of whom Blake had several, nowhere more clearly than in the devilish tone of the *Remarks*.

48

The picture which Fuseli designed for the title page of the booklet shows
Voltaire at the foot of a gallows from which the figures of Freedom and
Justice are hanging. Wearing a wig, Voltaire is seated upon the naked figure
of a wild man, who is crawling on all fours and eating grass. Voltaire digs his
spurs into the side of the savage and carries a whip. Off to the side, next to
an ivy-covered wall, Rousseau is depicted in his Armenian costume. From
his left hand is suspended a plumb line, symbolizing truth. With his right
hand he points to the activity of the *philosophe*. In his vicious letter ridicul-
ing Rousseau in the English press, "*Lettre de M. de V. au Docteur
Pansophe*," Voltaire parodied Rousseau's "return to nature" thesis by suggesting that the citizens of London should commune with nature by eating
the grass in Hyde Park.[39]

Frontispiece of Fuseli's *Remarks*, designed by Fuseli and
engraved by Charles Grignion. (By permission of the British
Library)

Frontispiece to Vol. III.

Cochin.

Orpheus.

Frontispiece of William Kendrick's translation of *Emile*. Fuseli must have been aware of this translation, published by Becket and de Hondt. Becket was a former apprentice of Millar. There is a crawling figure (eating grass?), which is almost identical to the crawling savage in Fuseli's design for the *Remarks*. (Library of Congress, Washington, D.C.)

Fuseli's Correspondence with Lavater from Italy
and his Interest in Lavater's Work

From Fuseli's letters to Lavater in 1769 we know that he had finally decided to make a career as an artist and that he was planning a trip to Italy to study. He promised Lavater in a letter of 24 August 1769 that he would be in Switzerland by September for a stay on his way to Rome.[1] This same letter is full of requests that Lavater obtain monetary support for the planned stay. Fuseli described his distaste at having to live off *"fremde Generosität"* and wrote that the burden of his obligations was so great that it had even driven him to thoughts of suicide.[2] He did not seem to have gotten any support from his family in Zurich, who were forever admonishing him with charges of irresponsibility and who, it would seem, did not lend much credence to his grandiose plans. In June of 1769 he protested to Lavater:

> *...wer mir nicht trauet, mag sich hier in England bei Sir Joshua Reynolds, Moser von Schaffhausen, itzt Keeper of the Royal Academy, Dr. Armstrong und, wenn ihr nötig habt, von zwanzig Andern, die ich euch nicht nennen will, erkundigen.*[3]

Nonetheless, in the fall of 1769, Fuseli still planned a stay in Zurich, and asked that his friend find him a quiet, simple lodging in his native city and in Lavater's neighborhood, where he could paint and sketch in peace for a while before his sojourn to Italy.[4] Fuseli's plans were drastically altered, however, by the fire in Johnson's apartments at the beginning of 1770. Lost in the flames were whatever work Fuseli had completed in translating Winckelmann's *Geschichte der Kunst des Altertums*; all of the Winckelmann letters which Fuseli's father had given him; all of his books, paintings, and sketches; two bank notes; fifty pounds sterling; a *Geschichte der Deutschen Literatur*, which had not been completed; and seven larger-than-life sketches of the Apostles and Saints, which he was preparing as designs for stained glass windows for the Ely Cathedral.[5]

After the disaster which left him with only *"den Rock und die Hosen, die ich anhatte,"* Fuseli gave up hope of getting help from Zurich and gave himself over completely to the generosity of Coutts, the wealthy banker who was to become his patron as long as he lived.[6] With the commissions he earned by painting three large historical paintings for Coutts, he was able to buy some clothes, settle his debts, and embark for a trip to Italy in the company of his good friend, Armstrong. His first letters to Lavater from Rome are again charged with bitterness against Fuseli's father and his brother; and, again, he protests against real or imagined disbelief that the fire really happened:

Du willst Verifizierung des Brandes haben; schreib nach London an Herrn Peyer von Schaffhausen, der nahe beim Brande in Paternoster Row lebet, oder an Herrn Moser in Craven Street, Drury Lane, und frage sie, ob nicht Johnsons Haus und was ich darin hatte abgebrannt![7]

Fuseli's bitterness against his father and his brother is ingrained in his attitude from this time on. He became more and more independent of Zurich and considered himself for the first time to be a painter. Fuseli's correspondence with Lavater for the eight years that he was in Italy is sketchy. Of the extant correspondence from Fuseli to Lavater, we have: 1770, four letters; 1771, one letter; 1773, two letters; 1774, two letters; 1775, one letter; 1777, one letter; and 1778, one letter. Lavater was, as ever, Fuseli's enthusiastic admirer; and he fully approved of his friend's daring choice to follow his own genius. Lavater's description of his friend in a letter to Herder in November 1773 gives the feeling of his enthusiasm and love for Fuseli:

Füssli in Rom ist eine der grössten Imaginationen. Er ist in allem Extrem—immer Original; Shakespeares Maler—nichts als Engländer und Zürcher, Poet und Maler....Einmal send' ich Dir seine originalen Briefe—Windsturm und Ungewitter.—Reynolds weissagt ihn zum grössten Maler seiner Zeit. Er verachtet alles. Er hat mich, der Erste, mit Klopstock bekannt gemacht. Sein Witz ist grenzenlos. Er handelt wenig, ohne Bleistift und Pinsel—aber wenn er handelt, so muss er hundert Schritte Raum haben, sonst würd' er alles zertreten. Alle griechischen, lateinischen und englischen Poeten hat er verschlungen. Sein Blick ist Blitz, sein Wort ein Wetter—sein Scherz Tod und seine Rache Hölle.[8]

It is clear that by 1773, when both Lavater and Fuseli were thirty-three years old, each had found himself, and that each would become absorbed in his own career: Fuseli as a painter, and Lavater as shepherd of Christ, minister of the afflicted, and, above all, *Menschenkenner*. It is in this last endeavor that Lavater was to become famous on the Continent, in England, and in America. During the early years that Fuseli was in Rome, Lavater was beginning his physiognomical studies that would lead to the publication of his *Physiognomische Fragmente*, the first three volumes of which appeared in 1775 in Germany. Although Lavater asked Fuseli for pictures to illustrate his *Fragmente*, the two argued over details. *"Warum soll ich dir aber Zeichnungen von Dingen schicken, die mich nicht rühren? Ich habe Versuche gemachet und weiss, dass sie dir nicht gefallen würden."*[9] Thus Fuseli replies to Lavater's repeated requests, especially for a head of Christ, which for Lavater would be the supreme human physiognomy. *"Es ist eben so unmöglich, Jesus Christus für einen Christen zu malen, als Gott für seinen Anbeter; Raphael und Michelangelo haben beides und mit Menschenwürde getan—Moses aber hat ihm doch besser nachgesehen."*[10] Lavater's perpetual search for the perfect *Christuskopf* was never rewarded to his satisfaction.[11] Lavater's biggest mistake in dealing with Fuseli, as Fuseli himself wrote him in 1771, was that he had preformed conceptions with which he tried to influence Fuseli's choice of subject:

Wisse, dass Invention die Seele des Malers und ein Maler ohne sie auf der Schuhmacherzunft ist.
Deine und meine Imagination mögen dieselbe sein;

Framingham State College
Framingham, Massachusetts

*aber um ihre Bilder auszuführen, muss sie in meinem
und nicht in deinem Kopfe aufflamen.*[12]

The result of their bickering was that Fuseli's work appeared only in the
fourth volume of the German edition, and then was represented only by one
picture.[13] When Fuseli first read the *Fragmente*, which he obtained in 1777,
he had much praise for Lavater and his work. Aside from a few
"*Kleinigkeiten*," Fuseli wrote Lavater that his work in the *Fragmente* was,
like Lavater himself, worthy of eternity. With his usual incisive critical sense,
Fuseli wrote Lavater:

> —*und wenn du nichts geschrieben hättest als das Kapitel über den Homer, und wenn du
> auch nichts getan hättest, als was du für mich tust—und zu tun hast—, so würde doch
> dein Name der erste deines Jahrhunderts sein.*[14]

The article on Homer had been written, in fact, by Johann Wolfgang von
Goethe, who at that time shared Lavater's enthusiasm for physiognomical
theory.

Perhaps because he was impressed with the German edition, and perhaps
in the expectation of seeing his beloved Lavater again, Fuseli began work on
a head of Christ as well as the heads of Satan and other physiognomical
sketches, which would eventually find their way into the expanded, French
version of the *Fragmente*, which was to appear in the Hague in 1781, 1783,
and 1786. In spite of his new spirit of cooperation with Lavater, he wrote:
"Den Christuskopf—und Jesus Christus helfe mir—habe ich angefangen."[15]
It was Henry Hunter's English translation of the French edition of the
Fragmente that Fuseli was to supervise, furnish with drawings, and contract
engravings for in London from the middle of the 1780s. The ambitious project of expanding the French version with additional illustrations in a magnificent quarto edition was overseen by Fuseli from the beginning until the project was completed in 1792.

Fuseli returned in the fall of 1778 to Zurich for a visit on his way from Rome
to England. There, he received several commissions from wealthy Zürcher
that he was to complete in London and send back to them. But the greatest
event of his return trip was an unhappy love affair with a niece of Lavater, Anna Landholt vom Rech. He was smitten with love as never before, but her
father refused his suit and caused his hasty retreat from Zurich in April 1779.
His letters back to Switzerland reveal a great loss and a great pain and signaled Fuseli's final separation from Switzerland. He was never to see his
native land again.

Part Two
Fuseli and Blake: Documentary Evidence of their Friendship

Watercolor portrait of Lavater by Markus Dinkel, dated 1790. Except for the absence of the skull cap and variations in the clothing, the painting is strikingly similar to Blake's engraving for Johnson. (From the Department of Prints and Drawings of the Zentralbibliothek, Zurich)

REV. JOHN CASPAR LAVATER

of Zurich. Born 1741. Died 1801.

Pub.ᵈ May 1.1800 by J. Johnson, in Saint Paul's Church Yard, London, from a Drawing in his possession, taken in 1787.

Blake's engraving of Lavater for Joseph Johnson (1800). The original source for this design might well have been a drawing based on a watercolor painting by Markus Dinkel (1762-1832), although the watercolor, which hangs in the Zentralbibliothek in Zurich, is dated "1790" and Johnson's caption indicated that the drawing from which this portrait was engraved was "taken in 1787." (From the Art Collection of the Folger Shakespeare Library, Washington, D.C.)

The Meeting of Fuseli and Blake (1781-1787?)

On October 8, 1779, William Blake became a full student of the Royal Academy. He showed his first picture there in May of the next year.[1] Fuseli returned to London from Rome in the spring of 1779. At first Fuseli took rooms at the home of John Cartwright, a painter with whom he had been acquainted in Rome.[2] He lived during this period from commissions for paintings that he had obtained in Zurich on his stop there on the way back from Rome, and he became a regular contributor to the exhibits at the Royal Academy. Thus it was that Blake and Fuseli, despite the differences in their ages, began their careers as artists at approximately the same time. Fuseli, his financial situation as precarious as ever, reinstated his relationship with the wealthy Coutts, rejoined the Johnson circle, and cultivated the patronage of Sir Joshua Reynolds.[3]

In the middle of 1781, Fuseli moved to Number 1 Broad Street.[4] At Number 28 Broad Street stood the house in which William Blake's family had resided since 1753.[5] Blake was born and reared there; and, although he probably spent most of his time at Besire's establishment during the period 1771-1779, in May of 1780 he gave the Broad Street address as his residence in the catalogue of *The Exhibition of the Royal Academy, M.DCC.LXXX.*[6] As close neighbors in 1781, Fuseli and Blake would have had opportunity to become acquainted as early as that year, though neither artist has left a record of any such meeting. Blake's biographers have noted the proximity of their lodgings during this period. Gilchrist simply states that Fuseli "became a neighbor" of Blake in 1780, but draws no more precise conclusion about the fact.[7] Mona Wilson's account suggests by inference that the two became acquainted at the time Fuseli moved to Broad Street, without mentioning any specific meeting: "He [Fuseli] returned in 1780 after a stay of some years in Italy, and lodged in Broad Street. With him Blake formed an enduring though chequered friendship...."[8]

Two associations that support the supposition that Blake and Fuseli became acquainted in the early eighties are Fuseli's friendship with Joseph Johnson and John Flaxman. It is a matter of record that Fuseli knew Flaxman in 1780, and the close relationship with Johnson was of long standing by that time.[9] From Fuseli's letters we know that the relationship with Johnson was more than a professional one. He refers to the publisher as *"mein Freund*

Johnson" in a letter to Bodmer as early as 1768, the year after Johnson had published the Rousseau pamphlet.[10] Blake was engraving for Johnson in 1780 and John Flaxman was his best friend at the time.[11] It is almost impossible to believe that their paths would not have crossed in the early eighties, at least casually; and it is likely that Blake, who had known of the "literary" Fuseli as the translator of Winckelmann since his teens, would have actively sought to become acquainted with the painter of the sensational "Nightmare," which appeared in 1781.[12] Both G.E. Bentley and Gert Schiff credit Fuseli for having introduced Blake into the Johnson circle, and for the fact that Blake was regarded in the eighties not merely as an engraver, but as an artist of some merit: "Through Fuseli, Blake probably got to know Johnson well..."; "Es ist wahr, dass Füssli ihn bei Johnson eingeführt habe...."13 The most precise statement as to when that might have occurred, however, is sometime "in the next decade" after 1779.[14]

The first recorded comment concerning the beginning of the period of intimacy between Fuseli and Blake is Blake's own reference in a letter written to Flaxman on September 12, 1800. In a poem of praise and love for Flaxman, Blake includes the following lines:

When Flaxman was taken to Italy,
Fuseli was given to me for a season. (K799)

It is known that Flaxman departed for Italy in 1787.[15] This is the same year that Blake engraved Fuseli's drawing for the frontispiece of his Lavater adaptation.[16] It is clear that by that time they were very good friends. Ruthven Todd's recent discovery of the original sketches that Fuseli made for that frontispiece suggests that Fuseli left much of the design to Blake himself, that he looked upon the younger man as a capable artist, that he chose Blake for the task, and that the design was more of a collaboration than has formerly been supposed.[17] Such a collaboration, especially for the egocentric Fuseli, who was jealous and scornful of most of the artists with whom he came into contact, indicates that Fuseli's having been given to Blake "for a season" in 1787 refers to a season of intense interaction and not necessarily to the beginning of their friendship.

Artistic Collaboration, Mutual Praise, and Documents of the Relationship of Fuseli and Blake (177?-1810)

Because of the lack of personal testimony or letters concerning the nature and duration of the friendship of Fuseli and Blake, collaborations, public and private critical defenses, and the ownership of a few books and engravings constitute the only empirical evidence we have. The following compilation represents an attempt to survey the documentation that does exist:

177?   Blake owns a copy of Fuseli's translation of five essays by J.J. Winckelmann under the title, *Reflections on the Painting and Sculpture of the Greeks* (London: J. Johnson, 1764). Blake's owner-ship of the volume has been established by the verification of the authenticity of his signature on the flyleaf.[1]

1787/88   Fuseli sketches the outlines for the design of the frontispiece of his Lavater adaptation, *Aphorisms on Man*. Blake completes the design and engraves the work.[2]

1788/89   Blake executes four engravings for the English edition of Lavater's *Physiognomische Fragmente*, which Fuseli was overseeing: *Essays in Physiognomy*, three volumes, bound in five (London: Henry Hunter, 1789). The designs are all in the first volume: (1) A small engraving identified by G.E. Bentley in 1972, probably designed by Blake himself;[3] (2) a decorative end-piece at the end of the "Fragments Nineteenth," probably also of Blake's own design; (3) "Head of Democritus," after Rubens; (4) a head of Spalding, Fuseli's old theology teacher. The designer of the Spalding por-trait is not known, but the work bears the characteristic stamp of Blake's own lines, and looks not unlike Blake himself.

1790/91   In Erasmus Darwin's *The Botanic Garden*, Fuseli supplies Blake again with a tentative sketch for an engraving, "The Fertilization of Egypt," which Blake completes and then engraves.

1790/91? An engraving by Blake after Fuseli, "*Falsa ad Coelum*," and "Head of a damned soul" from Dante's *Inferno*. An engraving published by Joseph Johnson, "Timon and Alcibiades," designed by Fuseli and engraved by Blake.

1795   An engraving in the 1795 edition of Darwin's *Botanic Garden*, "Tor-nado," published by Johnson.

1796   Blake is commissioned by a new publisher, James Edwards, to design and engrave the illustrations for a magnificent edition of Edward Young's *Night Thoughts*.[4] Coming to Blake when he was thirty-eight years old, this would have been the most significant commercial venture of his life, had the project been carried out as he expected. He designed and executed 537 watercolors for the book, some of which he showed in Edwards's book shops and in another print shop in Pall Mall. On June 24, 1796, Fuseli told Joseph Farington that Edwards was going to select 200 of the designs and that Blake would be allowed to engrave them. In the end, only forty-three of Blake's engraved designs were included in the edition that was published in 1797. There is a series of brief commentaries accompanying each plate. Gilchrist attributes the commentaries to Fuseli, but this has been questioned by Robert Essick in his recent commentary to a facsimile edition.[5] The preface to the edition was probably written with "Johnsonian swing" by Fuseli.[6] Gilchrist wrote that he suspected that Fuseli "had something to do with Edward's choice of artist...."[7] Blake's acquaintances considered the designs extravagant, and at least one of his friends considered Fuseli the "bad influence" on Blake's wildness of style.[8] Only nine of the "Nights" were published, and the edition did not sell well.

1798   Blake engraves designs by Fuseli for Charles Allen, *A New and Improved History of England* (London: J. Johnson, 1798).

Blake engraves designs after Fuseli for Charles Allen, *A New and Improved Roman History* (London: J. Johnson, 1798).

Fuseli writes Roscoe in an unpublished letter of August 6, 1798, that Moses Houghton, the young engraver who was to become Fuseli's "official" engraver in later years, ought to study Blake's engraving of "The Fertilization of Egypt," to see a good example of how to engrave drapery.[9]

1799   In the fifth edition of Darwin's *Botanic Garden* (London: J. Johnson, 1799), Blake executes a new engraving of "The Fertilization of Egypt."[10]

In a moment of dejection, Blake writes George Cumberland, "I am laid in a corner as if I did not Exist, & Since my Young's Night Thoughts have been publish'd, Even Johnson and Fuseli have discarded my Graver." (K795) But we find Blake engraving for Johnson the following year, perhaps with some support from Fuseli.

1800   Blake engraves a large (10-1/8 x 8-3/8 inch) profile of the head of Lavater for Joseph Johnson. Bentley designates the designer of the portrait as "unknown."[11] It clearly resembles, however, a portrait of Lavater executed by a Swiss artist, Markus Dinkel, in 1790.[12] The original drawing must have been made from that portrait. The skull cap in the engraving represents the only variation from the Dinkel portrait. Fuseli might have obtained the sketch from Lavater himself, or from someone else who made it after the Swiss engraving. Of course, Fuseli knew Lavater's features by heart. Two caricatures sketched on the margin of Fuseli's design for the Lavater frontispiece clearly depict Fuseli and his friend.[13] Another caricature on the verso of a design that Fuseli drew and which was later engraved by Blake shows Lavater's profile, closely resembling the Dinkel portrait. This caricature was published by Todd in 1972, but not identified by him.[14] This engraving was first catalogued by Archibald G.B. Russell in *The Engravings of William Blake* (London: Grant Richards, Ltd., MDCCCXII), who notes W.M. Rossetti's high opinion of its quality: "A superb and masterly example. As an engraver merely, Blake ranks high on the strength of this plate alone. The lines of the face are especially noteworthy for their skilful play, firmness and delicacy."[15]

Frederick Tatham related an amusing anecdote in connection with this engraving: "When aroused or annoyed he was possessed of a violent temper; but in his passions there was some method, for while he was engraving a large portrait of Lavater, not being able to obtain what he wanted, he threw the plate completely across the room. Upon his relating this he was asked whether he did not injure it, to which he replied with his usual fun: 'Oh! I took good care of that!'"[16]

To the year 1800 belongs also the famous letter written by Blake to John Flaxman on September 12, in which he writes: "When Flaxman was taken to Italy, Fuseli was given to me for a reason,..." (K799) This sentence is taken to refer to 1787, the year that Flaxman left for Italy, and Blake became close to Fuseli.

1801   Fuseli, in his *Lectures on Painting* (London: J. Johnson, 1801) includes an engraving that is thought to have been executed about the same time as the Lavater frontispiece (1787/89). This would explain the Lavater caricature on the verso of the original drawing. The drawing, a portrait of Michelangelo, is incomplete compared with Blake's final engraving. In the upper left corner is a pencil sketch of the legs of the figure, which in the drawing, only extends as far as the crotch. Todd, in company with David Bindman and Martin Butlin, attributes the pencil additions to the drawing to Blake.[17] Under the drawing are the following words, written by John Linnell: "Mich. Angelo by Fuseli/original drawing had from W. Blake."[18]

1805   Alexander Chalmer's *The Plays of William Shakespeare* (London: J. Johnson, 1805) contains two pictures designed by Fuseli and engraved by Blake: "Queen Catherine's Dream" and "Romeo and the Apothecary." These plates signal the revival of friendship between the two men. Blake had just returned from Felpham in 1803.

Cromek gives Blake a contract to illustrate Robert Blair's *The Grave*. Fuseli writes the foreword. There are 589 subscribers. Among them, Fuseli and other Royal Academicians. For some reason, Cromek, who is to become Blake's enemy, gives the job of engraving the designs to the fashionable Schiavonetti, who destroys the "Blakean" quality of the pictures in the process.[19] Robert Hunt, a critic hostile to Fuseli, attacked Blake's designs in *Bell's Weekly Messenger*, with harsh words also for Fuseli. In his *MS Note-Book* in 1808, Blake writes: "To H[unt]/You think Fuseli is not a Great Painter./I'm Glad: This is one of the best compliments he ever had." (K538)

1806   Richard Phillips, publisher of *The Monthly Magazine*, publishes Blake's fervent defense of Fuseli's "Ugolino," which had been attacked by Hunt in *Bell's Weekly Messenger*. In this letter is Blake's statement: "A gentleman who visited me the other day, said, 'I am very much surprised at the dislike that some connoisseurs shew on viewing the pictures of Mr. Fuseli; but the truth is, he is a hundred years beyond the present generation.' Though I am startled at such an assertion, I hope the contemporary taste will shorten the hundred years into as many hours; for I am sure that any person consulting his own eyes must prefer what is so supereminent; and I am as sure that any person consulting his own reputation, or the reputation of his country, will refrain from disgracing either by such ill-judged criticisms in future." (K864)

1809   In his *Descriptive Catalogue*, Blake shows himself to be familiar with the manuscript of Fuseli's *History of Art in the Schools of Italy*. He repeats several of Fuseli's judgments of the Italian artists.

1808/09   In his *Annotations to Sir Joshua Reynolds Discourses*, Blake defends Fuseli against the predominant taste which Reynolds represents for him: "O Society for Encouragement of Art! O King & Nobility of England! Where have you hid Fuseli's Milton? Is Satan troubled at his Exposure?" (K446) Further on in the same annotations, Blake again defends Fuseli's *Milton Gallery*, his most ambitious undertaking and his greatest financial failure: "The Neglect of Fuseli's Milton in a Country pretending to the Encouragement of Art is a Sufficient Apology for My Vigorous Indignation, if indeed the Neglect of my own Powers had not been. Ought not the Employers of Fools to be Execrated in future Ages? They Will and Shall! Foolish Men, your own real Greatness depends on your Encouragement of the Arts & your Fall will depend on [your *del.*] their Neglect & Depression. What you Fear is your true Interest. Leo X was advised not to Encourage the Arts; he was too Wise to take this Advise." (K452)

Blake is commissioned by Cromek to do engravings after a large fresco painting of the Canterbury Pilgrims of Chaucer. Stothard is told of the concept, executes his own design, and Cromek chooses his picture over Blake's.[20] Blake, feeling betrayed by all his friends, turns against all but Fuseli in his epigrammatic *Note-Book*. It is there that Blake penned his famous piece of doggerel concerning Fuseli:

The only Man that e'er I knew
Who did not make me almost spew
Was Fuseli: he was both Turk & Jew—
And so, [sweet *del.*] dear Christian Friends, how do you do?

(K551)

1810   In his *Public Address*, an Essay written in his *Note-Book*, and perhaps intended as raw material to be included in a catalogue for the showing of his "Canterbury Pilgrims," Blake writes: "Many People are so foolish [as] to think that they can wound Mr. Fuseli over my Shoulder; they will find themselves mistaken; they could not wound even Mr. Barry so." (K592) And later in the same essay, he places Fuseli's genius in the same category with Michelangelo, Shakespeare, and Milton: "I do not mean smooth'd up & Niggled & Poco-Piu'd, and all the beauties pick'd out [but *del.*] & blurr'd & blotted, but Drawn with a firm & decided hand at once [with all its Spots & Blemishes which are beauties & not faults *del.*], like Fuseli & Michael Angelo, Shakespeare & Milton." (K595)

Throughout these years, while Blake gave expression to his admiration for Fuseli's work, Fuseli himself left no evidence of how he felt about Blake's poetry, which he must have known. In a letter which Blake wrote to Thomas Butts on January 10, 1802, he complains that his living depends upon engraving for others and hints that his patrons have discouraged his original designs:

...As my dependence is upon Engraving at present,...& I find on all hands great objections to my doing anything but the mere drudgery of business, & intimations that if I do not confine myself to this, I shall not live; this has always pursu'd me. You will understand by this the source of all my uneasiness. This from Johnson & Fuseli brought me down here, & this from Mr. H. will bring me back again;..." (K812)[21]

Eudo Mason uses this line to elucidate some strange lines of verse that Blake wrote ten months later in another letter to Butts:

Poverty, Envy, old age & fear
Shall bring thy Wife upon a bier;
And Butts shall give what Fuseli gave,
A dark black Rock & a gloomy Cave. (K817)[22]

But the meaning of the "dark black Rock & gloomy Cave," although it indicates some tension in the relationship between Fuseli and Blake, is by no means a clear sign that Fuseli was discouraging Blake's own projects. Contemporary biographical accounts attest to the mutual admiration of one artist for the other, but fail to yield any specific information.

J.T. Smith's account of the nature of the friendship in his account of Blake's life suggests that Fuseli had high regard for Blake's own designs:

Blake's talent is not to be seen in his engravings from the designs of other artists,...; but his own engravings from his own mind are the productions which the man of true feeling must ever admire, and the predictions of Fuseli and Flaxman may hereafter be verified—That a time will come when Blake's finest works will be as much sought after and treasured up in the portfolios of men of mind, as those of Michel Angelo are at present.[23]

Writing in 1832, Frederick Tatham was even more definite about the closeness of the two:

Fuseli was very intimate with Blake, and Blake was more fond of Fuseli than any other man on earth. Blake certainly loved him, and at least Fuseli admired Blake and learned from him, as he himself confessed, a great deal. Fuseli and Flaxman both said that Blake was the greatest man in the country, and there would come a time when his works would be invaluable.[24]

No contemporary accounts can shed much light on what Mason calls the "friction and tension" of the relationship of Fuseli and Blake, but they do witness the affection and respect that existed between the two artists.

Fuseli's library, which was sold at Sotheby's soon after his death, contained the edition of Blair's *The Grave*: "(after Blake by Schiavonetti), and one [engraving] by Blake, rare, proofs."[25] It is significant that Blake had given Fuseli one of his own engravings of his design, executed in 1805. Fuseli owned a copy of both Stothard's and Blake's "Canterbury Pilgrims: The Canterbury Pilgrimage, after *Stothard* by *Schiavonetti, proof etching,* and the Canterbury Pilgrimage after *Blake*, by himself, *rare.*"[26] We know also that Fuseli owned a copy of Blake's emblem book, *For Children: The Gates of Paradise* (1793). His copy of this little book, which was printed by Johnson, but probably never offered for sale, is one of four extant copies. Fuseli gave it to the daughter of the family physician of one of his patrons in 1806. Because it was never really "published," it may be assumed that the book was given to Fuseli by Blake himself.[27]

The documentation surveyed here, although it sheds some light on the duration of Fuseli's association with Blake, cannot explain the kinship that they felt for each other. A more personal witness to their friendship is seen in one more piece of evidence that reveals more than any other: Blake's own copy of Fuseli's Lavater adaptation, *Aphorisms of Man*. The nature and importance of Blake's copy of this book will be given special treatment in Part V of this study, "Blake and Fuseli's Lavater."

Part Three
Blake and Fuseli's Winckelmann

Der Maler, der weiter denkt als seine
Palette reicht, wünscht einen gelehrten
Vorrat zu haben, wohin er gehen, und bedeutende
und sinnlich gemachte Zeichen von Dingen, die
nicht sinnlich sind, nehmen möchte.

—J.J. Winckelmann, 1775

The painter who thinks beyond his palette
longs for some learned apparatus by whose
stores he might be able to invest abstracted
ideas with sensible images.

—Fuseli's translation of
Winckelmann, 1765

Thank God, I never was sent to school
[To learn to admire the works of a Fool. *del.*]
To be Flog'd into following the Style of a fool.

—William Blake, MS. Note-book
1808-1811   (K550)

The Apprentice's Primer

Investigations of Henry Fuseli's influence upon William Blake generally begin with the year 1787: the year in which Blake's brother Robert died, in which Blake's closest friend John Flaxman went to Italy, in which "Fuseli was given me for a season" (K799). But there is evidence to suggest that even before that date, and before the well-known collaboration of Blake and Fuseli on Lavater's *Aphorisms on Man*, Fuseli might have influenced the young engraver's apprentice and poet.

This idea was first suggested by Sir Geoffrey Keynes in his article, "The Engraver's Apprentice" (1949).[1] Keynes speaks of Blake's reading during his early years and refers to a copy of Fuseli's translation of Winckelmann's *Reflections on the Painting and Sculpture of the Greeks (Gedanken über die Nachahmung der griechischen Werke in der Malerei und Bildhauerkunst)*, which Fuseli published in April 1764, only three months after his arrival in London. Blake's actual copy which belonged to Sir Geoffrey bears the earliest extant signature of the poet on the flyleaf. From the designation "William Blake, Lincoln's Inn" the signature can be dated as early as 1772 and not later than the end of July 1779—the tenure of Blake's apprenticeship to Basire on Great Queen's Street, across from Lincoln's Inn Fields.[2] The question of where Blake might have acquired a copy of Fuseli's translation becomes all the more intriguing in view of the fact that the book was a resounding failure in its day. Eudo C. Mason's painstaking research into the history and fate of the Winckelmann translation (1971) has shown that some earlier claims that Fuseli was instrumental in introducing Winckelmann to England have been exaggerated. Mason has provided evidence that the work did not sell well, if at all, and that it was virtually ignored.[3] The few critical notices of it in the contemporary press are entirely negative.[4]

A close reading of Fuseli's translation shows it to be an extravagantly embellished interpretation, which, although it is an essentially correct translation of Winckelmann's point of view, is so full of original metaphors and Fuseli's own rather bombastic style that it must be viewed not only as a translation, but as an original work as well. Mason has even been able to show that Fuseli's first published attempt in English is in manner of expression so derivative of his heroes and early "instructors" in the English language, Milton and Shakespeare, that many lines can be rearranged in blank verse.[5] The language in this translation reveals the same sort of emotional expressionism that characterizes Fuseli's German *Klagen* and his letters to Lavater. Writing in English, or what sometimes only appears to be English, Fuseli possessed an incredibly rich vocabulary and a tendency for startling phrases and neologisms. The strangeness of his expression cannot be explained away merely by the fact that as a foreigner he lacked sufficient grammar to express himself in a conventional manner, for he wrote the same way in German. Keynes's conjecture that "there are innumerable passages in this book which may have sown in Blake's mind seeds of some of the ideas that afterwards grew to the size, sometimes, of obsessions," invites further investigation of Fuseli's translation of Winckelmann and its importance in the formation of Blake's aesthetic.[6]

William Blake acquired the translation of Fuseli's Winckelmann sometime during his period of indenture to the antiquarian engraver, James Basire (1730-1802), between 1772 and 1779. Henry Fuseli was in Rome between 1770 and 1778 for a voluntary and self-directed apprenticeship in the school of great painting. The two artists were thus undergoing their years of training for their future careers during approximately the same period.

At this time there is no evidence of how Blake obtained a copy of Fuseli's Winckelmann translation. Blake was only eight years old when he is known to have had the translation in his possession. At that time Fuseli was in Rome, studying to be a painter. It is possible that Basire, who was executing many plates for the Society of Antiquities' *Sepulchral Monuments of Great Britain* at that time, might have provided his young apprentice with the work. It is equally possible, however, that Blake, who was fond of visiting bookstores in search of old prints, might have stumbled upon a copy of the book, which had been lying about unsold for eight or ten years.

Fuseli in Rome, as Cunningham reports, "lay on his back day after day, musing on the splendid ceiling of the Sistine Chapel.... He imagined, at all events, that he drank in as he lay the spirit of the sublime Michael, and that by studying in the Sistine, he had the full advantage of the mantle of the inspiration suspended visibly above him."[7] We know, too, that he was reading then the works of Shakespeare, Milton, Dante, and Petrarch in a new light. There in Rome, as he was later to report to Farington, he approached the literary giants to whom he had been introduced by Bodmer and Breitinger as for the first time, and "with inclination."[8] The trip to Rome, considered obligatory for any serious artist of the time, must have been planned by Fuseli very soon after his arrival in England. Knowles describes how Fuseli sought and obtained an interview with Sir Joshua Reynolds in 1767. Reynolds, much impressed with the drawings which Fuseli showed him, was amazed to discover that the young man had never been to Rome. According to Knowles, Sir Joshua exclaimed, sounding not a little like Fuseli himself, that "were he his age and endowed with the ability of producing such works, if any one were to offer him an estate of a thousand pounds a year, on condition of being any thing but a painter, he would without the least hesitation, reject the offer."[9] Fuseli himself wrote to Lavater a year and a half before he left for Rome: *"um der grösste Maler meiner Zeit zu sein, habe ich, sagt Reynolds, nichts zu tun, als für ein paar Jahre nach Italien zu gehen."*[10]

When he finally arrived in Rome in 1770, his academic training in the history and theory of art, which, under the supervision of his father and his teachers, had been a rigorous one, was behind him. Now he was to study the true book of art: the works of Michelangelo, Raphael, and the antique treasures he had known only from prints and engravings.

While Fuseli was in St. Peter's, Blake, who was "too simple" to deal with the tales and pranks of his "too cunning" fellow apprentices, was sent by Basire out from his shop on Great Queen's Street to make drawings in another holy sanctuary: Westminster Abbey. There, Gilchrist relates that the young William was covered by his own "mantle of inspiration":[11]

> Shut up alone with these solemn memorials of far off centuries,—for, during service and in the intervals of visits from strangers, the vergers turned the key on him,—the Spirit of the past became his familiar companion. Sometimes his dreaming eye saw more palpable shapes from the phantom past: one a vision of 'Christ and the Apostles,' as he used to tell; and I doubt not others. For, as we have seen, the visionary tendency, or faculty, as Blake more truly called it, had early shown itself.[12]

Like Fuseli, in addition to executing drawings and experiencing visions, Blake was reading. Literature and art, inseparable in the minds and works of both artists, were the sister muses for palette, graver and pen. Blake's early poems, privately published as the *Poetical Sketches* (1769-1778), suggest that he was an avid reader of poetry from an early age. Included in the hypothetical reading list which scholars have inferred from the *Poetical Sketches* are Collins, Chatterton, Percy, Spenser, Thompson—also a favorite of the young Fuseli—, as well as Shakespeare and Milton.[13] As for art history, the only work that is known for certain to have been among his readings during the apprenticeship was the Fuseli Winckelmann. "A curious relic," as Keynes called it, containing the earliest extant signature of William Blake.[14]

Though one can only conjecture how Blake came to possess the unsuccessful Fuseli translation, it is understandable that he would be interested in the subject matter. When he was but ten years old and still at Pars's Drawing School, he was sketching from plaster casts of antiquities. His father is said to have "bought for him the Gladiator, the Hercules, and the Venus of Medici, and various heads, hands and feet," during that time before he joined Basire.[15] Anthony Blunt has suggested that he might have had further exposure to ancient art by studying the portfolio of drawings which Henry Pars, the brother of William, brought back from Ionia, where he had been sent to "draw the remains of Greek sculpture and architecture."[16] This interest in "classical" art alone would have been enough to attract him to the title, *Reflections on the Painting and Sculpture of the Ancient Greeks*.

This small volume, which was written eight years before Fuseli translated it, contains not only praises and descriptions of ancient art, but also an evangelical message for the improvement of modern, specifically German, art. It might be said that at the time of his first essay, Winckelmann's more direct experience with European baroque art had as much to do, in a negative sense, with forming his aesthetic viewpoint as what he knew of classical art. The baroque tendencies that he saw in the collections of Dresden became synonymous with what art should not be, and served as a negative foil to what he perceived as perfection in the art of the ancient Greeks. But it was this inaugural essay, written from the distant vantage point of Dresden, that was to launch Winckelmann's fame and to prepare his reception by Mengs and the expatriated artist community in Rome. As Carl Justi pointed out in his masterly study of Winckelmann's life and work, Winckelmann was never to be aware of the actual scope of the treasures of antique art that were hidden away among the many acquisitions of Friedrich August II. Instead, he based his descriptions of Greek art in the *Gedanken* upon a few busts and gems, Roman burial figures which he mistook for vestals, and above all upon a plaster copy of the *Laocoön*, which belonged to the King.[17]

In his *Gedanken*, Winckelmann set forth seven requisites of ancient Greek art. Fuseli ordered the seven points under subject headings, which Winckelmann had not done in the original: Nature, Contour, Drapery, Expression, Workmanship in Sculpture, Painting, and Allegory. The *Gedanken* was, as the title suggests, a beginning and somewhat tentative statement of theories and attitudes which Winckelmann would express more dogmatically in later works. But this amazing essay contained, as Herder wrote, the seed of every idea that was to come from the pen of Winckelmann: "*einen reichen Keim alles dessen, was er nachher in seinen Werken entwickelt hat.*"[18]

In George Mills Harper's study, *The Neoplatonism of William Blake*, he fixes the span of Blake's "Grecian" period between 1783 and 1803 with his association with the neoclassical artists John Flaxman and George Cumberland, and, either directly or indirectly, through those two artists with the neoplatonic ideas of Thomas Taylor. Harper also names Fuseli among the acquaintances of Blake during that time who would have steered him in the direction of neoplatonic idealism and neoclassical aesthetics.[19] But Fuseli's Winckelmann, read by Blake before this "Grecian" period, could well have converted the young apprentice to the cult of the Greek way before he met Flaxman, Cumberland, or Fuseli. More recently, Anne Kostelanetz Mellor has devoted two pages of a chapter on "Romantic Classicism in Blake's Art" to suggestions of themes and even images that Blake might have found in his reading of the *Reflections*.[20] She bases the greater part of her discussion on the probability that when they became friends Fuseli and Blake discussed Winckelmann's *Geschichte der Kunst*.[21] Although there is no proof that Fuseli tutored Blake in Winckelmann's larger work, the intense relationship that evolved between the two artists as early as 1780 could only have encouraged the enthusiasm for the ancients that Fuseli had so vividly communicated in his translation.

Harper points out correctly that it is a mistake to take Blake's violent rejection of all things Greek after 1804 as an indication that the poet had abandoned concepts that he had discovered during the formative period in which he wrote that the "purpose for which alone" he lived was "to renew the lost Art of the Greeks." (K792) The vehemence with which Blake turns against the ancients "is evidence of the strength of his attachment to Greek metaphysical theories as they were manifested in the symbolism and mythology of art and literature."[22] This trait of protesting too much is equally telling in the case of Fuseli, who in 1801 in the "Introduction" to his *Lectures on Art* wrote:

"Winckelmann was the parasite of the fragments that fell from the conversation of Mengs, a deep scholar, and better fitted to comment a classic than to give lessons on art and style, he reasoned himself into frigid reveries and Platonic dreams on Beauty."[23] Fuseli was characteristically rebelling against the dogmatic authority which the ideas of Winckelmann had attained by the time those words were written, rather than rejecting the early premises outlined by Winckelmann in his *Gedanken*. The early essay had been full of the enthusiasm of discovery, but by 1801 Winckelmann's neoclassical precepts had taken on the appearance of rules, which Fuseli, the nonconformist stubbornly adhering to his own and no one else's style, had to refute:

> To him [Winckelmann] Germany owes the shackles of her artists, and the narrow limits of their aim; from him they have learnt to substitute the means for the end,and by a hopeless chace [sic] after that they call beauty, to lose what alone can make beauty interesting, expression and mind.[24]

The violence of Fuseli's rejection of Winckelmann is surprisingly close in spirit to Blake's condemnation of the Greeks three years later in the "Preface" to *Milton*: "Shakespeare & Milton were both curb'd by the general malady & infection from the silly Greek & Latin slaves of the Sword." (K480) The disclaimers made by both artists must be weighed against the tendency of each artist to borrow concepts, make them his own, and after having separated that which fit into his own system from that which did not, to reject the source altogether. Neither artist admitted adherence to any school of art or philosophy. "What distinguishes his learning," Kathleen Raine says of Blake in the introduction to her great study, *Blake and Tradition*, "is that he everywhere and at all times followed, in art, poetry, and philosophy, the traces, now clear, now almost lost, of tradition."[25] She also notes that his practice was "dictated by a belief in eclecticism for its own sake....He proceeded to draw in, to fuse and identify, gods and myths, symbolic terms and themes, from every source known or half-known to him.... He was fanatically eclectic."[26] Fuseli's Winckelmann was to be a primer for Blake in many of the aesthetic attitudes which were to stay with him throughout his life. What is of particular importance for this study is that Blake's first discovery of neoclassical ideas was, as British reviewers were fond of pointing out, tinged with "Teutonic" madness: they were given Blake through the medium of Fuseli's intensified and expressionistic language.

The examination of Fuseli's role in bringing Winckelmann's ideas to Blake will be treated thematically under three headings: (1) "Raphael the Sublime," the vision of the artist as genius, and the persona Blake created for Raphael in his works; (2) "Naked Beauty Displayed," the centrality of the naked human form to the work of Blake, and his interpretation of the neoclassical ideal; (3) "Allegory," Blake's concept of allegory and its relation to Winckelmann's conception of the subject matter and treatment of myth and reality in art.

Raphael the Sublime

The immediate inspiration for the *Gedanken* was Winckelmann's confrontation with Raphael's *Sistine Madonna*, the most precious painting in the *Gemäldegallerie* of Augustus III in Dresden. The treasure had been brought from the Duke of Modena in 1745, but it was not hung in the gallery until 1752, the same year that Winckelmann, the brilliant but penniless scholar and librarian, newly converted to Catholicism, arrived in Dresden with the promise of a position as librarian in the Vatican in Rome. Winckelmann visited the gallery for three successive days, searching with much difficulty for the source and definition of beauty in the famous painting.[1] Only after much reflection and long conversations with his friend, Martin Oeser, a painter with a wide knowledge of art history, did he reach his conclusion about the quality of greatness in Raphael:[2]

> *Die edle Einfalt und stille Grösse der griechischen Statuen ist das wahre Kennzeichen der griechischen Schriften aus den besten Zeiten, der Schriften aus Sokrates' Schule; und diese Eigenschaften sind es welche die vorzügliche Grösse eines Raffael machen, zu welcher er durch die Nachahmung der Alten gelangt ist.*[3] (W89)

Fuseli translates these lines:

> This noble simplicity and sedate grandeur is also the true characteristical mark of the best and maturest Greek writings, of the epoch and school of *Socrates*. Possessed of these qualities Raphael became eminently great, and he owed them to the ancients.[4]
> (FW34-35)

The prototype for this noble simplicity and sedate grandeur is the frozen, and for Winckelmann, dignified anguish captured in its pregnant moment by the sculptor of the *Laocoön*, which he had seen in Dresden in *"sehr fleissigen Abgüssen in Gips, die der König hat...."*[5]

The famous formulation, *Edle Einfalt und stille Grösse,* which was to have such an important impact on the history of taste and criticism in the eighteenth century, would not have seemed to Fuseli an outrageous or revolutionary perception at the time of his translation.[6] The face of the *Laocoön* becomes for Winckelmann a concrete symbol of the greatness of ancient Greek art. His description of the figure of the suffering priest of Apollo is a way of making visible the precepts of ancient aesthetics: it provides an example more instructive than chapters of academic theory. Like most such all-encompassing symbols, both the expression on the face of *Laocoön* and the motto that Winckelmann attaches to it are vague enough to be open to a wide range of interpretation. In the companion essay to the *Gedanken, Erläuterung der Gedanken,* Winckelmann writes of *Edle Einfalt und stille Grösse:* "*Dieser Ausdruck hat einen selten allgemeinen Beifall gefunden, und Künstler haben mit demselben allezeit viel gewagt"* (W133). Fuseli's editing of that statement in his translation is significant: "An expression which hath seldom met with general approbation, and never pronounced without hazard of being misunderstood." (W181)

Fuseli is quite sure that he understands what the expression means when he delivers his *Lectures on Painting* in 1801, even though by then he had been converted fully to the art of Michelangelo. Referring to the *Laocoön* as the archetype of mastery of expression in art, he writes:

> ...the prince, the priest, the father are visible, but absorbed in the man serve only to dignify the victim of one great expression; though poised by the artist, for us to apply the compass to the face of the *Laocoön* is to measure the wave fluctuating in the storm: this tempestuous front, this contracted nose, the immersion of these eyes, and above all, that long-drawn mouth, are separate and united, seats of convulsion, features of nature struggling within the jaws of death.[7]

William Blake's own drawings of the group, executed late in his career in 1815, some thirty-eight years after he first saw Winckelmann's description, similarly depict a dynamic expression of agony far removed from tranquility. But whatever interpretation was read into the face and body of *Laocoön,* they remained the touchstone of definition of ancient genius for a century thereafter. It is exactly that genius and not the statue itself which Winckelmann is attempting to describe in the famous sentence, the end of which Fuseli translates: "Possessed of these qualities Raphael became eminently great, and he owed them to the ancients." (FW35) "The true characteristical mark," "*Das wahre Kennzeichen,"* which one finds in Greek statues and writings are those qualities, which according to Fuseli's translation, Raphael *possessed.* For Fuseli during the period of this translation, and for Blake for the whole of his artistic career, the artist who inspired the *Gedanken,* Raffaello Santi, would be of more importance than any marble statue or plaster cast.

Raphael emerges from the pages of Fuseli's Winckelmann more god than painter. He is a philosopher possessed of a special soul which allows him to perceive the secret of the Greek ideal. Fuseli emphasizes this aspect of Winckelmann's thought in his translation. This is most clearly demonstrated in the last short essay in his book of Winckelmann essays, which he entitles "Instructions for the Connoisseur" ("*Erinnerungen über die Betrachtung der Alten Kunst,"* 1759). In this work, as in the other short piece taken from the fifth volume of the *Bibliothek der schönen Wissenschaften und der freyen Künste,*[8] Fuseli takes great liberties, sometimes going off on a tangent that is entirely his own. The phrases in italics in the following passage are not expressed by Winckelmann in the original:

> The second characteristic of works of art is Beauty. The highest object of man is man, *and for the artist there is none above his own frame.*
> *'Tis by moving your senses that he reaches your soul:* and hence the analysis of the bodily system has no less difficulty for him, than that of the human mind for the philosopher. I do not mean the anatomy of the muscles, vessels, bones, and their dif-

ferent forms and situations; nor the relative measure of the whole to its parts, and *vice versa: for knife exercises and patience may teach you these.* I mean the analysis of an attribute, essential to man, *but fluctuating with his frame, allowed by all, misconstrued by many, known by few:*—the analysis of beauty which no definition can explain, to whom heaven hath denied a soul for it. (FW258-259)

Das zweite Augenmerk bei Betrachtung der Werke der Kunst soll die Schönheit sein. Der höchste Vorwurf der Kunst für denkende Menschen ist der Mensch, oder nur dessen äussere Fläche, und diese ist für Künstler so schwer auszuforschen, wie von den Weisen das Innere desselben, und das schwerste ist, was es nicht scheint, die Schönheit, weil sie, eigentlich zu reden, nicht unter Zahl und Mass fällt. Ebendaher ist das Verständnis des Verhältnisses des Ganzen, die Wissenschaft von Gebeinen und Muskeln nicht so schwer und allgemeiner als die Kenntnis des Schönen, und wenn auch das Schöne, welches man wünscht und sucht, durch einen allgemeinen Begriff könnte bestimmt werden, so würde sie dem, welchem der Himmel das Gefühl versagt hat, nicht helfen. (W161)

Raphael was one to whom heaven had given the "soul for it," and the soul of Raphael is central to Winckelmann's view of his painting. Of the *Sistine Madonna,* he writes: "but still the soul, with which the painter inspired his godlike work breathes life through all its parts" (FW39); "*allein die Seele, welche der Schöpfer dem Werke seiner Hände eingeblasen, belebt es noch jetzt.*" (W92) The precept of Longinus that "sublimity is the echo of a noble mind," had been taught to Fuseli by Bodmer, for whom nobility of soul was the first immutable qualification of the artist.[9] Thus, the synthesis of the person and soul of the artist with the work of art itself came quite easily to him by the time he confronted the idea in Winckelmann. Whereas for Bodmer, Milton had been the renewer of classical greatness and a "Christian Homer," Raphael assumes a similar role in Winckelmann's pagan religion of beauty, where he becomes the "Apollo of Painters," (F183) "*Apollo der Maler*" (FW134).

This transfer of the greatness of the work of art to the person of the artist is not a distortion of Winckelmann's intention. Fuseli has not changed the meaning which Winckelmann intended in his accurate rendering of another description of Raphael in the *Gedanken:*

That great soul of his lodged in a beauteous body was requisite for the first discovery of the character of the ancients: he first felt all their beauties, and (what he was particularly happy in!) at an age when vulgar, unfeeling, and half-moulded souls overlook every higher beauty. (FW34-35)

Eine so schöne Seele, wie die seinige war, in einem so schönen Körper wurde erfordert, den wahren Charakter der Alten in neueren Zeiten zuerst zu empfinden und zu entdecken, und was sein grösstes Glück war, schon in einem Alter, in welchem gemeine und halbgeformte Seelen über die wahre Grösse ohne Empfindung bleiben. (W89)

Here, Raphael, beautiful of soul and of body, is the genius who was able to "feel" precociously the beauty of the ancients, which ability is denied lesser mortals. This "feeling" is given only to the chosen, and cannot be arrived at by study and academic copying. Despite the pragmatic message addressed to German artists in the *Gedanken*—"There is but one way for the moderns to become great, and perhaps unequaled; I mean by imitating the ancients," (FW2) "*Der einzige Weg für uns gross, ja, wenn es möglich ist, unnachahm-*

lich zu werden, ist die Nachahmung der Alten...'' (W62)—Winckelmann also believed in the innate nature of genius:

If ever an artist was endowed with beauty and deep innate feelings for it; if ever one was versed in the taste and spirit of the ancients, 'twas certainly Raphael. (FW263)

Ist ein Künstler mit persönlicher Schönheit, mit Empfindung des Schönen, mit Geist und Kenntnis des Altertums begabt gewesen, so war es Raffael, und dennoch stehen seine Schönheiten unter dem Schönsten der Natur.[10] (W126)

The persona of Raphael as developed by Winckelmann would have struck a sympathetic chord in the young Blake, who was to incorporate the work and character of the Italian artist into his own aesthetic system. In the *Concordance* there are four verse references to Raphael in works and letters of Blake, and fifty prose references, most of the latter occurring in Blake's defenses of his own system of art, or in polemical passages against other artists: *Annotations to Reynolds* (1808), thirty-one references; *A Descriptive Catalogue* (1809), twelve references; *Public Address* (1810), eight references; and the letters (1799-1806), nine references. All these, as well as scattered mention of Raphael in the verse and marginalia are in praise of his genius, and of all artists whom Blake admired, only Michelangelo's name occurs more often.[11]

Blake's admiration for Raphael would not in itself be remarkable if he had followed the predominant contemporary neoclassical taste. Raphael, along with Titian and Corregio, were held up as "supreme heroes" by the promulgators of a classical style in the early part of the eighteenth century.[12] But, in fact, Blake consistently rejects and criticizes Titian and Correggio, as well as the established academic taste which was represented for him by Sir Joshua Reynolds: "This Man was Hired to Depress Art." (K445) Blake remains faithful to Raphael, however, and views him in much the same spirit as he is presented in Winckelmann's early essays. From his earliest mention of the artist in his *Annotations to Lavater (circa,* 1788) to the manuscript *Vision of the Last Judgment* (1810). "Rafael Sublime, Majestic, Graceful, Wise" possesses those attributes which Blake ascribes to the persona of his own poet/self: powerful, touched with holiness, a wise prophet, despised by unfeeling and unknowing fools:

Rafael Sublime, Majestic, Graceful, Wise,
His Executive Power must I despite?
Rubens Low, Vulgar, Stupid, Ignorant,
His power of Execution I must grant?
Learn the Laborious stumble of a Fool,
and from an Idiot's Actions form my rule?
Go send your Children to the Slobbering School! (K547)

It was axiomatic among the eighteenth-century admirers of Raphael that his genius was not easy to grasp and that appreciation of his art could come only after rigorous study and contemplation. Winckelmann's own vigil in front of the *Sistine Madonna* is an example. Reynolds, also, had to search deeply for "the divine spark of Raffaelle's genius" (*Discourses,* K448). When Blake annotates Reynold's discourses around 1818, he uses Sir Joshua's academic approach to Raphael as a springboard to vent his rage against the idea that an artist might *acquire* genius: "I am happy I cannot say that Rafael

Ever was, from my Earliest Childhood, hidden from Me. I Saw & I Knew immediately the difference between Rafael & Rubens." (K447) There is an antagonism against the establishment in the arrogance of this and many other polemic statements in which Blake disagrees with Reynolds; but, as always in his annotations to his readings, there is the direct honesty of Blake conversing, or raging, with himself. One is inclined to take him at his word when he claims to have known and appreciated Raphael from "Earliest Childhood." Malkin reports that Blake's father provided him money to "buy prints" and allowed him to frequent the auction rooms of Langford and Christie.[13] When still a child he is said to have become a sort of mascot at such auction sales.[14] But the zeal with which Fuseli presented Winckelmann's admiration for the artist in his translation of the *Gedanken* and other essays, and the consistency with which Raphael is held up against the "Flemish" or "Dutch" styles must have had a profound effect in reinforcing Blake's natural inclination toward the style of the Italian artist.

Winckelmann's dislike for Rubens's corpulent figures and the "laboured" (*mühsamen*") style of the Dutch is exaggerated in Fuseli's translation: "We cannot conclude, from the Homeric shape which Zeuxis gave his female figures, that he raised them, like Rubens, into flesh-hills." (FW176) Winckelmann had only described Rubens's females as *"zu fleischig."* (W130)[15] Throughout his essay, Winckelmann faults the Dutch and Flemish painters for their imitation of common or vulgar nature:

> The imitation of beauty is either reduced to a single object, and is *individual*, or, gathering observation from single ones, *composes of these one whole.* The former we call copying, drawing a portrait, tis the straight way to Dutch forms and figures; whereas the other leads to general beauty, and its ideal images, and is the way the Greeks took. (FW18)

> *Die Nachahmung des Schönen der Natur ist entweder auf einen einzelnen Vorwurf gerichtet, oder sie sammelt die Bemerkungen aus verschiedenen einzelnen in eins. Jenes heisst eine ähnliche Kopie, ein Porträt machen; es ist der Weg zu holländischen Formen und Figuren. Dieses aber ist der Weg zum allgemeinen Schönen und zu idealischen Bildern desselben; und derselbe ist es, den die Griechen genommen haben.* (W76)

In praising the mastery of the *Sistine Madonna*, Winckelmann once more contrasts it to the deficiencies of northern art, though not with so much force as Fuseli in his translation:

> Let those that approach this, and the rest of Raphael's works, in hoping of finding there the trifling Dutch and Flemish beauties, the laboured nicety of *Netscher*, or *Douw*, flesh ivoried by *Van der Werf*, or even the licked [sic!] manner of some of Raphael's living countrymen; let those I say, be told, that Raphael was not a great master for them. (FW39)

> *Alle diejenigen, welche zu diesem und andern Werken Raffaels treten, in der Hoffnung, die kleinen Schönheiten anzutreffen, die den Arbeiten der niederländischen Maler einen so hohen Preis geben: den mühsamen Fleiss eines Netscher, oder eines Dou, das elfenbeinerne Fleisch eines Van der Werff, oder auch die geleckte Manier einiger von Raffaels Landsleuten unserer Zeit; diese, sage ich, werden den grossen Raffael in dem Raffael vergebens suchen.* (W92-93)

Blake was consistently vicious in his attacks on the Dutch and Flemish schools, much more so than Winckelmann, who allowed Rubens his greatness, but simply placed his work on a much lower order than Raphael's.

Blake complained of the English taste for the Dutch style: "The taste of English amateurs has been too much formed upon pictures imported from Flanders and Holland; consequently our countrymen are easily brow-beat on the subject of painting;..." (K864) This complaint, which is voiced in a letter to the publisher Richard Phillips in 1806, and which also contains an eloquent defense of Fuseli's work, is repeated in verse in the *Manuscript Notebook (circa* 1808-1811):

To English Connoisseurs
You must agree that Rubens was a Fool,
And yet you make him master of your School
And give more money for his slobberings
Than you will give for Rafael's finest Things
.... (K546)

In another epigram in the *Manuscript Notebook* Blake attacks the realism of Dutch paintings, with their detailed representation of common things, much in the spirit of Fuseli's embellishment of Winckelmann who decries those who "blundered through the dirt of vulgar forms" (F252), *"nach den ihm gewöhnlichen Formen gebildet"*(W157):

A Pretty Epigram for [those *del.*] the Entertainment
of those who [pay *del.*] have Paid Great Sums in the
Venetian & Flemish Ooze

Nature & Art in this together Suit:
What is Most Grand is always most Minute.
Rubens thinks Tables, Chairs & Stools are Grand,
But Rafael thinks A Head, a foot, a hand. (K547)

Winckelmann sees, in a similar manner, the inferiority of Dutch painters in the fact that they realistically depict such common objects, and allows them greatness in landscape painting alone.

In Winckelmann's discussion of Greek painting, known to him only from prints and engravings, he praises the bold outline which he saw as the predominant characteristic of Greek design. In the linear simplicity of vase decorations, coins, gems, and excavated frescoes, he discovers what he terms *"Kontur."* In his translation, Fuseli labeled the second section of the *Reflections*: "II, Contour," and consistently translates "contour," even when Winckelmann writes *"Zeichnung"* or *"Umriss."* Winckelmann saw this "line of beauty" in all Greek works; and, although he was disappointed with the frescoes that had been unearthed at Herculaneum, he could not accept that painting should not have been as sublime as sculpture in the age of the Greeks:

Greek painting perhaps shares all the praises bestowed upon their sculpture, had time and the barbarity of mankind allowed us to be decisive to the point. (FW52)

The science of beautiful proportions, of Contour and Expression, could not be the exclusive privilege of Greek sculptors alone. (FW54)

Alles was zum Preise der griechischen Werke in der Bildhauerkunst gesagt werden kann, sollte nach aller Wahrscheinlichkeit auch von der Malerei der Griechen gelten. Die Zeit aber und die Wut der Menschen hat uns die Mittel geraubt, einen unumstösslichen Ausspruch darüber zu tun. (W103-104)

From the evidence available to modern man, Winckelmann concludes:

All the Greek painters were allowed is Contour and Expression. (F52)

Man gesteht den griechischen Malern Zeichnung und Ausdruck zu; und das ist alles....
(W104)

Perspective, composition, and coloring were denied the Greeks; but, Winckelmann asserts, these discoveries of modern art are only adjunct to the first principles of art. Perspective and coloring might be learned from the observation of nature, but nature "could never bestow the precision of Contour, that characteristic distinction of the Greeks" (FW22). *"Könnte die Nachahmung der Natur dem Künstler alles geben, so würde gewiss die Richtigkeit im Kontur durch sie nicht zu erhalten sein; diese muss von den Griechen allein erlernt werden." (W79). The "noble and manly contour" that the ancient artist saw around him in the persons of his beautifully formed countrymen, together with the Greek tendency to make the beautiful more beautiful resulted in the line of beauty. Raphael's greatness is seen in this "Kontur" as well as in the expression characteristic to the Greeks. Fuseli* renders Winckelmann's praise of the *Sistine Madonna* with a curious mistranslation (in italics):

her face brightens with innocence; *a form above the female size,* and the calmness of her mien, makes her appear as already beatified: she has that silent awfulness which the ancients spread over their deities. How grand, how noble is her contour. (FW38)

Seht die Madonna mit einem Gesichte voll Unschuld und zugleich einer mehr als weiblichen Grösse, *in einer selig ruhigen Stellung, in derjenigen Stille, welche die Alten in den Bildern ihrer Gottheiten herrschen liessen. Wie gross und edel ist ihr ganzer Kontur!*
(W91-92)

Raphael, Poussin, and Michelangelo are singled out by Winckelmann as having captured this line. Winckelmann grudgingly gives Michelangelo the prize for having come closest to the Greeks in mastery of outline:

...only Michael Angelo may be said to have attained the antique; but only in strong, muscular figures, heroic frame; not in those of tender youth nor in female bodies, which, under his bold hand grew Amazons. (FW23)

[Michelangelo ist] vielleicht der einzige, von dem man sagen könnte, dass er das Altertum erreicht; aber nur in starken muskulösen Figuren, welche unter seiner Hand zu Amazonen geworden sind. (W80)

This association of Michelangelo with bold outlines would be significant for Blake, who always considered Michelangelo and Raphael together as champions for drawing and line against the "plagiaries of Venice and Flanders." (K525). Sharp distinction of line—"the bounding line"—is central to Blake's concept of artistic creation in poetry as well as in his engravings and paintings. In the *Descriptive Catalogue* of 1809 he writes:

The great and golden rule of art, as well as of life, is this: That the more distinct, sharp, and wirey the bounding line, the more perfect the work of art; and the less keen and sharp, the greater is the evidence of weak imitation, plagiarism, and bungling. Great inventors, in all ages, knew this: Protogenes and Apelles knew each other by this line. Raphael and Michael Angelo and Albert Dürer are known by this and this alone. The want of this determinate and bounding form evidences the want of idea in the artist's mind, and the pretence of the plagiary in all its branches. How do we distinguish the oak from the beech, the horse from the ox, but by the bounding outline? (K585)

For Blake, the enemies of the sharp, wiry, bounding line were the Rubens, Rembrandt, and artists who blurred and blotted their lines "by means of that infernal machine called Chiaro Oscuro, in the hands of Venetian and Flemish Demons." (K582) But added to this list were the successful and fashionable painters against whom he raged: "Reynolds & Gainsborough Blotted & Blurred one against another & Divided all the English World between them. Fuseli, Indignant, almost hid himself. I am hid." (K445) For Winckelmann, the destroyer of the line was Bernini, whose work he knew very little at the time of the *Gedanken*, but who personified for him all the distortions of baroque taste. In his *"Erinnerung über die Betrachtung,"* Fuseli's "Instructions for the Connoisseur," Winckelmann identifies Bernini with a prejudice as strong as Blake's: "Bernini, that destroyer of art," (FW260) *"Bernini, der Kunstverderber."* (W163) For Winckelmann, as for Blake, the "line of beauty" in art "has no abrupt or broken parts," (FW260) *"hat nicht unterbrochene Teile."* (W162) Bernini had broken the illusive line of genius, known to the Greeks, but not accessible to all, which is described by Winckelmann in the same essay:

> Beauty consists in the harmony of the various parts of an individual. This is the philosopher's stone, which all artists must search for, though a few only find it: 'tis nonsense to him, who could not have formed the idea out of himself. (FW259)

> The line which beauty describes is elliptical, both uniform and various: 'tis not to be described by a circle, and from every point changes its direction. All this is easily said—*there is the rub!* 'Tis not in the power of Algebra to determine which line, more or less elliptic, forms the divers parts of the system of beauty—but the ancients knew it; I attest to their works, from the gods down to their vases. (FW259)

> *Schöne besteht in der Mannigfaltigkeit im Einfachen, dieses ist der Stein der Weisen, den die Künstler zu suchen haben, und welchen wenige finden, nur der versteht die wenigen Worte, der sich diesen Begriff aus sich selbst gemacht hat. Die Linie, die das Schöne beschreibt, ist elliptisch, und in derselben ist das Einfache und einige beständige Veränderung. Sie kann mit keinem Zirkel beschrieben werden und verändert in allen Punkten ihre Richtung. Dieses ist leicht gesagt und schwer zu lernen: welche Linie, mehr oder weniger elliptisch, die verschiedenen Teile zur Schönheit formt, kann die Algebra nicht bestimmen. Aber die Alten kannten sie, und wir finden sie vom Menschen bis auf ihre Gefässe. (W162)*

Blake's conception of the innate knowledge of beauty as expressed in the *Annotations to Reynolds* is strikingly like the first six lines of Winckelmann's statement:

> Knowledge of Ideal Beauty is Not to be Acquired. It is Born with us. Innate Ideas are in Every Man, Born with him; they are truly Himself. The man who says that we have No Innate Ideas must be a Fool & Knave, Having No Con-Science or Innate Science. (K459)

And for Blake, also, this beauty is defined by the line.

Winckelmann's discussion of Greek painting, an example of which he had never seen, but which he knew about from Pliny, was not without precedent. In the *Erinnerungen...,* Fuseli's "Instructions for the Connoisseur," Winckelmann quotes George Turnbull, author of *Treatise on Ancient Painting* (1740). Turnbull, Winckelmann, and later, Fuseli in his lectures of 1801, refer to

Apelles and Protogenes synonymously with excellence in drawing. Blake, according to J.T. Smith, claimed Apelles "to have been his tutor." Appearing to him in visions, Apelles:

> was, he said, so much pleased with his style, that once when he appeared before him, among many of his observations, he delivered the following:—"You certainly possess my system of colouring; and I now wish you to draw my person, which has hitherto been untruly delineated."[16]

Raphael, Michelangelo, Apelles, Protogenes—all geniuses who were "born with the determinate organs" were able to see the line of beauty. In Blake's remarks about the talents of a child of his friend, Thomas Heath Malkin, Blake praises the drawings of the talented boy who died at the age of seven:

> They are all firm, determinate outline, or identical form. Had the hand which executed these little ideas been that of a plagiary, who works only from memory, we should have seen blots called masses; blots without form, and therefore without meaning. These blots of light and dark, as being the result of labour, are always clumsy and indefinite; the effect of rubbing out and putting in, like the progress of a blind man, or of one in the dark, who feels his way, but does not see it. These are not so. Even the copy from Raphael's Cartoon of St. Paul preaching, is a firm, determinate outline, struck at once, as Protogenes struck his line, when he meant to make himself known to Apelles. (K439)

There can be little doubt that Blake's conception of the artist, his early and consistent championing of the work and genius of Raphael against Dutch realism, and his preference for a linear style was influenced by Fuseli's Winckelmann. His later personal association with Fuseli, who himself was never to discard these enthusiasms of Winckelmann's early essays, could only have reinforced what the young apprentice read in Fuseli's Winckelmann. An amusing piece of doggerel that Blake wrote in his *Notebook* between 1808 and 1811 presents a "Blakified" synthesis of inspiration, genius, and outline distant from and yet close to the more somber ruminations of Winckelmann:

> All Pictures that's Painted with Sense & with Thought
> Are Painted by Madmen as sure as a Groat;
> For the Greater the Fool in the Pencil more blest,
> And when they are drunk they always paint best.
> They never can Rafael it, Fuseli it, nor Blake it;
> If they can't see an outline, pray how can they make it?
> When Men will draw outlines begin you to jaw them;
> Madmen see outlines & therefore they draw them. (K548-549)

Naked Beauty Displayed

Samuel Foster Damon's statement that Blake was the first English painter "who really understood that the nude is the basis of all art," is a bold and categorical assertion.[1] There can be no question that "nakedness," as Blake preferred to call the body divested of clothing, occupies an important position in Blake's aesthetic scheme from the beginning to the end of his artistic life. In his early reading of Fuseli's Winckelmann, he found beauty and expression inexorably connected with nudity, and there is a dimension to the concept of the glory of the nakedness of man in Blake's mythology which is similar to Winckelmann's own conception of a past and heroic age.

Winckelmann's controversial contention that the ancient Greeks were a more beautiful race, "prepared to beauty, by the influence of the mildest and purest skies," (FW4) *"Der Einfluss eines sanften und reinen Himmels wirkte bei der ersten Bildung der Griechen...,"* (W64) was one of the bases upon which his theory of classical beauty rests. Despite the derision and outrage with which this idea was met by English critics, for Winckelmann the idea was completely serious and profound. His insistence that the imitation of classics was not at odds with the imitation of nature rests upon two assumptions: (1) The Greeks had a more beautiful climate, geography, and nature surrounding them; (2) the benevolence of their environment together with their style of living produced more beautiful bodies and countenances: "perfectly elegant," (FW4) *"die edle Form."* (W64) For Winckelmann, it follows that having examples of beauty around them at all times and being taught to exercise the body to a state of perfect condition, the Greeks had more opportunity to contemplate the school of perfected physical nature, which:

> taught the Greeks to go on farther. They began to form certain general ideas of beauty, with regard to the proportion of inferior parts, as well as the whole frame: these they raised above the reach of mortality, according to the superior model of ideal nature. (FW12)

> *Diese häufigen Gelegenheiten zur Beobachtung der Natur veranlassten die griechischen Künstler noch weiter zu gehen: sie fingen an, sich gewisse allgemeine Begriffe von Schönheiten sowohl einzelner Teile als ganzer Verhältnisse der Körper zu bilden, die sich über die Natur selbst erheben sollten; ihr Urbild war eine bloss im Verstande entworfene geistige Natur. (W71)*

Winckelmann uses the phrase *"bloss im Verstande entworfen..."* twice in the *Gedanken*, once referring to *"Bilder,"* (W64) and once to *"Natur."* Fuseli translates the phrase only in one passage, where he writes: "brain-born images," (FW4) and identifies the source of the concept as Proclus's commentary on the *Timaeus* of Plato. In spite of this reliance on the *Timaeus*, Winckelmann does not project a strictly Platonic view of beauty in the *Gedanken* and does not place the ideal before nature, but depicts the ideal as having been perceptible in nature to the Greeks in parts, and after much exposure, having been gradually comprehended by the ancients in its totality. Thus, beautiful nature leads one to comprehend the ideal which is physically recreated as a unity by the artist in depictions of the perfected human form.

Winckelmann did not want to write yet another commentary on ancient aesthetics; he was attempting to say something new, to reinterpret the concept of the ideal for modern (German) artists, something more pragmatic and concrete than metaphysical. He viewed the Greeks with a curious mixture of rationalism and ecstatic *Schwärmerei*. His convoluted argument that the (more) beautiful nature of the Greeks came first, and then the perception of the ideal, was a way of being able to assert: "We observe, nevertheless, that the Greek artists...submitted to the law of the Thebans: 'To do, under a penalty, their best in imitating Nature'," (FW13) *"Bei allen diesen bemerkt man, dass das von den Thebanern ihren Künstlern vorgeschriebene Gesetz: 'die Natur bei Strafe aufs beste nachzuahmen'"* (W72); while at the same time observing that the work of the Greek artists was more ideal and beautiful than nature:

> But to form a "just resemblance," and, at the same time, "a handsomer one," being always the chief rule they observed.... They must of necessity, be supposed to have had in view a more beauteous and more perfect nature. (FW14)

> *Das Gesetz aber, "die Personen ähnlich und zu gleicher Zeit schöner zu machen," war allezeit das höchste Gesetz, welches die griechischen Künstler über sich erkannten, und setzt notwendig eine Absicht des Meisters auf eine schönere und vollkommenere Natur voraus. (W73)*

Winckelmann's vision of contemporary, more common, nature led him to a distaste for any realistic depiction of the modern natural world. Let the Greeks, who were schooled by perfect nature, lost forever to modern man, be the teachers of beauty. Copying vulgar nature can but lead the artist astray:

> Follows it not then, that the beauties of the Greek statues being discovered with less difficulty than those of nature, are of course more affecting: not so diffused, but more harmoniously united? and if this be true, the pointing to nature as chiefly imitable, is leading us into a more tedious and bewildered road to the knowledge of perfect beauty, than setting up the ancients for that purpose. (FW17)

> *Folgt nicht daraus, dass die Schönheit der griechischen Statuen eher zu entdecken ist, als die Schönheiten in der Natur, und dass also jene rührender, nicht so sehr zerstreut, sondern mehr in eins vereinigt, als es dieses ist? Das Studium der Natur muss also wenigstens ein längerer und mühsamerer Weg zur Kenntnis des vollkommenen Schönen sein, als es das Studium der Antiken ist.... (W76)*

The Greeks, having sorted out the maze of nature, can serve as guides for young artists. Winckelmann poses a test for this theory: to choose two youths of equal talents:

devoting one to antiquity, the other to nature, this would draw nature as he finds her; if Italian he might paint like Caravaggio; if Flemish and lucky, like Jac. Jordans; if French, like Stella: the other would draw like Raphael. (FW21-22)

...den einen das Altertum, den andern die blosse Natur studieren liesse. Dieser würde die Natur bilden, wie er sie findet: als ein Italiener würde er Figuren malen vielleicht wie Caravaggio; als ein Niederländer, wenn er glücklich ist, wie Jacob Jordaens; als ein Franzose, wie Stella: jener aber würde die Natur bilden, wie sie es verlangt, und Figuren malen, wie Raffael. (W79)

Blake took his training in the latter fashion, learning from prints of paintings by Michelangelo and Raphael, from plaster casts, and engravings of gems and marbles. Except for a few casual portraits, there is little evidence that Blake ever drew from *"blosser Natur."*

Convinced that the young artist trained in the school of the ancients would paint like Raphael, Winckelmann writes " *Figuren male, wie Raffael.*" Fuseli abbreviates the phrase: "draw like Raphael." The change in the translation is worth noting, because in every instance when Winckelmann thinks of beauty he has in mind *Figuren*. His entire concept of nature centers around the naked body of man, and *schöne Natur* in art is synonymous with representations of the human form. The broader, psychological nature of the later romantics is entirely absent from his aesthetic ken. Thus, for Winckelmann, the *Apollo Belvedere* becomes "a compound of the United Force of Nature, Genius, and Art," (FW19) *"was Natur, Geist und Kunst hervorzubringen vermögend gewesen...."* (W76) This perspective of the human body as the apex of beauty and expression marks the drawings, engravings and paintings of Blake, and links him to the neoclassical style, despite the valid notion that in many respects his art stands outside his time and anticipates much that was to come in romanticism. In the case of Winckelmann, the veneration of glorious bodies set in a vanished age of heroes does not lead back to nature, but away from, or perhaps more accurately, beyond physical nature. This is also the case in Blake's art.

From his earliest original engraving that has survived, Blake's "Glad Day," the naked body is splendidly displayed. This early work was to be embellished by Blake in later versions, and is a clear example of his use of images and designs that he borrowed and embued with his own special interpretation. Anthony Blunt suggested two possible sources for the design: Vitruvian man, the Renaissance commonplace of the ideally proportioned man within a circle, and two engravings showing the front and back views of a bronze figure, taken from *The Antiquities of Herculaneum.*[2] The figure is clearly idealized, yet because of Blake's treatment, it escapes the bounded, closed form of man measured within a circle. Winckelmann, himself, argued with the circle as the measure of man, probably thinking again of the cosmological myth in Plato's *Timaeus*, which Harper suggests "originated the Western symbolism of the perfection of the circle":[3]

The line which beauty describes is elliptical, both uniform and various: 'tis not to be described by a circle, and from every point changes its direction....'Tis not the power of Algebra to determine which line, more or less elliptic, forms the divers parts of the system into beauty—.... (FW259)

Die Linie, die das Schöne beschreibt, ist elliptisch, und in derselben ist das Einfache und einige beständige Veränderung. Sie kann mit keinem Zirkel beschrieben werden und

84

verändert in allen Punkten ihre Richtung...welche Linie,...kann die Algebra nicht bestimmen. (W162)

It is tempting to connect Blake's use of the circle as the limiting, "bounding sphere" in his mythology with this early reading of Winckelmann, as well as his insistence that beauty cannot be measured by mathematical proportions, which could only reduce the world to "the same dull round." Eight years after he executed the engraving "Glad Day" he wrote in *There Is No Natural Religion*:

Second Series

IV. The bounded is loathed by its possessor. The same dull round,
even of a universe, would soon become a mill with complicated wheels.

(K97)

Harper assigns Blake's use of the circle symbol to Blake's knowledge of Taylor's translation of Plato's *Timaeus*, which "did not become well known among English writers until the publication of Taylor's *Cratylus, Phaedo, Parmenides and Timaeus* in 1793."[4] But Blake had as early as 1777 read Fuseli's translation: "The human form allows of no circle, nor has any antique vase its profile semicircular," (FW259) *"So wie nichts Zirkelförmiges am Menschen ist, so macht auch kein Profil eines alten Gefässes einen halben Zirkel."* (W162) Without belaboring the point, it is safe to say that the *Reflections* and other essays in Fuseli's Winckelmann translation were Blake's first confrontation with ideas from the *Timaeus*. Fuseli's footnote would at the very least have acquainted the avid young reader with the name of the dialogue, which Harper has convincingly shown to be the source of many neoplatonic elements in Blake's thought. The "Glad Day" figure appears again in an engraving that Blake executed sometime between 1818 and 1820 for *Jerusalem*. There the figure, seen from the back, is "Albion adoring the Crucified Christ." The form is still naked, idealized, but now has become the symbol of heroic Albion. Like Winckelmann, Blake evokes a glorious past, not of ancient Greece, but of ancient Britain. Either naked or in clinging drapery, the prophets and characters drawn from Blake's imagination and from the poetry and scriptures he loved, exist in a timeless, ahistorical, indefinite realm.

The theme of nakedness in the poetry of Blake, which cannot be separated from his use of it in the graphics, is found in the early poems, often associated with innocence, or with the condemnation of prudery. In the beginning verses of "A Little GIRL Lost" Blake writes:

Children of the future Age
Reading this indignant page,
Know that in a former time
Love! sweet Love! was thought a crime.

In the Age of Gold,
Free from winter's cold,
Youth and maiden bright
To the holy light,
Naked in the sunny beams delight. (K219)

In Blake's later works, human "lineaments" are identified with sexual energy, the body is seen as the sensual definition of the soul. Thus speaks the polemical voice of the Devil in the *Marriage of Heaven and Hell:*

Plate 4

1. Man has no Body distinct from his Soul; for that call'd Body is a portion of Soul discern'd by the five Senses, the chief inlets of Soul in this age.
2. Energy is the only life, and is from the Body; and Reason is the bound or outward circumference of Energy.
3. Energy is Eternal Delight. (K149)

Plate 8

The nakedness of woman is the work of God. (K151)

"The lineaments of Gratified desire" is a phrase employed with irreverent and satirical turn in the verses in the *Notebook* of 1793:

40
Abstinence sows sand all over
The ruddy limbs & flaming hair,
But Desire Gratified
Plants fruits of life & beauty there.

41
In a wife I would desire
What in whores is always found—
The Lineaments of Gratified desire. (K178)

59
Several Questions Answered

What is it men in women do require?
The lineaments of Gratified Desire.
What is it women do in men require?
The lineaments of Gratified Desire. (K184)

But Blake retains the image and even incorporates it in his profound vision of Revelation and Apocalypse in *Milton:*

"These are the destroyers of Jerusalem, these are the murderers
"Of Jesus, who deny the Faith & mock at Eternal Life,
"Who pretend to Poetry that they may destroy Imagination
"By imitation of Nature's Images drawn from Remembrance.
"These are the Sexual Garments, the Abomination of Desolation,
"Hiding the Human Lineaments as with an Ark & Curtains
"Which Jesus rent & now shall wholly purge away with Fire
"Till Generations swallow'd up in Regeneration." (K533)

The hypocrisy and distortion of the modern attitude toward the body is found in Winckelmann: The Greeks perfected their bodies, which were from birth "undistorted by swaddling clothes," (FW5) *"niemals in Windeln einge-schränkt gewesen."* (W64) Further, writes Winckelmann:

In their dress they were profound followers of nature. No modern stiffening habit, no squeezing stays, hindered nature from forming easy beauty. (FW7)

Zudem war der ganze Anzug der Griechen so beschaffen, dass er der bildenden Natur nicht den geringsten Zwang antat. Das Wachstum der schönen Form litt nichts durch die verschiedenen Arten und Teile unserer heutigen pressenden und klemmenden Kleidung.... (W66)

Speaking of the schools where the youths exercised unhampered by clothing, Winckelmann continues:

> Here, beautiful nakedness appeared with such a liveliness of expression, such truth and variety of situations, such a noble air of the body, as it would be ridiculous to look for in any hired model of our academies. (FW10)

> *Die schönste Nacktheit der Körper zeigte sich hier in so mannigfaltigen, wahrhaften und edlen Stellungen, in die ein gedungenes Modell, welches in unseren Akademien aufgestellt wird, nicht zu setzen ist.* (W69)

Not only among the Greeks was this freer attitude the practice:

> During certain solemnities the young Spartan maidens danced naked before the young men: strange as this may seem, but will appear more probable, when we consider that the Christians of the primitive church, both men and women, were dipped together in the same fount. (FW11)

> *...die jungen Mädchen in Sparta an einem gewissen Feste ganz nackend vor den Augen der jungen Leute tanzten. Was hier fremd scheinen könnte, wird erträglicher werden, wenn man bedenkt, dass auch die Christen der ersten Kirche ohne die geringste Verhüllung, sowohl Männer als Weiber, zu gleicher Zeit und in einem und ebendemselben Taufsteine getauft oder untergetaucht worden sind.* (W70)

In the *Descriptive Catalogue*, Blake's commentary on a painting in his exhibit, "The Ancient Britons," he speaks of the responsibility of the artist in preserving the past and shows his vision of the "warlike naked Britons." Unfortunately, the painting as well as any other eyewitness description of it is lost, for Blake's exegesis of it is a digression on mythology, aesthetics, and the relation of the human form to beauty that belongs to the same genre as Winckelmann's *Gedanken*:

> The Britons (say historians) were naked civilized men, learned, studious, abstruse in thought and contemplation; naked, simple, plain in their acts and manners; wiser than after-ages. They were overwhelmed by brutal arms, all but a small remnant; Strength, Beauty, and Ugliness escaped the wreck, and remain for ever unsubdued, age after age.
>
> The British Antiquities are now in the Artist's hands; all his visionary contemplations, relating to his own country and its ancient glory, when it was, as it again shall be, the source of learning and inspiration. (K577)
> . . . .
> It has been said to the Artist, "take the Apollo for your model of your beautiful Man, and the Hercules for your strong Man, and the Dancing Fawn for your Ugly Man." Now he comes to his trial. He knows that what he does is not inferior to the grandest Antiques. Superior they cannot be, for human power cannot go beyond either what he does, or what they have done; it is the gift of God, it is inspiration and vision. He had resolved to emulate those precious remains of antiquity; he has done so and the result you behold; his ideas of strength and beauty have not been greatly different. (K579)

Indeed, Blake's conception of ideal forms was not greatly different from those he studied in engravings and casts of antiquities. Nowhere is this more clearly shown than in the centrality of the human body to Blake's idea of beauty. In this he is every bit as much a neoclassicist as Winckelmann:

> The Beauty that is annexed and appended to folly, is a lamentable accident and error of the mortal and perishing life; it does but seldom happen; but with this unnatural mixture the sublime Artist can have nothing to do; it is fit for the burlesque. The Beauty proper for

sublime art is lineaments, or forms and features that are capable of being the receptacles of intellect; accordingly the Painter has given in his beautiful man, his own idea of intellectual Beauty. The face and limbs that deviates or alters least, from infancy to old age, is the face and limbs of greatest Beauty and perfection. (K579-580)

Blake's ancient Britons are seen in harmony with their landscape and nature

The flush of health in flesh exposed to the open air, nourished by the spirits of forests and floods in that ancient happy period, which history has recorded, cannot be like the sickly daubs of Titian, or Rubens. Where will the copier of nature, as it now is, find a civilized man, who has been accustomed to go naked? Imagination only can furnish us with colouring appropriate, such as found in the Frescos of Rafael and Michael Angelo: the disposition of forms always directs colouring in works of true art. (K580-581)

How reminiscent are these ancient Britons of Winckelmann's Greeks:

from their earliest youth, the happy inhabitants of Greece were devoted to mirth and pleasure, where narrow spirited formality never restrained the liberty of manners, the artist enjoyed nature without a veil. (FW9)

In Griechenland aber, wo man sich der Lust und Freude von Jugend auf weihte, wo ein gewisser heutiger bürgerlicher Wohlstand der Freiheit der Sitten niemals Eintrag getan, da zeigte sich die schöne Natur unverhüllt zum grossen Unterricht der Künstler. (W68-69)

Blake expresses the same idea more bluntly:

As to modern Man, stripped from his load of clothing he is like a dead corpse. Hence Rubens, Titian, Correggio and all of that class, are like leather and chalk; their men are like leather and their women like chalk;... (K581)

Blake's strongest statement concerning the use of nudity in art is inscribed around his engraving of the Laocoön, which he executed toward the end of his career, forty-one years after he read Winckelmann's enraptured description of the statue: "Art can never exist without Naked Beauty displayed." (K776)

It is curious that Blake waited so long to engrave the group, and that when he did so it was because he had been commissioned for a print for Rees's *Cyclopaedia.* Sometime after the engraving of 1815, he drew a pencil interpretation of the *Laocoön.* The only other mention recorded in the *Concordance* of the famous statue in Blake's work is in a defense of his own indifference to accuracy in costuming in a picture which has been lost:

I understand that my Costume is incorrect, but in this I plead the authority of the ancients, who often deviated from the Habits to preserve the Manners, as in the instance of Laocoön, who, though is a priest, is represented naked. (K583)

Winckelmann's description of the figure of Laocoön notes this same discrepancy, and, in fact, makes of it an example of the use of the body in the expressiveness of the work of art:

Had Laocoön been covered with a garb becoming an ancient sacrificer, his sufferings would have lost one-half of their expression. (FW31)

Unter einem Gewande, welches der Künstler dem Laokoon als einem Priester hätte geben sollen, würde uns sein Schmerz nur halb so sinnlich gewesen sein. (W87)

By the time Blake engraves the *Laocoön* and embellishes his private copy with crowded inscriptions, the priest of Apollo becomes the Urizen/God/Jehova/Christ of his complex mythology. Yet the symbol of Laocoön as the noble soul in strife remains the same: Blake makes use of the "allegory" of Laocoön, to use Winckelmann's special term for symbolical images in art. And although in the original pencil interpretation the central figure is clothed, the strong, muscular body still stands forth under the clinging drapery, "which is formed alone by the Shape of the Naked." (K462) Blake's Urizen/Laocoön is God made in flesh with noble contours. Critics objected to Blake's imbuing spirits with real bodies, and he responds in A Descriptive Catalogue with the authority of the ancient art to which he had been directed by Fuseli's Winckelmann:

> The connoisseurs and artists who have made objections to Mr. B.'s mode of representing spirits with real bodies, would do well to consider that the Venus, the Minerva, the Jupiter, the Apollo, which they admire in Greek statues are all of them representations of spiritual existences, of Gods immortal, to the mortal perishing organ of sight; and yet they are embodied and organized in solid marble. (K576)

Allegory

The idea of allegory forms a central part of Winckelmann's *Gedanken* and is the subject of a larger essay in 1764: *Versuch einer Allegorie, besonders für die Kunst.* Next to the idea that the modern artist must be as familiar with the Greek arts as with a friend, the concept of the necessity of profound or sublime allegory in the plastic and graphic arts was Winckelmann's most fervently held theory. The seminal thoughts in the *Gedanken*, as seen in the intensified light of Fuseli's translation, foreshadow the elaborate and eclectic mythopoeic system developed by William Blake over the course of his artistic life.

Any discussion of Blake's use of allegory must be approached with some caution. In the later works, the word becomes a negative label associated with the poet's ostensible rejection of the classical tradition. Blake often sees allegory as a device for hiding truth, "Vision," or "Imagination" is the vehicle by which the poet/prophet reveals truth. Thus in the *Note-Book*, in the essay to which D.G. Rossetti gave the title *Vision of the Last Judgment*, Blake writes in 1810:

> The Last Judgment is not Fable or Allegory, but Vision. Fable or Allegory are a totally distinct & inferior kind of Poetry. Vision or Imagination is a Representation of what Eternally Exists, Really & Unchangeably. Fable or Allegory is Form'd by the daughters of Memory. Imagination is surrounded by the daughters of Inspiration, who in the aggregate are call'd Jerusalem. Fable is Allegory, but what Critics called The Fable, is Vision itself. The Hebrew Bible & the Gospel of Jesus are not Allegory, but Eternal Vision or Imagination of all that Exists. (K604)

For Blake, "Vision" and "Imagination" are the immediate, real revelations that are seen by the poet, as by the biblical prophet "with their imaginative and immortal organs; the Apostles the same; the clearer the organ the more distinct the object. A Spirit and a Vision are not, as the modern philosophy supposes, a cloudy vapour, or a nothing: they are organized and minutely articulated beyond all that the mortal and perishing nature can produce." (K576) The Bible, as an eternal and perpetually renewed revelation, remains vision, but the Greek fables, "which originated in Spiritual Mystery & Real Visions" are "lost & clouded in Fable and Allegory." The real vision, seen in the most ancient time, when not renewed and experienced directly, can then be preserved only in the memory. Hence the consistent juxtaposition in Blake's aesthetic system between art and poetry inspired by "The Greek Muses...the daughters of Mnemosyne, or Memory and not of Inspiration or

Imagination...." (K565-566) and original and theophanous works of direct inspiration. But Blake's insistence upon the visionary nature of the images and figures in his art, which was taken as canon by his early admirers and critics, does not alter the fact that his poetry and art abounds with allegory, and specifically that sort that he despises as having been "Begat on Mnemosyne." (K605) His visions, however real they might have been, were furnished by his "making many Finish'd Copies both of Nature & Art & of whatever comes his way from Earliest Childhood." (K455). Throughout his lifetime, Blake was to stock his mind with images, designs, mythology, and metaphysical conceptions which were stored in his prodigious memory for future use, often far removed from the context in which he first encountered them.

The matter is further complicated by the fact that in his famous letters to Thomas Butts in 1803, Blake, probably speaking of his *Milton,* writes on April 25:

> ...for I have in these three years composed an immense number of verses on One Grand Theme, Similar to Homer's Iliad or Milton's Paradise Lost, the Persons & Machinery intirely new to the Inhabitants of Earth (some of the Persons Excepted). (K823)

and on July 6th:

> Thus I hope that all our three years' trouble Ends in Good Luck at least & shall be forgot by my affections & only remember'd by my Understanding; to be a Memento in time to come, & to speak to future generations by a Sublime Allegory, which is now perfectly completed into a Grand Poem. I may praise it, since I dare not pretend to be other than the Secretary; the Authors are in Eternity. I consider it as the Grandest Poem that this World Contains. Allegory address'd to the Intellectual powers, while it is altogether hidden from the Corporeal Understanding, is my Definition of the Most Sublime Poetry; it is also somewhat in the same manner defin'd by Plato. This Poem shall by Divine Assistance, be progressively Printed & Ornamented with Prints & given to the Public. (K824-825)

Thus, on the one hand, the word allegory is used for all poetry which is not inspired, and on the other hand, Blake uses the term "Sublime Allegory" to describe his greatest prophetic work. The puzzle of this seeming paradox, which led S. Foster Damon to call this one positive allusion to "Sublime Allegory" a "slip of the pen,"[1] has been clarified by Northrop Frye, who differentiates between "the most sublime poetry," demanding commentary, and the "Spenserian" or "continuous" allegories.[2] In Blake's identification of the creative imagination of the poet with the creative power of God, his poetry is for Frye not "allegorical but mythopoeic."[3] More recently, Joseph Anthony Wittreich has seen in Blake's two conceptions of allegory—the literal and the critical—the key to understanding Blake's concept of himself as a poet, and of his place within the tradition of epic and prophetic writing. Wittreich develops Blake's view of himself as the Miltonic poet "...an allegorist, a symbolist, who looks back for his aesthetic not to Homer or to Vergil but to the Bible. Milton's allegories are not simplistic but complex,..."[4]

Winckelmann clearly distinguishes between two classes of allegory in a more secular vein:

> Viz. the *sublime* and the *more vulgar.* Symbols of the one might be those by which some mythological or philosophical allusion, or even some unknown mysterious rite, is ex-

pressed. Such as are more commonly understood, *viz.* personified virtues and vices & c. might be referred to the other. (FW201-202)

Man könnte die allegorischen Bilder der Alten unter zwei Arten fassen und eine höhere und gemeinere Allegorie setzen, wie überhaupt in der Malerei dieser Unterschied stattfinden kann. (W143)

The sublime allegory of which Winckelmann writes must always have something in it for the spirit of man, must be in some way inspired and intrinsically related to the thing or idea to which it alludes. He recognizes the emptiness of allegories which have, because of time and distance, lost that essential element and have become mere clichés or decorative forms devoid of intellectual content:

Indeed the sublime allegory of the ancients has not been transmitted to us, without the loss of its most valuable treasures: it is poor, when compared with the second kind [of vulgar allegory] which is often provided with several symbols for one Idea. (FW206)

Die höhere Allegorie der Alten ist freilich ihrer grössten Schätze beraubt, auf uns gekommen, sie ist arm in Ansehung der zweiten Art. Diese hat nicht selten mehr als ein einziges Bild zu einem einzigen Ausdruck. (W145)

Yet, for the artist who has immersed himself in the beauty of ancient poetry, the source has not been cut off:

However the remains of ancient allegory are not yet worn out; there are still many secret stores: the poets and other monuments of antiquity, afford numbers of beautiful images. (FW211)

Unterdessen sind die übriggebliebenen Allegorien von Künstlern neuerer Zeiten noch nicht insgesamt verbraucht. Es sind vielen unter ihnen hier und da einige unbekannt geblieben, und die Dichter und die übrigen Denkmale des Altertums können noch allezeit einen reichen Stoff zu schönen Bildern darreichen. (W146)

Wittreich names Fuseli among the renewers in the eighteenth century of a tradition of allegory "which took shape during the Renaissance," and as "one of those voices which when raised, were generally disregarded as they are generally disregarded still; yet they seem to be the voices that Blake in this theoretical statement echoes and in his poems follows."[5] Fuseli's "voice" in this matter is inexorably tied to his activities as a transmitter and translator of Winckelmann's thought. In 1764, shortly before he left Berlin, he collaborated with Sulzer on seven articles in his *Allgemeine Theorie der schönen Künste.* Among these articles was the entry on "Allegorie." The Fuseli/Sulzer exposition on allegory refers to Winckelmann's ideas on the subject, and repeats some concepts from the *Gedanken,* a copy of which he had brought with him from Switzerland.

Fuseli's later descriptions of allegory in his *Aphorisms on Art* and his lectures do not differ in any substantial way from the ideas he first read and translated in the *Gedanken.* This point is important for the lasting influence of Winckelmann's ideas on Fuseli; for, among his German readers, Winckelmann's thoughts on allegory were the most coolly received aspect of his famous early writings. Schlegel was later to criticize the manner in which all aspects of pictorial and rhetorical allusion had been confounded by Winckelmann under one rubric.[6] While it is true that Winckelmann's aesthetic pronouncements are wide, sweeping, and sometimes indistinct, it is also true that his purpose was to discover and reform taste among the artists of his country rather than to write a discourse on the distinctions of genre, form, and typology. The inclusion of mythology and religion with allegory, which is characteristic in the *Gedanken*, could be seen as synthesis rather than confusion in Blake's own heterodox metaphysical system: "Their personal theology was quite allegorical; and so is ours," (FW195) *"Die Göttergeschichte aber ist nichts als Allegorie und machet den grössten Theil derselben auch bei uns."* (W13) It is also important to note that Winckelmann's discussion of allegory does not limit itself only to its use in painting, but is central to his idealistic conception of the creative act itself. When he speaks of allegory in painting, he is speaking about the very soul of art.

> There is another important step left towards the atchievement [sic] of the art: but the artist, who, boldly foresaking the common path, dares to attempt it, finds himself at once on the brink of a precipice, and starts back dismayed. (FW56)

> *Zur Erweiterung der Kunst ist noch ein grosser Schritt übrig zu tun. Der Künstler, welcher von der gemeinen Bahn abzuweichen anfängt, oder wirklich abgewichen ist, sucht diesen Schritt zu wagen, aber sein Fuss bleibt an dem jähesten Orte der Kunst stehen, und hier sieht er sich hilflos.* (W107)

Typically, Fuseli's artist expressively "starts back dismayed" where Winckelmann's stands in bewilderment. But Fuseli has captured the spirit of Winckelmann's meaning, and in the following important exposition of the idea of allegory, he translates with an admirable economy of words:

> The subject matter of modern artists—the fables, the saints, and metamorphoses—have been repeated over and over again until every tolerable judge grows sick at them. The Judicious artist falls asleep over a Daphne and Apollo, a Proserpine carried off by Pluto, and Europa &c. he wishes for occasions to shew himself a poet, to produce significant images, to paint allegory. (FW57)

> *Die Geschichte der Heiligen, die Fabeln und Verwandlungen sind der ewig und fast einzige Vorwurf der neueren Maler seit einigen Jahrhunderten. Man hat sie auf tausenderlei Art gewandt und ausgekünstelt, so dass endlich Überdruss und Ekel den Weisen in der Kunst und den Kenner überfallen muss.*

> *Ein Künstler, der eine Seele hat, die denken gelernt, lässt dieselbe müssig und ohne Beschäftigung bei einer Daphne und bei einem Apollo, bei einer Entführung der Proserpina, einer Europa und dergleichen. Er sucht sich als einen Dichter zu zeigen, und Figuren durch Bilder, das ist, allegorisch zu malen.* (W107)

For Winckelmann, whose experience in literature at the time he wrote this essay far surpassed his knowledge of sculpture and painting, poetry was the measure by which the visual arts were to be described and judged. If Winckelmann discovered the essence of Raphael's greatness by tracing his inspiration back to the ancients, he arrived at the Laocoön with Homer as his guide. There was nothing in this approach that would have offended Fuseli's sensibilities. It was the approach of Bodmer, Breitinger, and Sulzer. Fuseli's orientation to the plastic and graphic arts was outspokenly literary. The "confusion" of the requirements of the media, central to Lessing's "correction" or explication of Winckelmann's theory of expression, was almost doctrine to Fuseli. In one of the first articles that he wrote for Johnson's *Analytical Review*, concerning the history and state of the arts in England, Fuseli writes:

The analogy between Poetry and Painting has been admitted in the earliest of ages. Painting is silent Poetry and Poetry is a speaking picture—Simonides. Men of superior minds see nature through the medium of a fine imagination, so that however different the mere machinery of their art and the quality of their materials they will have a general resemblance in the ideal and make very similar impressions. The painter's colours are his diction. The excellence of pictures or language consists in raising clear, complete, and circumstantial images, and turning readers into spectators. A stile [sic] in painting is the same as writing; be it words or colours, they convey sentiments. Every epithet used by a good writer paints its objects and paints it distinctly.[7]

For Blake, who valued the one side of his double talent no less than the other, Winckelmann's discussion of allegory must have been the first intellectualization of his dual vision of himself as poet/painter. The painter "wishes to shew himself a poet," *"er sucht sich als einen Dichter zu zeigen":* this phrase alone perhaps best explains what Winckelmann has in mind when he speaks of allegory. The painter must be as the sublime poet: learned in great literature, religions, mythologies.

Winckelmann is actually calling for some sort of encyclopaedic catalogue upon which the modern artist, "lost in a desart," (FW58) *"wie in einer Einöde,"* (W108) could draw in order to give pictorial representation of abstracted ideas:

The painter who thinks beyond his palette longs for some learned apparatus, from whose store he might be enabled to invest abstracted ideas with sensible and meaning images. Nothing has been published of this kind, to satisfy a rational being; the essays hitherto made are not considerable, and far beneath this great design. (FW58)

Der Maler, der weiter denkt als seine Palette reicht, wünscht einen gelehrten Vorrat zu haben, wohin er gehen, und bedeutende und sinnlich gemachte Zeichen von Dingen, die nicht sinnlich sind, nehmen könnte. Ein vollständiges Werk in dieser Art ist noch nicht vorhanden: die bisherigen Versuche sind nicht beträchtlich genug und reichen nicht bis an diese grossen Absichten. (W108)

Here, as elsewhere in the *Gedanken,* the pragmatic aspect of the essay might seem to reduce Winckelmann's message to the tone of a pedantic textbook on how to become a great artist:

The artist would require a work, containing every image with which any abstracted idea might be poetically invested: a work collected from all mythology, the best poets of all ages, the mysterious philosophy of different nations, the monuments of the ancients on coins, utensils, &c. This magazine should be distributed into several classes, and, with proper application to peculiar possible cases, adapted to the instruction of the artist. (FW60)

Der Künstler hat ein Werk vonnöten, welches aus der ganzen Mythologie, aus den besten Dichtern alter und neuerer Zeiten, aus der geheimen Weltweisheit vieler Völker, aus den Denkmalen des Altertums auf Steinen, Münzen und Geräten diejenigen sinnlichen Figuren und Bilder enthält, wodurch allgemeine Begriffe dichterisch gebildet worden sind. Dieser reiche Stoff würde in gewisse bequeme Klassen zu bringen und durch eine besondere Anwendung und Deutung auf mögliche einzelne Fälle, zum Unterricht der Künstler, einzurichten sein. (W110)

What seems pedantry in this part of the essay, however, might actually have provided Blake with the stimulus to stock his mind early with "the mysterious philosophy of different ages, the monuments of the ancients on coins, utensils, &c." Ruthven Todd (1946) was the first to discover Blake's debt to just such a source book: Jacob Bryant's *New System, or an Analysis of Ancient Mythology* (1774-1776).[8] Blake was engraving plates for the *New System* at the same time he acquired Fuseli's Winckelmann. Geoffrey Keynes has also studied Blake's use of images in Bryant, which he first encountered as a boy-apprentice and held in his remarkable memory for forty years.[9] In fact, Blake uses Bryant in exactly the manner Winckelmann called for. No matter that what was a Greek artifact in Bryant becomes an apocalyptic symbol in *Jerusalem*, Bryant provides Blake with a "learned apparatus by whose stores he might be enabled to invest abstracted ideas with sensible and meaning images." Kathleen Raine, in her extensive study of Blake's use of Bryant, calls the *New System* "the *Golden Bough* of its day," and she points out that "Blake cites it as authoritative in all matters of mythology."[10] Winckelmann's call for a book with images "from all mythology" seems realized in Bryant's eclectic work which dealt not only with Greek and Roman mythology, but with Egyptian, Eastern, and biblical myths.[11]

The call for a source book must not be extrapolated, however, out of the context in which Winckelmann viewed the creative process. For him the sublime realization of abstract ideas had been achieved above all in the poetry and philosophical literature of the ancients. The poet is the first translator of the unfathomable in life. The poet connects ideas to images; and, insofar as he is touched with genius, he is able to make these associations with such strokes of wit and inspiration that the idea and the image become one in the consciousness of the reader. Homer, above all poets, has done this:

> Homer, as Cicero tells us, has transformed man to God: which is to say, he not only exceeded the truth, but, to raise his fiction, preferred even the impossible, if probable, to the barely possible. In this Aristotle fixes the very essence of poetry, and tells us that the pictures of Zeuxis had that characteristic. (FW191)

> *Homer hat aus Menschen Götter gemacht, sagt Cicero; das heisst, er hat die Wahrheit nicht allein höher getrieben, sondern er hat, um erhaben zu dichten, lieber das Unmögliche, das wahrscheinlich ist, als das bloss Mögliche, gewählt. Aristoteles setzt hierin das Wesen der Dichtkunst und berichtet uns, dass die Gemälde des Zeuxis diese Eigenschaft gehabt haben.* (W140)

Like poetry, painting cannot be restricted to depictions of common nature alone:

> Painting goes beyond the senses: there is its most elevated pitch, to which the Greeks strove to raise themselves, as their writings evince. (FW57)

> *Die Malerei erstreckt sich auf Dinge, die nicht sinnlich sind; diese sind ihr höchstes Ziel, und die Griechen haben sich bemüht, dasselbe zu erreichen, wie die Schriften der Alten bezeugen.* (W108)

But having attained this elevated pitch, the artist in the ecstasy of creation finds himself at a loss in his desire to convey the most eminent prerogative of art: "The representation of invisible, past and future things," (FW62) *"die Vorstellung unsichtbarer, vergangener und zukünftiger Dinge."* (W112) Winckelmann's requirement for the artist is rigorous and formidable. This did not pass unnoticed by the British reviewer of the translation who complained that Winckelmann was calling for the painter to be "a knight errant...the very pink of perfection in all arts and sciences." Blake's vision of the poet/prophet is similar, though couched in metaphysical terms:

Hear the voice of the Bard!
Who Present, Past & Future, sees;
Whose ears have heard
The Holy Word
That walk'd among the ancient trees. (K210)

To reach the height of epic and tragic poetry, painting must spring from the same sort of visionary conception as the sublime poet possesses. Winckelmann writes:

If it not be a contradiction to stretch the limits of painting as far as those of poetry, and consequently, to allow the painter the same ability of elevating himself to the pitch of poet as the musician enjoys; it is clear that history, though the sublimest branch of painting, cannot raise itself to the heights of the tragick or epick poetry by imitation alone. (FW191)

Truth, lovely as it is in itself, charms more, penetrates deeper, when invested with fiction: fable, in its strictest sense, is the delight of childhood; allegory that of riper years. And the old opinion, that poetry was of earlier date than prose, as unanimously attested by the annals of different people, makes it evident, that even in the most barbarous times, truth was preferred, when appearing in this dress. (FW192)

Es scheint nicht widersprechend, dass die Malerei ebenso weite Grenzen als die Dichtkunst haben könne, und dass es folglich dem Maler möglich sei, dem Dichter zu folgen, wo wie es die Musik imstande ist zu tun. Nun ist die Geschichte der höchste Vorwurf, den ein Maler wählen kann, die blosse Nachahmung aber wird sie nicht zu dem Grade erheben, den eine Tragödie oder ein Heldengedicht, das Höchste in der Dichtkunst, hat. (W140)

Die Wahrheit, so liebenswürdig sie an sich selbst ist, gefällt und macht einen stärkeren Eindruck, wenn sie in eine Fabel eingekleidet ist; was bei Kindern die Fabel, im engsten Verstande genommen, ist, das ist die Allegorie einem reifen Alter. Und in dieser Gestalt ist die Wahrheit in den ungesittetesten Zeiten angenehmer gewesen, auch nach der sehr alten Meinung, dass die Poesie älter als Prosa sei, was durch die Nachrichten von den ältesten Zeiten verschiedener Völker bestätigt wird. (W141)

Blake, like Winckelmann, places "historical" painting above all other branches of the art. In his own explications of his "Poetical and Historical Inventions" in the *Descriptive Catalogue* he presents a strikingly similar argument against what Winckelmann calls "*blosse Nachahmung.*" Here, he is describing a tempera painting, "The Bard," after a poem by Gray, quoting first from Gray's poem:

The Bard, from Gray

"On a rock, whose haughty brow
"Frown'd o'er old Conway's foaming flood,
"Robed in the sable garb of woe,
"With haggard eyes the Poet stood;
"Loose his beard, and hoary hair
"Stream'd like a meteor to the troubled air.

"Weave the warp, and weave the woof,
"The winding sheet of Edward's race."

Weaving the winding sheet of Edward's race by means of sounds of spiritual music and its accompanying expressions of articulate speech, is a bold, and daring, and most masterly conception, that the public have embraced and approved with avidity. Poetry consists in these conceptions; and shall Painting be confined to the sordid drudgery of facsimile representations of merely mortal and perishing substances, and not be as poetry and music are, elevated into its own proper sphere of invention and visionary conception? No, it shall not be so! Painting, as well as poetry and music, exists and exults in immortal thoughts. (K576)

These "immortal thoughts" of which Blake speaks are no less bound to truth and history because they are clothed in allegory, fiction, or allusion. He sees the "reasoning historian"—one who deduces truth from recording events—as the antithesis of the poet, who alone can see historical fact in its "poetical vigour":

In this Picture, believing with Milton the ancient British History, Mr. B. has done as all the ancients did, and as all the moderns who are worthy of fame, given the historical fact in its poetical vigour so as it always happens, and not in that dull way that some Historians pretend, who, being weakly organized themselves, cannot see either miracle or prodigy; all is to them a dull round of probabilities and possibilities; but the history of all times and places is nothing else but improbabilities and impossibilities; what we should say was impossible if we did not see it always before our eyes. (K578)

George Mills Harper's discussion of Blake's concept of allegory mentions the similarity between Winckelmann's discrimination between vulgar and sublime allegory and Blake's concept of allegory, and Harper notes that Blake's allegory "'addressed to the intellectual powers'...certainly does not fit the conventional definition, and the relationship of his own meaning to the doctrine of obscurity is important."[12] In Winckelmann's essay clarity is the quality to be striven for in art; and, at the same time, he implies that the allegory must not be obvious:

The last rule of the ancients was to beware of signs too near a-kin to the thing signified. Let the young allegorist observe these rules, and study them, jointly with mythology, and the remotest history. (FW216)

Endlich waren die Alten bedacht, das Bezeichnete mit seinem Zeichen in ein entferntes Verhältnis zu stellen. Nebst diesen Regeln soll die allgemeine Beobachtung bei allen Versuchen in dieser Wissenschaft billig sein, die Bilder, womöglich, aus der Mythologie und aus der ältesten Geschichte zu wählen. (W148)

The more intellectual, the more striking and unusual the analogy, the more permanently it remains in the mind of the observer:

Every idea increases in strength, if accompanied by another or more ideas, as in comparisons; and the more still as they differ in kind: for ideas, too analogous to each other, do not strike:.... Hence the power of discovering a similarity, in the most different things, is what we call wit; Aristotle's 'unexpected ideas'; and these he requires in an orator.... The more you are surprized by a picture, the more you are affected; and both those affects are to be obtained by allegory, like to fruit hid beneath the leaves and branches, which when found surprizes the more agreeably, the less it is thought of. (FW193)

Eine jede Idee wird stärker, wenn sie von einer oder mehr Ideen begleitet ist, wie in Vergleichungen, und um so viel stärker, je entfernter das Verhältnis von diesen zu jener ist. Denn wo die Ähnlichkeit derselben von selbst darbietet,...erfolgt deine Verwunderung. Das Gegenteil ist dasjenige, was wir Witz, und was Aristoteles unerwartete Begriffe nennt: er fordert eben dergleichen Ausdrücke von einem Redner. Je mehr Unerwartetes man in einem Gemälde entdeckt, desto rührender wird es, und beides erhält es durch Allegorie. Sie ist wie eine unter Blättern und Zweigen versteckte Frucht, welche desto angenehmer ist, je unvermuteter man sie findet;... (W142)

Blake, who had no less interest in truth and clarity than Winckelmann, was also firmly convinced that, like all prophetic writers, he would not be understood by all. But the care and intricacy with which he wove his mythopoeic system from the threads of his various readings suggests that he fervently desired to be understood by men of vision. He strove to show that wit, that Imagination and Invention which would enable him to use tradition in a new way, in the spirit of Milton. Thus, as Wittreich suggests, the poet becomes "an architect of new forms, a generator of values nobler than those his culture already possessed, a maker of new myths rather than a recorder of old ones."[13] In his famous letter to Dr. Trusler of August 23, 1799, Blake writes of his vision:

> I see Every thing I paint In This World, but Every body does not see alike. To the Eyes of a Miser a Guinea is more beautiful than the Sun & a bag worn with the use of Money has more beautiful proportions than a Vine filled with Grapes. The tree which moves some to tears of joy is in the Eyes of others only a Green thing that stands in the way. Some See Nature all Ridicule & Deformity, & by these I shall not regulate my proportions; & Some Scarce see Nature at all. But to the Eyes of the Man of Imagination, Nature is Imagination itself. As a man is, So he Sees. As the Eye is formed, such are its Powers. (K793)

With the weight of his sacred ancient authorities behind him, and in his own unpoetical way, Winckelmann had said much the same thing in his defense against critics of the figure of Jesus in the *Sistine Madonna*:

> This is no easy matter to convince a critick, conceited enough to blame the Jesus of the Madonna, that he is mistaken. Pythagorus, says the ancient philospher, and Anaxogorus look at the sun with different eyes; the former sees a god, the latter a stone. (FW183)

> *Ein angeblicher Richter der Kunst, der das Kind in den Armen der Madonna so elend findet, ist so leicht nicht zu belehren. Pythagoras sieht die Sonne mit andern Augen an als Anaxagoras: jener als einen Gott, dieser als einen Stein, wie ein alter Philosoph sagt.* (W135)

Winckelmann, toward the end of his thoughts on allegory, admits the mystery of sublime allegory and the fact that for many it is inaccessible. Again, Plato is his guide:

> Allegory, as Plato says, of poetry in general, has something enigmatick in itself, and is not calculated for the bulk of mankind. And should the painter, from the fear of being obscure, adapt his performance to the capacity of those, who look upon a picture as upon a tumultuous mob, he might as well check every new and extraordinary idea. (FW231)

> *Aber die ganze Allegorie hat, wie Plato von der Dichtkunst überhaupt sagt, etwas Rätselhaftes und ist nicht für jedermann gemacht. Wenn die Besorgung, denen undeutlich zu sein, die ein Gemälde wie ein Getümmel von Menschen ansehen, den Künstler bestimmen sollte, so würde er auch alle ausserordentlich fremden Ideen ersticken müssen.* (W150)

In his eloquent defense of his own symbolism Blake uses an argument in complete agreement with Winckelmann's definition of allegory:

> You say that I want somebody to Elucidate my Ideas. But you ought to know that What is Grand is necessarily obscure to Weak men. That which can be made Explicit to the Idiot is not worth my care. The wisest of the Ancients consider'd what is not too Explicit as the fittest for Instruction, because it rouzes the faculties to act. I name Moses, Solomon, Esop, Homer, Plato. (K793)

Winckelmann advises his reader that the pencil of the artist should be "impregnated with reason," so "that after having satiated the eye, he may nourish the mind: and this he may obtain by allegory; investing, not hiding his ideas"; (FW63-64) *"in Verstand getunkt sein…Er soll mehr zu denken hinterlassen, als was er dem Auge gezeigt, und dieses wird der Künstler erhalten, wenn er seine Gedanken in Allegorien nicht zu verstecken, sondern einzukleiden gelernt hat."* (W113) He did not intend to imply that the artist was bound to use only borrowed allegory:

> then, whether he chuse [sic] some poetical object himself, or follow the dictates of others, he shall be inspired by his art, shall be fired with the flame brought down from the heaven by Prometheus, shall entertain the votary of art, and instruct the mere lover of it. (FW64)
>
> *Hat er einen Vorwurf, den er selbst gewählt oder der ihm gegeben wurde, welcher dichterisch gemacht oder zu machen ist, so wird ihn seine Kunst begeistern und wird das Feuer, welches Prometheus den Göttern raubte, in ihm erwecken. Der Kenner wird zu denken haben, und der blosse Liebhaber wird es lernen.*(W113)

In her chapter on Tiriel, Kathleen Raine poses a rhetorical question: "What will be the result if into a world of Swedenborgian, Ossianic, and Nordic myth there breaks the "Grecian light and glory" that was in such works as Stuart's and Revett's *Antiquities of Athens* and Winckelmann's *Reflections on the Painting and Sculpture of the Greeks*, culminating in 1804 in the bringing to England of the Elgin marbles.[14] Her own research on Blake provides the best answer to that question insofar as his borrowing of themes and images from the classical tradition is concerned. What Blake found in his early reading of Winckelmann is not direct images which he could transfer to his designs, not themes for his poetry. He found there aesthetic attitudes toward the nature of the artist himself and the creative act, toward the presentation of the ideal in the human form, the intimate and inexorable relationship of poetry and visual arts, and the uses of sublime allegory in the "representation of invisible, past, and future things." (FW62)

Part Four
Blake and Fuseli's Rousseau

—And is a man guilty of this enormous
lump of *errors*, or *worse*—to be
defended, and his pernicious maxims to
be scattered abroad by you—who
imbibed religion, and constitutional
sentiments, with your mother-milk?

—Henry Fuseli
*Remarks on the Writing
and Conduct of J.J.
Rousseau*

An Angel came to me and said: "O pitiable foolish young man! O
"horrible! O dreadful state! consider the hot burning dungeon thou
"art preparing for thyself to all eternity, to which thou art going in
"such career."

—William Blake
*The Marriage of
Heaven and Hell*

The Negative Evidence in the Very Early Works: 1770-1784

Close reading of the *Poetical Sketches* and manuscript fragments written by Blake before 1788 fails to yield any convincing indication that Blake read Fuseli's *Remarks* before that time. There does seem to be a superficial resemblance between Blake's allegorical version of the origin of man's suffering in the manuscript fragment, "Then She Bore Pale Desire" (circa 1770), and the cultural pessimism of Rousseau's *First Discourse*. In his allegory, Blake traces the genealogy of vice back to Curiosity, through Pride, Shame, and Ambition, and relates how Reason, "once fairer than light, till foul'd in Knowledge's dark house" finally "drove sweet innocence away." (K41-42) Fuseli's exposition of Rousseau's treatise on the effects of the arts and sciences on society emphasizes that the origin of tyranny and slavery is concomitant to the discovery of knowledge, and that knowledge is born of vice and not virtue.[1] But Blake's early prose allegory is an abstract compendium of man's folly, and knowledge is just one of the evils which participates in this secularized version of the fall of innocence. "Then She Bore Pale Desire" is Blake's first tentative attempt to philosophize and expresses a precocious pessimism for one yet in his teens. Although it presents no indication of a knowledge of Rousseau's social theories, this prose fragment reflects a discontent with the world that will find more mature expression a decade later.[2]

The absence of any direct or veiled mention of Rousseau or Fuseli in Blake's outrageous satire of his own intellectual circle, *An Island in the Moon* (circa 1784), seems to indicate that Blake did not have access to the *Remarks* and that he was not intimate with Fuseli before that period. In the burlesque manuscript novel in which Blake makes fun of so many fads and intellectual trends of the day, he expressly uses Voltaire as a butt.[3] The characters are "quarreling and having a bit of fun with him." (K45) It is significant that Rousseau's name is not mentioned here, given the constant pairing of the two philosophers in the later works. No character in *An Island in the Moon* vaguely resembles Fuseli, who, with his blistering hatred of Voltaire, would have been a colorful addition to the eccentric group which convened on the island.[4] That Blake was reading philosophy, or at least discussing it, during this period in his early twenties is clear from the fact that he names characters "The Pythagorean" and "The Epicurean." But only one short passage can be tied to any Rousseauistic train of thought. The character Quid (Blake) says of the young student, Aradobo:

> There's Aradobo in ten or twelve years will be a
> far superior genius.
> Ah! said the Pythagorean, "Aradobo will make a very
> clever fellow."
> "Why," said Quid, "I think that [a *del.*] any
> natural fool would make a clever fellow, if he was
> properly brought up."
> "Ah, hang your reasoning!" said the Epicurean.
> "I hate reasoning. I do everything by my feelings." (K50)

This general allusion to educational theory and preference for feeling over reason is, however, too slender a thread to connect *An Island in the Moon* to Rousseau or Fuseli.

It is in 1788 that William Blake annotated an unbound copy of Fuseli's adaptation of Lavater's *Vermischte unphysiognomische Regeln...* (1787-1788). We are brought up to the period during which we know Blake and Fuseli were closely associated. In addition to partially designing and engraving the frontispiece for the Aphorisms, Blake was engraving pictures for the grand English edition of Lavater's *Physiognomy*, the translating and editing of which Fuseli was closely overseeing. It is during this period that Blake seems to have read philosophy and it is then that it is likely that Fuseli gave him a copy of the *Remarks*. In his last entry of notes in his unbound copy of the Fuseli-Lavater *Aphorisms*, Blake makes his first direct statement of philosophical point of view and for the first time he identifies himself as a philosopher:

> But as I understand Vice it is a Negative. It does not signify what the laws of Kings &
> Priests have call'd Vice; we who are philosophers ought not to call the Staminal Virtues of
> Humanity by the same name that we call the omissions of intellect springing from pover-
> ty. (K88)

"We who are philosophers" stand behind man and not law, dogma or doctrine. As adversary to King and Priest, Blake has steeped himself in the deistic doctrines of his day and is preparing to state his own view of religion. The philosophers have seen much, but the philosophers must be corrected. Blake's lifelong battle with materialism has begun. He sees that the best manner in which to demonstrate the failure of a rationalist philosopher to define man satisfactorily is to outline the tenets of a materialistic definition and to see what sort of creation one is left with. This is what he sets about to do in his first experiment in illuminated printing, the engraved series *There Is No Natural Religion* and *All Religions Are One* (1788). In these series of engravings, Blake makes a straightforward statement of his belief—the only such statement that he will ever make that is not confounded or illuminated with myth, satire, and veiled allusions. Many of the objections to materialism and deism that Blake makes in the two tractates *There Is No Natural Religion* are strikingly close in spirit to the objections stated by Rousseau's Savoyard vicar in *Emile*. The vocabulary is radically different from the quieter confession of the good priest, but the weaknesses of materialism are seen in the same points. Fuseli's own theological views, which are expressed by him in the *Remarks*, are in close harmony with Rousseau's. It is possible that Fuseli brought the Savoyard to Blake at a time when the younger man was struggling to find the proper expression of his own religious ideas. What Blake would have found there was not a theology upon which he would base his own system, but a theology against which he could react and which his special vision would enable him to set right.

Fuseli, Blake, and the "Two Rousseaus"

In speaking of Rousseau and Blake, one must differentiate between the persona-Rousseau that Blake creates in his poetry and the possible influence of the writings and theories of the Genevan thinker on Blake's intellectual development. In his entry on Rousseau in *A Blake Dictionary*, Damon writes: "Blake always associated Rousseau and Voltaire as the mainsprings of the French Revolution. He attacked their Deism and particularly disbelieved in Rousseau's virtuous Natural Man, the height of perfection until corrupted by civilization."[1] Damon is here clearly speaking of the persona-Rousseau, and is emphasizing the negative role assigned to him by Blake in the poems after 1800. Similarly, Jean Hagstrum states: "On the side of vengeance he regularly placed the Deists, the classics, Voltaire, Rousseau, Gibbon, Hume. On the side of forgiveness and the religion of Jesus, he placed Wesley, Whitefield, the humble monks, and the medieval unknown religious."[2] Again, the reference is to the figure of Rousseau which appears in the later poems. The persona-Rousseau emerges for the first time in Blake's fragment, *The French Revolution* (1791) and is not there seen negatively, but heroically. In his imaginative history of the earliest stages of the Revolution, Blake includes the names of historical participants in the political events in France with characters and events purely of his own invention. He intends to show the tyranny of the aristocracy, the defiance by the commons, and the atmosphere of apocalypse that he sees in these events. Toward the end of the fragment, "Gleams of fire streak the heavens and of sulphur the earth," the heroic La Fayette calls forth the troops of liberty:

> Over his head the soul of Voltaire shone fiery; and over the army
> Rousseau his white cloud
> Unfolded, on souls of war, living terrors, silent list'ning toward
> Fayette.
> His voice loud inspir'd by liberty, and by spirits of the dead, thus
> thunder'd:
>
> "The Nation's Assembly command that the Army remove ten miles
> from Paris;
> "Nor a soldier be seen in road or in field, till the Nation command
> return." (K147)

Four or five years later, the figure of Rousseau appears in Blake's writing again, linked, as on the first occasion, with Voltaire in *The Song of Los*. In the mythic history of the world and the development of human thought that

Blake gives in the section of his poem called "Africa," he traces the spread of civilization, reason, and law which binds man more and more to the earth. The vision of man is restrained, locked in the static materialism of Newton and Locke. Rousseau and Voltaire then appear as somewhat ominous participants in the "howl" that will "rise up from Europe," but again, they are seen as revolutionary firebrands:

> Clouds roll heavy upon the Alps round Rousseau & Voltaire,
> And on the mountains of Lebanon round the deceased Gods
> Of Asia, & on the desarts of Africa round the Fallen Angels
> The Guardian Prince of Albion burns in his nightly tent. (K246)

Erdman has shown that in 1795 Blake's hopes for the revolution have not yet soured and that "these Alpine figures are pillars of fire, if not light, in the 'European darkness'."[3]

When Blake does turn his wrath on Voltaire and Rousseau in 1803, it is because the revolution has failed to crush the "Purple Tyrant." "The iron hand crush'd the Tyrants' head/And became a Tyrant in his stead": *Pickering Manuscript*, 1803 (K431). Thus it is that the persona-Rousseau, who with his other half, Voltaire, had promised to chase away much suffering and ignorance, becomes in the later poems one of the failed twin prophets of false promise: the enemy of religion and the human race. But as in the case of Blake's vehement rejection of the classics, which occurs at the same crucial period in his life, the very passion with which he condemns Rousseau is implicit evidence that he is rejecting what he once held dear, that he is railing at his own false direction as well. Rousseau, like Voltaire, Gibbon, and the heroes of antiquity, becomes a war monger among men and an instrument of destruction:

> Titus! Constantine! Charlemagne!
> O Voltaire! Rousseau! Gibbon! vain
> Your [mocks & scorn *del.*] Grecian mocks & Roman sword
> Against this image of his Lord. (K420)

The joining together of Voltaire and Rousseau in the poetry of Blake, first as positive spirits, and then as "Pharisees & Hypocrites" (K682) reflects Blake's own conversion from the exploring and rather free-thinking period of the middle eighties through the nineties to the more radical and revelationary Christocentric vision of *Milton* (1804-1808) and *Jerusalem* (1804-1820).[4] By then the Deists and followers of Natural Religion become the murderers of Jesus. For, having cast them first in the role of banishing superstition and priestly hypocrisy, he came to see them as having killed faith in the process. They become symbolic scoffers and mockers in the enemy camp of science, as Blake announces in one of his most famous poems from the *Note-Book* (1800-1803):

> Mock on, Mock on Voltaire, Rousseau:
> Mock on, Mock on: 'tis all in vain!
> You throw the sand against the wind,
> And the wind throws it back again.
>
> And every sand becomes a Gem
> Reflected in the beams divine;

Blown back they blind the mocking Eye,
But still in Israel's paths they shine.

The Atoms of Democritus
And Newton's Particles of light
Are sands upon the Red sea shore,
Where Israel's tents do shine so bright. (K418)

It is not necessary to assume that the constant pairing of the two figures of Rousseau and Voltaire demonstrates Blake's lack of a deep understanding of the vast differences in their philosophical or theological stands: fairness and accuracy have little place in polemical battles. It is certain, on the contrary, that anyone close to Fuseli and sympathetic to his view would know that Rousseau was not Voltaire and that Voltaire was not Rousseau. In a sense, Rousseau and Voltaire represent "Contraries," in the Blakean sense of the word: the one, precise, rational, coldly cynical; the other, vague, sentimental, hopeful for man in the end.

This is what Fuseli is so eager to demonstrate in his *Remarks*. But as enemies of priestcraft and powerful warriors against the old order; and above all, as secularizers of evil, they were, as Blake understood, one. Rousseau, as Fuseli ironically presents him in the *Remarks*, is one of the blaspheming devils destined to be condemned by the Church in all of its manifestations. Voltaire, in the vicious portrait that Fuseli draws, is a no less dissenting, if evil and misanthropic, genius. They were brought to Blake from the Continent by a fiery son of *Sturm und Drang*.

As the one among Blake's friends who was the most knowledgeable about the person and theories of Rousseau, Fuseli is of importance also in the second aspect of the Rousseau-Blake connection: the extent to which Blake was actually acquainted with the works of Jean-Jacques Rousseau. Since scholars have begun to study Blake's thought within the context of history, and to perceive the poet, in the words of Mark Schorer,"as a man in the world," and not outside of it,[5] the unmistakable, if unacknowledged, strain of Rousseau's thought in Blake's writing has been identified by Schorer, David Erdman, Kathleen Raine, Jacob Bronowski and others.[6] Erdman, who has given the most complete treatment of the development of Blake's thought against the background of 18th century intellectual trends and events, has pointed to the positive strains of influence in *Tiriel*, Songs of Innocence, The French Revolution, the "Lambeth prophecies," and the scattered marginalia.[7] Erdman identifies Rousseau as "Blake's modern source" of political vision in the Lambeth books, and calls him a "reader of Rousseau."[8] In several instances, Erdman suggests that Fuseli, whom he calls a "Jovial son of the Enlightenment," might have been the intermediary between Blake and Rousseau: "...his coming to Blake as a spiritual comforter after the death of Robert and the departure of Flaxman implies a more sober sympathy between the two men, such as have been established by Fuseli's interest in Rousseau and Lavater."[9]

Erdman's supposition had been stated with much less reservation in European studies several decades before the appearance of his monumental work. As early as 1922, Ernst Wirz in his unpublished but invaluable dissertation "Die literarische Tätigkeit des Malers J.H. Füssli," traced the circumstances surrounding Fuseli's rare pamphlet, and gave a somewhat exaggerated picture of Fuseli as a disseminator of Rousseauism in England. But the first published suggestion that Fuseli was Blake's tutor in the ideas of

Rousseau came in 1947 from Henri Roddier, who in his pioneering study, *J.-J. Rousseau en Angleterre au XVIIIe Siècle*, stated: *"Mais le grand intermédiaire entre Rousseau et Blake nous parait être ici Henri Fuseli, qui presente avec Blake de si étranges affinities."*[10] Jacques Voisine, who continued the work begun by Roddier in his *J.J. Rousseau En Angleterre A L'Epoque Romantique* (1956), reinforces this role of Fuseli, "fervent rousseauiste zurichois," and devotes several pages to Fuseli's role as intellectual mentor to Blake.[11]

Kathleen Raine, who is strongly convinced of a Rousseau influence in Blake's *Songs of Innocence* and *Tiriel*, suggests that Rousseau "came to him through Mary Wollstonecraft."[12] Raine has in mind themes of innocence, childhood, and education in the works of Blake; and, in this respect, Wollstonecraft, "a true daughter of Rousseau," is a likely candidate as intermediary.[13] Although there is no record of any personal association between Blake and Wollstonecraft, he certainly knew of her and her writings by 1790, when he was commissioned by Johnson to engrave Chodowiecki's illustrations for her translation of Salzmann's *Elements of Morality*.[14] Although a general Rousseauistic influence of Wollstonecraft's writings upon Blake's thought is not to be discounted, it in no way conflicts with Fuseli's role in the matter, for Wollstonecraft and Fuseli had different perceptions of Rousseau. It is not without significance that Mary's husband Godwin saw Fuseli as a rather bad influence upon her: "If Mary derived improvement from Mr. Fuseli, she may also be suspected of having caught the infection of some of his faults."[15] Among his faults, Godwin refers to the fact that Fuseli "has not had the leisure to bring the opinions of his youth to a revision," and that "Smitten with Rousseau's conception of the perfectness of the savage state, and the essential abortiveness of all civilization, Mr. Fuseli looks at all our little attempts at improvement with a spirit that borders perhaps too much on contempt and indifference."[16] Godwin ends his assessment of Fuseli's influence on Mary gloomily: "I believe that Mary came something more of a cynic out of the school of Mr. Fuseli, than she went into it."[17] Godwin had reason to dislike Fuseli on other than philosophical grounds, for it was well known that Mary fell hopelessly in love with the Swiss artist and that her feelings were more than platonic.[18] That Fuseli schooled Wollstonecraft in the more cynical implications of Rousseau's cultural pessimism is not to be precluded. For it is not Rousseau, the protector of childhood, goodness,and innocence, which Fuseli brought to England. His interest in Rousseau was far removed from the popular and sentimental images of childhood that were current in the mid-eighteenth century. What little Fuseli has to say about children in his writings treats them as aesthetic objects. For Fuseli, children are subjects of immediate charm, like sketches or lyric poetry, characterized by quickness, motion, and brief spontaneity.[19] When he discusses *Emile* in the *Remarks*, he does not dwell on theories of education, but on the political and theological issues which are contained in the work. When he speaks of the vulnerability of the "infant bloom of nature," he has less in mind the repressing of infant joy than he does the controversy which led to the burning of *Emile* in Paris and Rousseau's reply to Archbishop Beaumont: Rousseau's refusal to condemn man in the cradle to the onus of original sin.[20]

The exploration of the impact of Rousseau's theories on Blake's opus is a large subject which has not yet been exhausted and one which is outside the scope of this study. What is of importance here is the light in which the philosopher was presented to Blake by Fuseli in the 1780s, and the role that Fuseli's "image" of Rousseau plays in Blake's initial interest and enthusiasm for liberal philosophy in that period of his life. Like the version of classicism that emerges from Fuseli's Winckelmann, the character and posture of Rousseau in the *Remarks* is expanded, modified, and intensified by Fuseli's own singular world-view. It is a view of dissenting and scorned genius seen through the imaginative eye of Fuseli.

Erdman was the first to see Fuseli's *Remarks on the Writing and Conduct of J.J. Rousseau* as a direct textual influence on Blake's writing and thought.[21] His suggestions, in footnotes, invite closer investigation of the works of both men, to determine the extent of Fuseli's role in reinforcing Blake's own satirical and increasingly ironical view of his age and his increasingly defiant and indignant view of himself as an artist.

Like any investigation into the sources of Blake's learning during the period in which he was getting established as an engraver, meeting with the Johnson circle, and beginning to write his own ambitious works, the problem of the Fuseli/Rousseau/Blake connection is compounded by the lack of any substantial documentation. We have no copy of the *Remarks* that is known to have belonged to Blake, and he mentions the work nowhere in his correspondence or other writings. Evidence must be extrapolated from the texts themselves.

Fuseli, Blake, and the Savoyard Vicar

Fuseli was well aware when he wrote the *Remarks* that the controversial aspect of Emile was theological and not pedagogical. The furor that broke out concerning the profession of Rousseau's Savoyard priest in Geneva in 1762 was the spark which fired the young Heinrich Füssli and his friend J.C. Lavater to launch their attack against the corruption of the infamous Grebel. The profession of the vicar was only the preface, as Fuseli understood, to the religious ideas that Rousseau subsequently expressed in his *Lettres de la Montagne*. Thus, in his chapter on *Emile*, Fuseli declares himself, in his anonymous pose, on the side of the "blasphemous" Rousseau as the enemy of the "reasonable adorers of God."[1] This designation for the pious rationalist defenders of the faith is consistently and even bitterly ironic in the *Remarks*. They are those who would demonstrate religion by reason and science. For Fuseli, faith is by definition confined and destroyed when translated into dogma and sect. All arguments concerning the material proof of Christianity and investigations of religious revelation are dismissed by him as philistine. The mystery is not to be penetrated by reason:

> Approach the sanctuary of mysteries, guided by reason, but remember that its feeble light can only make darkness visible:—and him who without a letter of credence, and an authentic key from St. John, not in his head or heart, but in his hand, crams his emetic trash down your throat, under the pretence that it will dulcify your stomach, unveils the Babylonian whore, or discovers the merchants of Tyrus in the East-Indian company—him set down among the victims of grim superstition, and sour-brained dotage.[2]

Fuseli's love of the Bible and admiration for its imagery makes him all the more intolerant of those who would explicate miracles and images by reason or in terms of current events. For him, the key of David must be carried in head or heart. It is of significance to note Fuseli's fondness of the book of Revelation, Job, and Ezekiel in his letters and writings. His knowledge of and interest in religious matters is far greater than is generally recognized and is important in the story of his relationship with Blake.[3] A miracle is, Fuseli writes with reference to Rousseau's *Letters from the Mountain* "an exception from the pre-established laws of nature, is by its own definition indemonstrable to man, or any being acquainted with the full extent, number, modifications of these laws."[4] In Fuseli's introduction to the *Remarks*, Rousseau is presented as one who "...though living upon the immortality of the soul, yet thinks it not geometrically demonstrable."[5] Fuseli had read *Emile* in Switzerland, he was familiar with Rousseau's likening of the materialists to a deaf man who denies the existence of sounds because they are not perceptible to him. Fuseli does not present Rousseau as a rationalist, but as an inspired genius.

If, as it appears, Fuseli brought Rousseau's theological ideas to Blake, it is likely that the younger man was inspired to read the writings that Fuseli discusses in the *Remarks*, especially the profession of the Savoyard priest in *Emile*. A reissue of Kendrick's translation of *Emilius and Sophia* was published in 1783.[6] Since Blake is not known to have read French at this time, it is Kendrick's translation that he would have read.[7] To investigate the possibility that Blake was reading and reacting to the Savoyard vicar at the time Fuseli's influence over him was strongest, it is necessary to look for evidences in the texts Blake was writing at the time for parallels to ideas in the *Remarks* or in Rousseau's own writings. The citations from Rousseau's "The Profession of Faith of a Savoyard Curate" are from the 1767 reprint of Kendrick's translation.

In the first series of *There Is No Natural Religion*, Blake draws the conclusion:

> *Conclusion.* If it were not for the Poetic or Prophetic character the Philosophic & Experimental would soon be at the ratio of all things, & stand still, unable to do other than repeat the same dull round over again. (K97)

What leads him to this conviction is the static and limited image of the universe that emerges from viewing man as limited to perception through the five senses of rational philosophy:

> *The Argument.* Man has no notion of moral fitness but from Education. Naturally he is only a natural organ subject to Sense.
> I. Man cannot naturally Percieve but through his natural or bodily organs.
> II. Man by his reasoning power can only compare & judge of what he has already perciev'd.
> III. From a perception of only 3 senses or 3 elements none could deduce a fourth or fifth.
> IV. None could have other than natural or organic thoughts if he had none but organic perceptions.
> V. Man's desires are limited by his perceptions, none can desire what he has not perciev'd.
> VI. The desires & perceptions of man, untaught by any thing but organs of sense, must be limited to objects of sense. (K97)

Thus, Blake's reading of philosophers who would teach that man is bounded by the five senses tells him that philosophy in its attempt to define man, restricts and binds him to the circular, repetitive wheel of the sensible universe. The Poetic and the Prophetic character of man is the only dynamic and liberated aspect of existence, and as such, must be at odds with the Philosophic and Experimental.

In *Emile* Rousseau's priest had approached his struggle with faith through the route of philosophy, and had found only disillusionment. Philosophy lacks any consistent measuring device of man:

> I conceived that the weakness of the human understanding was the first cause of the prodigious variety I found in their [the philosophers'] sentiments, and that pride was the second. We have no standard with which to measure this immense machine [the universe]; we

cannot calculate its various relations; we neither know the first cause nor the final effects; we are ignorant even of ourselves.[8]

Despairing of ever learning from the feuding philosophers, the Savoyard priest turned in upon himself for the answer, relying on the senses. He then learns that his intellect allows him not only to perceive things, but also to make comparisons and judgments:

> To perceive is only to feel or be sensible of things; to compare them is to judge of their existence: to judge of things and to be sensible of them are very different. Things present themselves to our sensations as single, and detached from each other, such as they barely exist in nature: but in our intellectual comparison of them they are removed, transported, as it were, from place to place, disposed on and beside each other, to enable us to pronounce concerning their difference and similitude. The characteristic faculty of being an intelligent, active being, is, in my opinion, that of giving a sense to the word exist.[9]

Unfortunately, the meaning of existence is not to be found, as the vicar discovers in his rambling dissertation on matter, motion, and will, through the roads of reason. He has gone through a process similar to Blake's six tenets. He is forced to despair that he, "a simple, honest man" who "has no system to maintain," will not answer the questions of God and existence by exploring the senses or the relation of things one to another and drawing abstract conclusions from those comparisons—Blake's "ratio":

> II. Man by his reasoning power can only compare & judge of
> what he has already perciev'd. (K97)

The vicar's God, which the apparent order of the nonhuman universe shows to be benevolent, remains illusive. Not to be proved by science and experimentation, it seems that he must be intuited sentimentally—"I adore the supreme power, and melt into tenderness at his goodness."[10] Some vague "internal voice"[11] cries out to be heard: this, for Rousseau is the voice of religion:

> The more I reflect on our capacity of thinking, and the nature of human understanding, the greater is the resemblance I find between the arguments of our materialists and that of...a deaf man. They are, in effect, equally deaf to that internal voice, which, nevertheless, calls them so loud and emphatically. A mere machine is evidently incapable of thinking, it has neither motion nor figure productive of reflection: whereas in man there exists something, perpetually prone to expand, and to burst the fetters by which it is confined. Space itself affords not bounds to the human mind: the whole universe is not extensive enough for him; his sentiments, his desires, his anxieties, and even his pride, take rise from a principle different from that body within which he perceives himself confined.[12]

But unlike Blake, Rousseau is not prophet, and only confesses not to understand this "something" which wishes to burst out of the confines of the material body. Blake's second series of *There Is No Natural Religion* contains the audacious refutation of the six tenets of the first series. Here the voice of the "Poetic and Prophetic character" overturns the restrictions that the vicar understands and accepts passively:

> I. Man's perceptions are not bounded by organs of perception;
> he percieves more than sense (tho' ever so acute) can discover.
> II. Reason, or the ratio of all we have already known, is not the
> same that it shall be when we know more.
> III. [*This proposition has been lost.*]

IV. The bounded is loathed by its possessor. The same dull round, even of a universe, would soon become a mill with complicated wheels.

V. If the many become the same as the few when possess'd, More! More! is the cry of a mistaken soul; less than All cannot satisfy Man.

VI. If any could desire what he is incapable of possessing, despair must be his eternal lot.

VII. The desire of Man being Infinite, the possession is Infinite & himself Infinite.

Application. He who sees the Infinite in all things, sees God. He who sees the Ratio only, sees himself only.

Therefore God becomes as we are, that we may be as he is. (K97-98)

It is Blake's reading of Rousseau and other philosophers who attempted to take away fear and superstition from religious speculation and to love truth before dogma that forms the background of Blake's own system. In the best discussion of Blake's relation to the "deism of natural religion which he professed to despise," Mark Schorer has identified aspects of Enlightenment theology that Blake incorporated into his own thought.[13] Among these are religious tolerance, hatred of any dogma, the fallibility of intuitions, cosmopolitanism and the universality of religious truth in all faiths and nations. Despite his reputation for hidden prophecies and obscurity, Blake does not see himself as a mystic. He is a Poet-Prophet of revealed experience and all his visions are of the "faculty which experiences." (K98) In *All Religions Are One* Blake expresses the cosmopolitan idea of the universality of truth in his own visionary way. Rousseau's vicar sees the disparity and enmities between different religions as the fault of the priests:

Ever since men have taken it into their heads to make the Deity speak, every people make him speak in their own way, and say what they like best. Had they listened only to what the Deity hath said to their hearts, there would have been but one religion on earth.[14]
. . . .
Let us not confound the ceremonials of religion with religion itself. The worship of God demands that of the heart; and this, when it is sincere, is ever uniform; men must entertain very ridiculous notions of the Deity, indeed, if they imagine he can interest himself in the gown or cassock of a priest, in the order of the words he pronounces, or the gestures and genuflections he makes at the altar.[15]
. . . .
Now, either all religions are good and agreeable to God, or if there be one which he hath dictated to man, and will punish him for rejecting, he hath certainly distinguished it by manifest signs and tokens, as the only true one. These signs are common to all times and places, and are equally obvious to all mankind, to the young and old, the learned and the ignorant, to Europeans, Africans and Savages.[16]

Blake is no less convinced than Rousseau of the universality of religious truths, but he sees the common denominator in the perception of that truth in what he calls Poetic Genius. Poetic Genius is not mysticism; it is immediate experiential revelation of the Poet Prophet:

The Voice of one crying in the Wilderness

The Argument. As the true method of knowledge is experiment, the true faculty of knowing must be the faculty which experiences. This faculty I treat of.

PRINCIPLE 1St. That the Poetic Genius is the true Man, and that the body or outward form of Man is derived from the Poetic Genius which by the Ancients was call'd an Angel & Spirit & Demon.
PRINCIPLE 2^d. As all men are alike in outward form, So (and with the same infinite variety) all are alike in the Poetic Genius.
PRINCIPLE 3^d. No man can think, write, or speak from his heart, but he must intend truth. Thus all sects of Philosophy are from the Poetic Genius adapted to the weaknesses of every individual.
PRINCIPLE 4th. As none by travelling over known lands can find out the unknown, So from already acquired knowledge Man could not acquire more: therefore an universal Poetic Genius exists.
PRINCIPLE 5th. The Religions of all Nations are derived from each Nation's different reception of the Poetic Genius, which is every where call'd the Spirit of Prophecy.
PRINCIPLE 6th. The Jewish & Christian Testaments are An original derivation from the Poetic Genius; this is necessary from the confined nature of bodily sensation.
PRINCIPLE 7th. As all men are alike (tho' infinitely various), So all Religions &, as all similars, have one source.
The true Man is the source, he being the Poetic Genius. (K98)

Thus Blake adds to the concept of universality a qualification: "The Religions of all Nations are derived from each Nation's different reception of Poetic genius, which is everywhere call'd the Spirit of Prophecy." The true Man may perceive religion differently, but the source is the same. The perversion of the true genius of every race occurs in the hands of priests. In *The Marriage of Heaven and Hell,* which Blake wrote a few years later, he traces the birth of Priesthood—an evil to him at this time:

Plate 11

The ancient Poets animated all sensible objects with Gods or Geniuses, calling them by the names and adorning them with the properties of woods, rivers, mountains, lakes, cities, nations, and whatever their enlarged & numerous senses could percieve.
And particularly they studied the genius of each city & country, placing it under its mental deity;
Till a system was formed, which some took advantage of, & enslav'd the vulgar by attempting to realize or abstract the mental deities from their objects: thus began Priesthood;
Choosing forms of worship from poetic tales.
And at length they pronounc'd that the Gods had order'd such things.
Thus men forgot that All deities reside in the human breast.
(K153)

In Fuseli's Rousseau pamphlet, the theme of universality is evoked in an ironical manner by contrasting the ideal with the reality of organized religion: the whole catalogue of sins brought on by religious bigotry, adherence to dogma and the persecution of one sect by another:

Had it not—to give a few *modern* instances— had it not been for these paroxysms of his, could *Luther* have indulged himself quietly in the fat luxury of a convent—*Leon's* golden age of literature and taste had not been overrun by the armies of Fanaticism; *Charles, Philip,* and *Alba* not turned their red-hot furies loose on *Europe*; the bells of *Bartholomew's* night had not been rung; *Smithfield, Merindol, Cabrieres,* and *Thoulouse,* would have not have blazed; the *Henrys,* the *Louis',* the ****, would not have been stabbed—abominated—expelled; no *Holy Tribunal* would smother the howlings of

humanity—nor earthquakes shake a throne; Truth—the wretched victim of itself—had
not been torn to tatters under the hands of its defenders;—and the Father, Son and Holy
Ghost—the Virgin—and their host of black, white and grey—had not been darted upon
Luther—Luther had not damned *Zwingli—Calvin* had not burnt *Servet—*a Bishop might
have signified something above a paper mitre—no sneaking, praying, psalmsinging,
scripture-expounding villain would have been called a dissenter—The *Moravians* would
not have adored their ass in the dark—no spirit had whipt into a maid's head—the
Quakers would not work their damnation with fear and trembling—in short—we might be
all of one mind—jolly fellows—and peaceably enjoy each our *rib of the word made
flesh,*—as Boccaccio says.—[17]

Fuseli's reverence for Christ was as sincere as his hatred of conventional
"christianism," as he refers to conventional confessions. He writes to
Lavater from Rome in 1770:

...und ob ich gleich weniger ein Christ als du bin (weil es mir vorkommt, dass die Religion
Jesu Christus noch vor des Paulus Zeit untergegangen war), so wird doch der göttliche
Mensch [Christ] meinem Kopfe und Hand immer die stärkste Begeistrung einwehen. Ver-
dammnis denke ich nicht, weil ich Gott liebe und einsames Denken an ihn mir Tränen der
Wollust auspresst, die ich noch keiner, auch der geistigsten Weiberliebe nicht bezahlt
habe.[18]

Fuseli, who obviously loved to shock the pious, was particularly fond of
stating that Christ's religion preceded him to the tomb, for he related the
same idea to Knowles sometime between 1805 and 1825, at least twenty-five
years after the letter to Lavater. Knowles quotes Fuseli as saying: "There are
no real Christians, for the religion of Christ died with its great author; for
where do we witness in those who bear his name the self abasement and
charity of their master, which qualities he not only taught, but practiced."[19]
Although he recognized the sincere and fervent faith of Lavater, Fuseli could
never quite comprehend such a pious attitude, and remained sceptical about
the mass of the churchgoing devout. In the *Remarks,* he characterizes the ordinary believer as more motivated by greed than any other impulse: He even
makes the blasphemous suggestion that the pagans of former days accepted death with considerably more grace than the followers of Christ:

But if ever an effect diametrically opposite to the cause, has amazed observation, 'tis,
that as long as immortality was no more but a guess of conjecture, man hugged it with the
most restless ardour: death was the victory of virtue, the most exalted reward of
benevolence, a complete atonement for affliction.—Since Jesus Christ has brought it to
light, we'd all jump the life to come.—[20]

In a footnote to that same statement, in which he contrasts the nobility of
Socrates and Cato with the horrors and fears depicted in Shakespeare's
"Christian" tragedies, Fuseli notes:

The truth is, there are few who do not grind their taste for beauty on gross appetite, and
fewer who build virtue on conscience; we all practise or love it, as the divines say, *sub in-
tuitu boni.* And if it is certain, that a child prefers a bit of sugar in the hand, to a shop of
sweetmeats to-morrow, we are likelier to do what is right for fortune in this life, than for
happiness in the next. Let a miser meeting misery from church, imagine howling—or
hallelujah as long as you please—the halfpenny lies snug;—let him remember the next
lottery, 'twill perhaps be given. Go on from these dregs of human nature to its most
generous juices—and you'll find that we all hate to serve God for nothing, or worse than-
nothing,—death—immortality—.[21]

"General and abstracted ideas form the source of our greatest errors," Rousseau's vicar says. "The jargon of metaphysics never discovered one truth; but it has filled philosophy with absurdities of which we are ashamed, as soon as they are stript of their pompous expressions."[22] The negative value placed on abstraction appears in Blake's annotation to Fuseli's Lavater *Aphorisms*, when he reacts to two aphorisms which he will borrow with modification for the second series of *There Is No Natural Religion*. The Lavater aphorisms read:

I.

Know, in the first place, that mankind agree in essence, as they do in their limbs and senses.

2.

Mankind differ as much in essence as they do in form, limbs, and senses—and only so, and not more. (K65)

Blake responds approvingly to Aphorism 2:

This is true Christian philosophy far above all abstraction. (K65)

In his own modification, the aphorism becomes:

PRINCIPLE 2^d. As all men are alike in outward form, So (and with the same infinite variety) all are alike in the Poetic Genius. (K98)

The attraction that Blake felt for Lavater's aphorisms and also for the "science" of physiognomy is based, in part, on Blake's absolute insistence upon the "real," homocentric, and concrete vision of religion and the spiritual world.

Blake's use of the term Poetic Genius, which he equates with the Lord in his annotations to Swedenborg's *Divine Love,* appears for the first time in the notes to Fuseli's Lavater aphorisms, and for the last time in *Milton*. It is a term, Damon suggests, "used by Blake when he discovered the central importance of the Imagination."[23] Blake sees the prophets as perceptors and revealers of God and religion because they are possessed of Poetic Genius. It is of significance that Blake begins to develop his idea of this concept at the time of his close association with Fuseli. Fuseli had first encountered the idea of original and divine genius when he read the *Urdichter,* Milton and Shakespeare, under the tutelage of Bodmer in Switzerland. There is a similarity in Bodmer's vision of the mission of the poet as bringer of lost or hidden truths to man and Blake's conception of himself as a poet. Fuseli's aesthetic orientation was strongly influenced by what he learned in his youth. Poetry, painting, music are conceived in the same spirit, and have as their task the revelation of inner truths. If Fuseli's orientation was more secular than that of his teacher, the aesthetic principle remained the same. Fuseli's view of Rousseau is colored by the point of view that the genius must be one who is able to see what others cannot. This was seen in the Winckelmann translation, where the artist-genius is depicted as one outside the realm of consensus and acquired knowledge. Genius is intuitive, and Fuseli defends Rousseau against those who decry the emotionalism of his writings with the typical expression of his definition of Genius:

Rousseau, you say, should propose coolly, and plead without passion.—There are in the walks of science certain characteristics of true genius.—Suppose it even employed in the highroads of argument or composition—there is a light of method, a chain of truths, a nerve of expression, so candid a manner, the stile glows so genially, palpitates so warmly, faints away so pallid, or mixes so meltingly with your heart—that you cry out, "There is more than head, art, memory—there is truth, sentiment, soul!" Such is the language of genius; and do you think it employs another, when virtue is the theme? Nothing is so easily found out as moral copies and originals.—Memory is not ideas—in that soil genius grows not: the same ink that burnt the paper under *Aretin's* pen, will freeze when used by *Parthenio Etyro*. 'Twas the heart, 'twas the strength of mind, 'twas the enthusiasm of benevolence that scattered flowers over Emile.[24]

Blake's consistent juxtaposing of the "Daughters of Memory" to Inspiration, which has been noted in the chapter on Winckelmann, is entirely consistent with the manner in which Fuseli uses the juxtaposition of acquired learning and intuitive genius in his evaluation of Rousseau. In his chapter on the *First Discourse,* Fuseli gives a digression on genius that is particularly close to Blake's conception of the term, especially when he is being polemic, as in the *Annotations to Reynolds.* Fuseli, arguing that learning should be restricted to "Genius," writes:

The rudiments of science should never have been levelled with those whom nature made, to crawl; their ruggedness, a kind of subsultory method, even a conciseness bordering upon obscurity, presupposing much, implying much—might have been the test of real genius. The gravitation of minds varies to infinity, and Providence has probably in most of her subjects combined inclination and capacities—their united endeavours may be supposed equal to the opposition they meet with in their objects.—There is a kind of intuition in genius—'twas *Raphael's,* 'twas *Pascal's.*
. . . .
...As it is not very difficult by dint of memory, and compendiums, to conquer your tracts of divinity, law, and physic, (for it does not require more head, than to be a clever cobler or brush-maker) why should Thickskull be afraid to enter the breach, through which brother Jack has brayed and kicked himself into a chariot, an office, or a bishoprick?[25]

The inevitable concomitant to such a view of genius is that the masses of the non-genius order will not be able to understand or appreciate the truths brought to them. In their own personal and artistic lives, both Fuseli and Blake saw themselves in this light. Rousseau, in his persecution, was the prototype for Fuseli of the misunderstood genius. This role will be filled by *Milton* in his later life. Blake, in his defenses of himself, of Fuseli, and of all whom he saw as bearers of hidden truths, expresses an idea very close to Fuseli's own. His first ironical treatment of Genius occurs in *The Marriage of Heaven and Hell,* which he wrote in 1790.

Pernicious Maxims and Truth-Bringing Devils

Blake's *Marriage of Heaven and Hell* is usually recognized as a satire on Swedenborg, which marks Blake's movement "from some feeling of affinity with Swedenborg to a strong sense of outrage."[1] Although the connection with Swedenborg is attested to by the title, style, and format of the work, Blake's polemical intention in the *Marriage of Heaven and Hell* must go beyond, in the words of John Howard, "a desire to ridicule a man long passed away," and "must be addressed to somebody."[2] In his long article, "An Audience for the Marriage of Heaven and Hell," Howard suggests that the satire is not confined to Swedenborg himself, but is addressed to "an audience composed of members of the New Jerusalem Church and the Joseph Johnson circle."[3] Noting Blake's familiarity with Fuseli's adaptation of Lavater's *Aphorisms on Man*, and Fuseli's nickname, "Principal Hobgobblin-Painter to the Devil," Howard states: "The association of aphorisms, the Johnson-devil metaphor, and the opposition of the principles of the Johnson group to those conservative Swedenborgians, form a background for Blake's liberal corrosive proverbs of Hell."[4] If the devils in the satire are seen as the liberals in the Johnson circle: Priestley, Paine, and Fuseli; and the religious angels frightened almost blue by the wisdom of the devils as Blake's Swedenborgian friends, *The Marriage of Heaven and Hell* becomes more comprehensible. The work is thus placed within a political and social context as well as a theological one. But there is an aspect of what Northrop Frye calls Blake's "blistering ridicule of the wisdom that dwells with prudence"[5] that suggests that Fuseli provided Blake with a model that went beyond his reputation as painter to the devil.

The first critic to recognize that "some of M HH is in the mocking tone of Fuseli's *Remarks on Rousseau*" was Erdman.[6] Erdman relegates his observation of similarity of tone in the two works to a footnote which tantalizes and invites further investigation for textual parallels.

Fuseli's Rousseau pamphlet is couched throughout in the language of irony and is laced with bitterness against religious intolerance, sects, and hypocrisy. It must be remembered that in 1767 the scandal of the Rousseau-Hume affair had placed the unequivocal hero of Fuseli's youth in the center of a vicious controversy. Fuseli himself was enraged and somewhat disappointed by the attacks in the English press and the reports of Rousseau's erratic behavior towards Hume and his English guests. To one reading the work in the late 1780s in the months before the initiation of the French

Revolution, Fuseli's pamphlet would provide an impassioned and well-informed image of the philosopher in whom a new interest was awakened by political events. Rousseau's *Confessions,* the first six books of which had been published in English translation in 1783 about a year after their publication in French in Geneva, and the subsequent publication of the last six books in London in 1790 caused renewed interest not only in the works, but in the character of Jean-Jacques.[7] Fuseli's early pamphlet addresses both the works and the character of the problematic Genevan.

The Hume affair and the personality of Rousseau are addressed in the last three chapters of Fuseli's work. The other seven are concerned with stating what Rousseau did and did not say in his important works to 1767 and how he had been abused and misunderstood by established authorities, in short: how his truth had been perverted and rejected by "Kings" and the philistine religious. Fuseli's indignation at Rousseau's treatment at the hands of the mob had been registered in the Dälliker letter two years before he wrote the *Remarks*; and the theme with which he opens his pamphlet is already on his mind when he tells Dälliker that, judging from the consequences of telling the truth:

> *Ich sehe denn aber auch nicht, warum Jesus Christus den dogmatischen und mysteriösen Teil seiner Religion in die weite Welt hinausgesandt hat, da derselbe, ich appelliere an seinen Richterstuhl, bis itzo zum Teile die Quelle aller Schismen, Lästerungen, Rasereien, Lächerlichkeiten, Blutvergiessungen, Greueln der Kreuz bezeichneten war und ist, zum Teile die Anhänglichkeit an seine göttliche Moral entkräftet.*[8]

Fuseli's seemingly blasphemous statement never doubts the truth of Christ's vision, only the ability of the world to understand it. Out of the hands of genius, truth becomes fanaticism and turns on its author, it becomes the exclusive property of sects and cults. After meeting with Rousseau in 1766, Fuseli writes to Bodmer that the philosopher and the theologian alike must hate him on principle, for he is against all systems.[9] At the time that Fuseli writes the *Remarks*, Christ, Socrates, and Rousseau are seen in the same light. This does not mean that Fuseli reduces the divinity of Christ so much as that he elevates the revelation of the others to the same plane: they are all attuned to truth, which is divine.

Persecution follows genius. Fuseli grows to see himself more and more in company with genius rebuked and despised, especially after the failure of his Milton Gallery in 1790.[10] As a fellow genius, and Fuseli has no doubt that he is one, he expressed his indignation in the *Remarks.* It is this "tone" of indignation that Blake echoes in *The Marriage of Heaven and Hell.* In his "Preface" to the *Remarks* Fuseli launches his cynical diatribe concerning the futility of truth-bringing in a wild, epigrammatic style:

> And first—because it has been decided by the voice of the world, "That truth is not to be told."—Throw a glance on society—open the annals of time—Truth has been—and is—the destroyer of peace—and the parent of revolution—And will be so—for this plain reason—because it is of epidemic nature—because a man cannot see, or fancy to see its most transient spark—but with a dogstar rage he will pursue it through thick and thin—sink the mob at his heels in the quagmires which the jack-a-lanthorn dances o'er,—or at their head break thro' all the barricades of power, nets of politics, and cobwebs of speculation—tear at the cordage of interest—nay spare not even the silken ties of temper and affection, to come at it.[11]

The fictitious editor of the *Remarks* thus faults Rousseau for having spoken, when, like Christ, he would have been better advised to keep revelation to himself. This ironical method is repeated throughout the *Remarks*: defend the thesis by stating its antithesis, and then demolish the antithesis with irony. As Erdmann has shown, Blake uses much this same technique in *The Marriage of Heaven and Hell* by employing Swedenborg's theosophical analytics, which he then transcends by contradiction.[12]

In Blake's rejection of Swedenborg or the adherents of the Swedenborgian New Church, there is an implied rejection of all who claim exclusive right to truth. This is the fault of Swedenborg, that he has sought to expose the hypocrites and the folly of churches, but in so doing he has only "conversed with Angels who are all religious, & not with Devils who all hate religion." (K157) As in the series *There Is No Natural Religion* he has corrected the philosophers, he now corrects the religious. The Devils are doubters and scoffers,but in their challenge of dogma there is much to be learned. They are not to be identified with Blake any more than the Devils are. Neither group speaks for Blake's heart and soul, though they seem to be fighting for both. In his reading of Rousseau, his acquaintanceship with Fuseli, Blake has conversed with Devils who have refined his vision; and although he is not one himself, he seems to enjoy their company more than that of the blandly pious. In his ironical "remonstrance against this enterprize," Fuseli has the outraged editor of the *Remarks* define Rousseau as just such a devil:

Has he not disputed on self-murther?—Has he not blasphemed man into a being naturally good? Has he not, to the abhorrence of every good schoolmaster, affirmed, that the idea of God can have no meaning for a boy of ten years; that to him Heaven is a basket of sweetmeats, and Hell—a school?—Does he care for original sin? he, who despises the eternity of hell pains;—and though living upon the immortality of the soul, yet thinks it not geometrically demonstrable? If he seems to allow of a free determination of the will, he thinks of the interventions of private Providence, as the diseased patchwork of a Geneva watch. —And is man guilty of this enormous lump of *errors*, or *worse*—to be defended, and his pernicious maxims to be scattered abroad by you—who imbibed religion and constitutional sentiments, with your mother-milk?[13]

And Fuseli brings the blaspheming devil concept to direct expression in an ironic reference to Voltaire:

—I would have you to know that *Arrouet* believes in God;—and to give the due praise of disinterestedness and generosity to his faith—believes in God, though he has proved that *his* God is the Devil.—[14]

Blake's Devil in the last "Memorable Fancy" of Heaven and Hell speaks like a humanist to an appalled Angel:

Plates 22-24

Once I saw a Devil in a flame of fire, who arose before an Angel that sat on a cloud, and the Devil utter'd these words: "The worship of God is: Honouring his gifts in other men, each according to his "genius, and loving the greatest men best: those who envy or "calumniate great men hate God; for there is no other God." (K158)

The Angel, beside himself with rage and turning first blue, then yellow, and "at last white, pink & smiling," replies:

"Thou Idolater! is not God One? & is not he visible in Jesus
"Christ? and has not Jesus Christ given his sanction to the law of
"ten commandments? and are not all other men fools, sinners, &
"nothings?" (K158)

At this point, the Devil replies in a manner which ironically posits questions which "condemn" Christ in a manner strikingly similar to Fuseli's mock condemnation of Rousseau:

The Devil answer'd: "bray a fool in a morter with wheat, yet shall
"not his folly be beaten out of him; if Jesus Christ is the greatest
"man, you ought to love him in the greatest degree; now hear how
"he has given his sanction to the law of ten commandments: did he
"not mock at the sabbath, and so mock the sabbath's God? murder
"those who were murder'd because of him? turn away the law from
"the woman taken in adultery? steal the labor of others to support
"him? bear false witness when he omitted making a defence before
"Pilate? covet when he pray'd for his disciples, and when he bid
"them shake off the dust of their feet against such as refused to lodge
"them? I tell you, no virtue can exist without breaking these ten
"commandments. Jesus was all virtue, and acted from impulse, not
"from rules." (K158)

In the humorous conclusion to the dialogue, the Angel is converted by the Devil's argument:

Note: This Angel, who is now become a Devil, is my particular
friend; we often read the Bible together in its infernal or diabolical
sense, which the world shall have if they behave well.
I have also The Bible of Hell, which the world shall have whether
they will or no.

One Law for the Lion & Ox is Oppression.

(K158)

Though Blake might not be a Devil, he continued to read the Bible in its "diabolical sense" for the rest of his life, challenging any sort of orthodox thought. This is nowhere more clearly demonstrated than in Blake's insistence upon "divine humanity" and his grappling with the nature of evil and the Fall.

In the *Remarks,* Fuseli, understanding that Rousseau had sought to avoid theological condemnation by positing his exposition on the origin of evil outside the context of the second chapter of Genesis, presents Rousseau's thesis on the subject in a natural and not a supernatural state. This state of nature is not the state of Adam and Eve envisioned by "the despotic systems of the moralists, built by reason and inhabited by passions."[15] Fuseli understands well how Rousseau sought in the *Second Discourse* to avoid the moralistic commonplace that sin and vice led natural man down—sin and vice being for Rousseau the result or effect and not the cause of man's misfortune. Rousseau leaves open the question of when and in what phase of man's evolution his hypothetical state of nature is to be placed, but suggests that it might be in some vague realm outside the theological Garden of Eden. Fuseli paraphrases from Rousseau's introduction to the *Second Discourse:*

Most of those that have written on this subject, mistook the effect for the cause. "Talking of nothing but wants, keen desires, oppression, pride they transported the ideas of society into the realms of nature. —Most have not even doubted the once existence of a state of nature, tho' it be evident from the scriptures, that the first man, immediately inspired and instructed by God, was not in that state himself," etc. Disc. Intro. Oeuv. t. iii.[16]

Rousseau's tracing of man "back to the nipple of nature" is, Fuseli writes, to imagine him outside of a social context, isolated and stripped of all metaphysical or supernatural gifts he might have received from God. Rousseau found his hypothetical man "wrapped up in instinct,—taught his lore by appetite and fear—harmless because content—content because void of comparative ideas—solitary, because without wants,—snatching the moment on the wing, from the past and future ones. —Yet even in this wilderness of nature he stamps him with the sovereignty of vegetation and instinct; behold him free, improveable, compassionate."[17] How came then the strong to become enslaved by the weak? Whence the origin of injustice and inequality? Fuseli writes that Rousseau's *Second Discourse* has the purpose of marking the moment "when in the progress of things, right succeeded to violence, nature received the yoke of law,..."; in short, how man, born free, ended up everywhere in chains. Blake obviously has in mind some sort of parody of Rousseau's image of man in chains when he writes:

> The Giants who formed this world into its sensual existence, and now seem to live in it in chains, are in truth the causes of its life & the sources of all activity; but the chains are the cunning of weak and tame minds which have power to resist energy; according to the proverb, the weak in courage is strong in cunning. (K155)

These antediluvian Giants in this "Memorable Fancy" are part of a secular Genesis, and not too removed from Rousseau's savages, who, in the end are enslaved by those weaker, but more cunning, than they. Although giants play a more defined role in Blake's later works, it is interesting to note that Fuseli, in his chapter "On the Origin of INEQUALITY among MANKIND, and if the law of NATURE authorises it," makes a puzzling reference to Giants, which does not seem to refer to Rousseau's use of the word and which might have been his own metaphor for strength and weakness:

> Such are the random outlines of a work which you might call the triumph of conjecture—compared with others. Rousseau, like his own giant, with every enormous stride measures only his superiority over the dwarf that pants behind him. — You laugh to hear the dwarf deny the existence of provinces he cannot explore; and why would you rave at the brood of interest and dullness, for their attempts to drown the oracles of nature in their hisses, at seeing them strut forth with their carpenter's rule to measure the regions of probability—?[18]

It could be, too, that the Giant and dwarf are allegories for Rousseau and Voltaire, respectively, since in the next paragraph Fuseli launches a violent attack on Voltaire. The reference to the dwarf's trying to measure probability with a rule would have also appealed to Blake.

The Marriage of Heaven and Hell is Blake's first philosophical examination of the problem of good and evil. He has not yet reached the complexity of his fourfold symbolism of the androgynous man of premundane existence. Unsatisfied with moralistic explanations of man's behavior, Blake attacks the conventional perspective of "the religious" and develops his theories of "Contraries." Blake's statement in *Plate 3:*

> Without Contraries is no progression. Attraction and Repulsion,
> Reason and Energy, Love and Hate, are necessary to Human
> existence. (K149)

reveals the mind of one who, much like Rousseau, is trying to comprehend man, the psychological and physical phenomenon, and not man, the theologically condemned or saved soul. In a sense, the argument of *Heaven and Hell* is Blake's own attempt to secularize notions of good and evil and to divest them from the garments of judgmental moralism. The writings of Swedenborg, which Blake might once have found attractive, he now sees as "the linen clothes folded up." Swedenborg is "the Angel sitting at the tomb." (K149) The contraries are dynamic, the dogmas are folded, static. The contraries have been misinterpreted by the Angels:

> From these contraries spring what the religious call Good & Evil.
> Good is the passive that obeys Reason. Evil is the active springing
> from Energy.
> Good is Heaven. Evil is Hell. (K149)

The idea of contraries, as J.G. Davis has said, is not peculiar to Blake.[19] Almost every philosopher who observes human nature comments upon the contradictions in human impulses. But there is something in the intense and polemic conviction in which Blake sets forth his definitions of the sources of good and evil that suggests that he might be reacting to some specific idea set forth by another. Rousseau's Savoyard priest, who sets about to study man by studying himself, discovers these contraries in himself as a kind of dualism:

> In meditating on the nature of man, I conceived that I discovered two distinct principles; the one raising him to the study of eternal truths, the love of justice and moral beauty, bearing him aloft to the regions of the intellectual world, the contemplation of which yields the truest delight to the philosopher; the other debasing him even below himself, subjecting him to the slavery of sense, the tyranny of passions, and exciting these to counteract every noble and generous sentiment inspired by the former.[20]

Thus far, Rousseau sounds very much like a moralizing angel. But in the next lines he uses terms remarkably like Blake's, but with reversed values:

> When I perceived myself hurried away by two such contrary powers, I naturally concluded that man is not one simple and individual substance. I will, and I will not, I perceive myself at once free and a slave; I see what is good, I admire it, and yet I do the evil: *I am active when I listen to my reason, and passive when hurried away by my passions*; while my greatest uneasiness is, to find, when fallen under temptations, that I had the power of resisting them.[21] (My italics)

The phrase is the antithesis of Blake's: "Good is the passive that obeys Reason. Evil is the active springing from Energy." There is even more reason to believe that Fuseli had led Blake to read his favorite profession of religious views, when one reads the closing lines of the vicar's confession of the contrary impulses that govern his behavior: "...let those, who imagine him [man] to be a simple uncompounded Being, reconcile these contradictions, and I will give up my opinion and acknowledge him to be one substance."[22] It seems as if Blake might be reacting directly to the challenge made by Rousseau's spokesman. In *The Marriage of Heaven and Hell* Blake is announcing that he has joined the ranks of the philosophers he has been reading. Like them, he is answering the question, "What is Man?" To be sure, Blake was to spend a lifetime in pursuit of that question. The highly satirical *Heaven and Hell* stands at the beginning of his search. Rousseau's vicar had told him:

> Avoid all those, who, under pretence of explaining natural causes, plant the most destructive doctrines in the hearts of men; and whose apparent scepticism is an hundred times more dogmatical and affirmative than the decisive tone of their adversaries. Under the haughty pretext of being the only persons who are truly enlightened, honest and sincere, they subject us imperiously to their magisterial decisions, and give us for the true principles of things, only unintelligible systems, which they have raised in their imaginations.[23]

Blake says in *The Marriage of Heaven and Hell:* "I have always found that Angels have the vanity to speak of themselves as the only wise; this they do with a confident insolence sprouting from systematic reasoning." (K157) The English poet was to distrust systems based on reason throughout his life: "I must Create a System or be enslav'd by another Man's. I will not Reason & Compare: my business is to Create." (K629) These lines written in *Jerusalem* are preshadowed by the argumentative dialogues in *The Marriage of Heaven and Hell,* where Blake was still forming his system, trying to separate the Angels from the Devils, the Prolific from the Devourers, and trying to discern the wise man from the learned.

Fuseli had opened the first chapter of the *Remarks* with a statement of his motive in writing the piece:

> The motives which produced the following remarks on the writings and conduct of John James Rousseau are gratitude, humanity, indignation.
> If to give instruction grace, is the great duty of genius, Rousseau has done his—
> If the first object of man is man—if his nature has such titles as not to know endangers and dishonors, 'tis supine brutality to slight them, to mistake the spurious for the genuine—Humanity is your great prerogative—then whether you sway society, or guide the plough, whether you scatter passions round ye, or anatomise the prism of a moth—whether you write a book or read one—be humane.
> If truth is called error, and argument a dream; if Vice mobs Virtue, and Quackery pins her mantle to the back of Simplicity—indignation is merit.[24]

In Blake's *Marriage of Heaven and Hell,* when Blake depicts himself dining with the prophets Isaiah and Ezekiel, he asks them how they "dared so roundly to assert that God spoke to them; and whether they did not think at the time that they would be misunderstood, & so be the cause of imposition." The prophet Isaiah replies:

> "I saw no God, nor heard any, in a finite organical
> "perception; but my senses discover'd the infinite in every thing, and
> "as I was then perswaded, & remain confirm'd, that the voice of
> "honest indignation is the voice of God, I cared not for consequences,
> "but wrote." (K153)

It is certain that the voice of indignation spoke to Fuseli and Blake very early in life, it is equally certain that each recognized that voice in the other. Both artists are full of contradiction and seem to defy classification according to style or aesthetic movement. But the search for truth was equally important to both. Fuseli ends the first chapter of the *Remarks* by saying:

> We have the good-nature at our expense to confound the learned with the *wise* man—who centers all his midnight cares in *action*; this was the principle of ancient philosophy, as strength was the design of their gymnastick exercises; but we seem made to talk. —We call science with them the individuation of ideas—our corollaries may be trifles, or worse, provided we, with Milton's Satan,
>
> > O'er bog or steep, thro' strait, rough, dense or rare,
> > With head, hands, wings, or feet, pursue our way;
> > And swim, or sink, or wade, or creep, or fly—[25]

During the period from 1788 to 1800 the painter from Zurich and the printer from London came together, and both benefited from the association. They were to go their different paths to genius, often altering and rejecting attitudes which they had formerly held dear. In the third "Memorable Fancy" an Angel has laid before Blake the horrors of Hell-fire and damnation, saying

> O
> "horrible! O dreadful state! consider the hot burning dungeon thou
> "art preparing for thyself to all eternity, to which thou art going in
> "such career."

But after all the horrors are shown the young Blake, presumably by friends who saw his association with liberal free-thinkers as the road to perdition, the Angel retreats, and Blake finds himself sitting on a pleasant bank, "hearing a harper who sung to the harp; & his theme was: 'The man who never alters his opinion is like standing water, & breeds reptiles of the mind'." (K156) The identity of this harper is disputed by critics; it might well have been Fuseli, who wrote in 1789: "Genius without bias, is a stream without direction: it inundates all, and ends in stagnation."[26] One of Blake's "Proverbs of Hell" is "Expect poison from standing water." (K152)

Part Five
Blake and Fuseli's Lavater

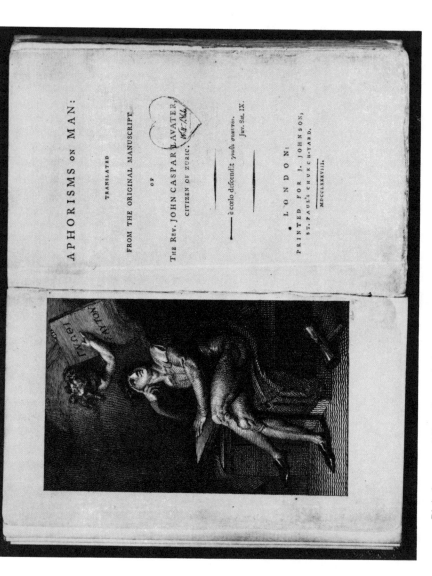

Blake's copy of Fuseli's rendering of Lavater's *Regeln*. Blake wrote his name inside the heart with which he encircled Lavater's name. (This item is reproduced by permission of *The Huntington Library, San Marino, California*)

Blake's Copy of the *Aphorisms on Man*

Blake's annotated copy of the *Aphorisms on Man* is the most important extant written documentation of his close relationship with Fuseli in the 1780s. The engraving that accompanies the title page, the design of which had long been attributed to Fuseli and which is signed by Blake, was shown conclusively to be Fuseli's design when his original drawing for the engraving was discovered in 1970.[1] Study of the variation between Fuseli's incomplete sketch and the final state of the engraving shows that Fuseli and Blake were collaborators in the project of the engraving. The closeness with which they worked and the fact that Fuseli left the details of the final state of the engraving to Blake show that "Fuseli, although sixteen years older than Blake, must have felt the bond of sympathy between them to be strong enough for him to leave the fuller development of his indicated desires to the younger artist, with confidence that the final engraving would express his original version."[2] Gert Schiff includes the engraving in his definitive *Oeuvrekatalog*, and the engraving is now fully accepted as one of Fuseli's designs.[3] Todd's important article, in which he lists all Blake's known engravings for Fuseli, gives the most complete survey of the subject and supports the supposition that "for a short period, roughly from late 1787 to early 1792, the men were in closer contact and enjoyed more absolute sympathy with each other than at any other time during their friendship."[4] As Todd has shown that there is more of Blake in the engraving that accompanies Fuseli's Lavater adaptation than the hand of an engraver engaged to copy the design of another, it can also be shown that Fuseli's rendering of the *Regeln* of his dearest friend is far more than a mechanical translation. In the case of the *Aphorisms*, Fuseli's role of intellectual intermediary to Blake is clearly demonstrable. Support for this view is seen in the external evidence of Blake's copy as well as in the stylistic influence of the text.

The volume owned by Blake is now in the Huntington Library. It represents the first preliminary printing and was obtained by Blake with the pages unbound. This is indicated by the fact that Blake's handwritten notes run far into the margins of the pages, and that several words were thus cut off in the process of binding at a later date.[5] Erdman has noted that ink blots which were transferred from adjacent pages at the time of annotation demonstrate that when Blake was making his notes the pages were stacked in random order.[6] The publication notice reads: "London, J. Johnson, St. Paul's Church Yard, MDCCLXXXVIII," and the book carries the same dedication from

Lavater to Fuseli and Fuseli's "Advertisement" that were to appear in at least two other editions published by Johnson and in numerous American editions.[7] After the title page, there is a list of fourteen *errata*, six of which appear to have been corrected in the text by someone other than Blake.[8] A peculiarity of this edition is that the aphorisms are misnumbered after aphorism 189, going from 189 to 200, thus making the total number of aphorisms appear to be 643. This fault was corrected in Johnson's editions of 1789 and 1794, both of which show 632 aphorisms.

That Blake obtained the work unbound and in a preliminary state is sure evidence that he was given the little volume as soon as it came from Johnson's press. Blake's emotional comments in the margins show that he was truly touched by what he found there. His encircling of Lavater's name (with a heart containing his own name) on the title page shows the affection that he felt for the book and its author. On the end-page of his copy, Blake explains his comments of approval, disapproval, and "uneasy" perceptions of Lavater's wisdom:

> ...For I write from the warmth of my heart, & cannot resist that impulse I feel to rectify what I think false in a book I love so much & approve so generally.

> Man is bad or good as he unites himself with bad or good spirits: tell me with whom you go & I'll tell you what you do.

> As we cannot experience pleasure but by means of others [so we are *del.*], who experience either pleasure or pain thro' us, And as all of us on earth are united in thought, for it is impossible to think without images of somewhat on earth—So it is impossible to know God or heavenly things without conjunction with those who know God & heavenly things; therefore all who converse in the spirit, converse with spirits. [& they converse with the spirit of God. *del.*]

> For these reasons I say that this Book is written by consultation with Good Spirits, because it is Good, & that the name Lavater is the amulet of those who purify the heart of man. (K88)

Fuseli's deep friendship with Lavater and his intimate knowledge of his thought and work must have influenced Blake's high opinion of the Swiss theologian. Gilchrist tells us that Blake showed his annotations to Fuseli, "who said that one could read their writer's character in *them*."[9] It has been the tendency of scholars commenting on Blake's notes on Lavater to emphasize the poverty of thought in Lavater's sayings in invidious comparison to the mystic Swedenborg, whose works Blake was reading at the same time. This tradition begins with Gilchrist, who calls Lavater "the Swiss enthusiast," and Fuseli's version of his sayings an "...imposing scroll of fervid truisms and haphazard generalities, as often disputable as not, if often acute and striking." Gilchrist admits that it was "like all his [Lavater's] other writings, warmly welcomed in this country," but that "it does not impress one as an elixir of inspired truth...."[10] This sort of disdain has continued in modern scholarship with Damon's assessment that the *Aphorisms* "are mild, shrewd sentences consigning true Christians to Heaven and condemning the intemperate in thought or action as vipers to be stamped upon."[11] Blake was as fond of branding vipers of his own definition as was Lavater, and the book's "complete lack of mysticism" would have attracted Blake rather than have repelled him at this time.[12] While the influence of Swedenborgian mysticism in Blake's "System" has been well established by scholars, it is often overlooked that Blake's unconventional morality, as expressed in *The Marriage of Heaven and Hell*, has the same sort of zealous and didactic flavor as Lavater's book of "rules to live by." Whether or not Lavater's reputation as a physiognomist, philosopher, and *Menschenkenner* has withstood the test of time, the fact remains that Fuseli's eccentric friend, extremely famous in his day, was probably considered by Blake to be every bit as profound a thinker as the Swedish metallurgist.[13] It is interesting to note that, after absorbing much from Swedenborg's philosophy, Blake turns against him in *The Marriage of Heaven and Hell*:

> Thus Swedenborg boasts that what he writes is new; tho' it is only the Contents or Index of already publish'd books. (K157)

Fuseli's Lavater adaptation, on the other hand, was to remain one of Blake's "most favourite volumes."[14] Gilchrist's statement is corroborated by a letter from Blake to Tatham on August 4, 1824, from which G. E. Bentley has identified a statement in the closing lines as a partial quote from Aphorism 69: "The humble is formed to adore."[15] Thus, we see Blake consulting his copy of the *Aphorisms* twenty-seven years after the time of his closest association with Fuseli, and only three years before his death. After Blake's death, his annotated copy of the *Aphorisms* went to his friend, Samuel Palmer, was later in the library of Robert Hoe, and was sold in 1911 to the Huntington.[16]

Vermischte
unphysiognomische

K e g e l n

zur

Menschen-
und
Selbstenntniß.

Von

[signature]
Johann Caspar Lavater
zu Gaben bey Hrn. Heren.

1 7 8 8.

Vermischte
unphysiognomische

R e g e l n

zur

Selbst-
und
Menschenkenntniß.

Von

Johann Caspar Lavater.

1 7 8 7.

Title pages of the two volumes upon which Fuseli based his translation/adaptation of Lavater's *Regeln*. (Special Collections Division, The Milton S. Eisenhower Library, The Johns Hopkins University, Baltimore, Maryland)

The Epigrammatic Style

Because of the value and insight into Blake's thought provided by the quickly scribbled *notes* in the *Aphorisms*, Fuseli's rendering of his friend's rules is the most often read of any of the Swiss painter's English literary undertakings—perhaps the only thing to come from his pen which has been read continuously from the time of its first publication until today. It is one of the many ironies of their relationship that Blake's latter-day fame has rescued the literary career of the once-famous Keeper of the Royal Academy from obscurity.

In his biography of 1880, Gilchrist devoted a short chapter, "Meditation: Notes on Lavater," to the comments Blake recorded in the margins of his copy of *Aphorisms of Man*.[1] Gilchrist apologized for having quoted from Lavater's rules "perhaps too copiously, the reader may think, for their intrinsic merit."[2] Although other commentators on the marginalia have echoed Gilchrist's low opinion of Lavater as a philosopher, the fact remains, as Gilchrist realized, that these epigrams and Blake's notes to them are invaluable for at least two reasons. First, more than any other writings of Blake during the crucial eighties, they reveal what he was thinking and contain the seeds of many of the ideas that he was to develop in his mature works. This aspect of the marginalia has been established with authority by scholars such as Jacob Bronowski, Mark Shorer, David Erdman, and Morton D. Paley.[3] Second, it appears that Blake's confrontation with the *Aphorisms* provided the direct impetus for his "Proverbs of Hell" in *The Marriage of Heaven and Hell* and his fondness for the epigrammatic style in general. Gilchrist saw the stylistic influence of Lavater's work as an "external accident," and S. Foster Damon states somewhat more generously: "Blake used the stimulating form of these apothegms to teach his own doctrines, which are radically different in thought."[4] While both aspects of the influence of the *Aphorisms* on Blake are pertinent to the study of Fuseli's role as a transmitter of ideas to Blake, the focus here is less on the philosophical impact of Lavater's thought and more on the style in which Fuseli gave those thoughts an "English dress."

In November 1787, Lavater published the first volume of his rules under the title, *Vermischte unphysiognomische Regeln zur Selbst- und Menschenkenntniss*. A year later, a second volume appeared with a slightly changed title, *Vermischte unphysiognomische Regeln zur Menschen- und Selbstkenntniss*.[5] The small, pocket-sized books appeared with no publisher's name as limited and "autographed‘ editions.[6] A month before the publication of the first volume, Lavater sent a manuscript version of his "rules" to Fuseli in London. Accompanying the manuscript was a letter, which Fuseli included as the "Dedication" of the *Aphorisms on Man*:

To

HENRY FUSELI, A.M.

TAKE, dear observer of men, from the hand of your unbiassed friend, this testimony of esteem for your genius.

All the world know that this is no flattery; for, in an hundred things, I am not of your opinion; but, in what concerns the knowledge of mankind, we are nearer to one another than any two in ten thousand.

What I give here is the result of long experience, matured and confirmed by various and daily application. It will be found, I hope, an useful book for every class of men, from the throne to the cottage. All is not, cannot be, new; but all ought to be true, useful, important; and much, I trust, is new and individual.

I give you liberty not only to make improvements, but to omit what you think false or unimportant.

The number of rules may appear large, yet it is small compared to what might have been written: in the mean time you and I, as well as our readers, may find ample employment in studying these.

J.C. Lavater.

Zuric, October 13, 1787.[7]

Fuseli made full use of Lavater's permission to edit and amend, as any attempt at a quantitative comparison of the German and English texts demonstrates. With few exceptions, Fuseli strove to keep the intrinsic meaning and flavor of Lavater's saying, even if his imagery and diction strayed far afield from the original. R.J. Shroyer counts sixty-five aphorisms in Fuseli's translation for which no German equivalents can be found in either the 1787 or the 1788 volumes published by Lavater.[8] While one may judge the degree of originality exercised by Fuseli by comparison of the language of the *Aphorisms* with that of the *Regeln* where they can be matched, there is no way of determining with any authority the degree to which Fuseli exercised his license to edit in the case of aphorisms which can be found only in the English text. Without presuming too much on the basis of the negative evidence of the "missing" *Regeln*, it is nonetheless tempting to suggest Fuseli himself might have been the author of some of them. Given the absence of the original manuscripts from which the German and the English versions were compiled, one can only conjecture whether Fuseli, in fact, inserted some gems of his own among the wise sayings of his friend.

There can be no question, however, that *Aphorisms on Man* and Lavater's two volumes are based essentially on one body of work. It is possible to find German equivalents for almost ninety percent of the English aphorisms and the first fifty-one of the English aphorisms match the first fifty-one *Regeln* in the 1787 volume. Thereafter, however, the sayings as they appear in Fuseli's text have been shortened, combined, and, in some cases, significantly altered and must be searched out in the two volumes of German sayings. Again, what is important here is the degree to which the *Aphorisms* exerted a stylistic influence on Blake. Lavater's German style is heavy and cluttered with tortured wordplay. Fuseli, who was working at this time on his own aphorisms on art, attempted to transform his friend's homey sayings into terse and precise epigrams and to give a conscious and consistent style to the wisdom that rolled fluently and randomly from Lavater's pen over a period of several months.

As in the case of the Winckelmann translations, it is difficult to tell in *Aphorisms on Man* where translation leaves off and invention begins. In his "Advertisement," Fuseli states that the maxims do not represent an anthology selected by him, but rather that they are Lavater's "effusions" exactly as given to Fuseli in the form of a spontaneously and rapidly executed manuscript. At the end of this "Advertisement," Fuseli declares his intention of publishing within the year another volume of aphorisms as a companion piece to the work at hand, "not, indeed, by the same author." His projected work was, in fact, to constitute Volume II of the "translation."

ADVERTISEMENT.

IN the following collection of Aphorisms, the reader is not to expect a set of maxims compiled from the author's own, or by him selected from the works of others; but an original, meditated and composed in the series here offered during the autumn of 1787, and transmitted in the author's own manuscript to the publisher.

Notwithstanding the rapidity that attended this work, (and the world know that all this author's works are effusions); it will be found to contain what gives their value to maxims—verdicts of wisdom on the reports of experience. If some are truisms, let it be considered that Solomon and Hippocrates wrote truisms: if some are not new, they are recommended by an air of novelty; if whim should appear to have dictated others, it was the whim of humanity; and what may be deemed rash will be found to flow from the fervour of indignant honesty, or the exultations of benevolence. Acute and perspicuous, they are not infected by the cant of sects, or circumscribed by local notions, but general as the passions and feelings of the race.

It is the intention of the editor to add another volume of APHORISMS ON ART. WITH CHARACTERS AND EXAMPLES, not indeed by the same author, which the reader may expect in the course of the year.

May, 1788.[9]

These *Aphorisms on Art with Characters and Examples*, the manuscript of which Fuseli himself was composing simultaneously with his translating for Lavater, never were to appear from Johnson's press as intended. As chance would have it, another fire in Johnson's shop destroyed the impression. Knowles reports: "In conformity with his intention, one sheet was worked off [by Johnson] and corrected by him; but an accidental fire having taken place on the premises of the printer, the whole impression was destroyed, and Fuseli could never bring himself to undergo the task of another revision."[10] It fell to Knowles to edit and publish the aphorisms, which Fuseli had expanded in manuscript over the next two decades, in his posthumous *Life and Writings of Henry Fuseli, Esq., M.A. R.A.* (Volume III, 1831).[11] Fuseli's intended Volume II of the Aphorisms is important to the topic at hand, for it tells us that Fuseli was particularly immersed in the aphorism as a literary form at the time that he is known to have been most closely associated with Blake. For the most part, the aphorisms that Knowles published concerned art, genius, and the attainment of the sublime, and when read together with the Lavater *Aphorisms*, they provide interesting contrasts. As in his rendition of Lavater's *Regeln*, Fuseli's own aphorisms strive for elegance and are far removed from the comfortable and homey tone of Lavater's style. Lavater had intended his rules "for every class of men, from the throne to the cottage." There is no evidence that Fuseli ever intended to be understood by the inhabitants of the cottage, as the following series of his transformations of Lavater's words demonstrates:

Lavater No. 18

Die Menschenkenntnis soll dir das zeigen, was in Andern Vereinbares und Unvereinbares ist mit dir selbst. Sie zeigt dir das in dem Andern, was dich existenter und harmonischer mit dir selbst und mit allem Guten um dich her, macht. Selbstkenntniss zeigt dir, was dich Andern geniessbar und ungeniessbar macht (p. 15).[12]

Fuseli No. 18

The study of man is the doctrine of unisons and discords between ourselves and others (p.9)

Lavater No. 29

Wie die Zudringlichkeit, so die Ueberlästigkeit; Der sehr Ueberlästige für Andere ist sehr überlästig sich selbst; Jeder ungestümm Neugierige ist lär und unbeständig und heftig in Allem. Neugierige Zudringlichkeit erregt durchaus den Verdacht eines kleinen, leidenschaftlichen und zweydeutigen Charakters—So wie ruhig warme Lernbegierde immer einen guten Charakter vermuthen lässt (pp. 23-24).

Fuseli No. 29

Who forces himself on others, is to himself a load. Impetuous curiosity is empty and inconstant. Prying intrusion may be suspected of whatever is little (p. 14).

Lavater No. 107

Wer mehr seinen Sinn hat für das Positife, ist ein positifer Mensch; Ein negatifer, wer mehr schnellen seinen Sinn hat für das Negatife (p. 61).

Fuseli No. 104

Some characters are positive, and some negative (p.40).

Lavater No. 207

Wer Grössere sucht, als er ist, und sich an ihrer Grösse weidet, sich in ihrer Grösse gefällt, seine grössten Eigenschaften in ihren grössern vergisst, ist selbst schon wahrhaft gross (p. 104).

Fuseli No. 203

Who seeks those that are greater *than himself, their greatness* enjoys and *forgets his* greatest qualities in *their greater ones, is* already *truly great* (p. 72).
[Blake underlines and comments in the margin: "I hope I do not flatter my self that this is pleasant to me" K71.]

Lavater No. 248

Wer das Schönste nicht schön, das Mittelmässige elegant nennt, hat sicherlich keinen Geschmack (pp. 117-118).

Fuseli No. 228

Whom mediocrity attracts, taste has abandoned (p. 79).

Lavater No. 255

Misstrauen ist immer ein grosses Soll gegen das Haben *im Punkte der Grösse* (p.120).

Fuseli No. 235

Suspicion bids futurity disavow the present (p. 81).

Lavater No. 312

Wie geistiger das Medium, oder Mittel ist, wodurch ein Mensch in der unbemerktesten Einsamkeit existiert, desto edler, heiliger, göttlicher ist er (p. 148).

Fuseli No. 282

The *more there is* of mind in your *solitary employments,* the more *dignity there* is in your *character* [Blake underlines: K73.] (p. 99).

Lavater No. 316

Wer das erlaubteste und unerlaubteste Vergnügen mit gleicher Weisheit und Ge-lassenheit zu entbehren weiss, der naht sich der Erhabenheit (p. 150).

Lavater No. 337

Der ist einer sehr verderblichen Eigenliebe noch nicht abgestorben, der bitter fröm-melnd neckt (p. 160).

Fuseli No. 285

He, *who can at all times* sacrifice *pleasure to duty,* approaches *sublimity* [Blake underlines: K73] (p. 100).

Fuseli No. 301

He has not a little of the devil in him who prays and bites [Blake comments: "There is no other devil, he who bites without praying is only a beast" K73] (p. 106).

In his annotations, Blake used the book exactly in the manner that Lavater had intended: to expose the nature of the reader himself. At the top of the first aphorism, Blake writes: "For the reason of these remarks see the last aphorism" (K65). The last aphorism states:

643

If you mean to know yourself, interline such of these aphorisms as affected you agreeably in reading, and set a mark to such as left a sense of uneasiness with you; and then shew your copy to whom you please (K65).

In accordance with his faith in the intuitive nature of truth and genius, Lavater had written down his gems of wisdom as they occurred to him, supposedly with little reflection or editing. The purpose of the little vademecum was to provide an instant psychological profile of the reader. The subject was to read the *Regeln* through in one sitting, and record his instant and unpremeditated reaction in the margins, or by marking. From these signs, the reader could then read himself or give the book to a friend for an interpretation. "Know thyself" was not only the motto on the title page, but was also the purpose of the exercise. That Lavater had some insight into human nature is evidenced by the revealing responses that Fuseli's adaptation elicited from Blake. It appears that Blake did make his notes in the rapid, immediate manner suggested. Although there are some notations that appear to have been added by him later in pencil, most were written on the unbound pages, with the same pen and at the same time. The pleasure and the mischief with which Blake responded to Lavater's challenge may have also been the direct impetus for his habit thereafter of carrying on argumentative dialogues with Swedenborg, Bishop Watson, Sir Joshua Reynolds, Spurzheim, and Wordsworth, in the margins of books which he owned.[13]

We do not know whether Blake saw the aphorisms that Fuseli was composing himself at this time, but he must have known of them. It is very possible that the two men exchanged epigrams during this period. A random sampling of Fuseli's own *Aphorisms on Art* shows how close in tone they are to his Lavater adaptation and how they would have appealed to Blake:

3. Art, like love, excludes all competition, and absorbs the man (p. 63).[14]

9. The fiery sets his subject in a blaze, and mounts its vapours; the melancholy cleaves the rock, or gropes through thorns for his; the sanguine deluges all, and seizes none; the phlegmatic sucks one, and drops off with repletion (p. 64).

20. Reality teems with disappointment for him whose sources of enjoyment spring in the elysium of fancy (p. 68).

33. He has powers, dignity, and fire, who can inspire a trifle with importance (p. 73).
41. Beauty, whether individual or ideal, consists in the concurrence of parts to one end, or the union of the simple and the various (p. 76).
56. —The copious is seldom grand (p. 81).
57. Glitter is the refuge of the mean (p. 81).
62. All mediocrity pretends (p. 82).
131. Next to him who can finish, is he who has hid from you that he cannot (p. 110).
137. Genius knows no partner. All partnership is deleterious to poetry and art: one must rule (p. 112).

Fuseli's preference for aphorisms and his pride and skill in that classical device went so far as to alienate his correspondents and colleagues, who found this manner of expression quaint and old-fashioned. Joseph Farington records in his diary on February 13, 1805:

Lawrence remarked that Fuseli's letters were written in an *Epigrammatic style*, in which much sense and knowledge was condensed in a small compass, That His manner of writing was not agreeable to those authors & readers of the present day, who are captivated by a stile woven out & very different from his. Were *His matter* expressed in the manner which suits their taste, they would be enchanted by it.[15]

It seems very likely that, among Fuseli's acquaintances, Blake was "enchanted" or, at least, challenged by this epigrammatic style. After reading the *Aphorisms*, Blake was inspired to give vent to his own version of such rules in *The Marriage of Heaven and Hell*. In every way, Blake's aphorisms, "The Proverbs of Hell," bear the spark of his own genius. His intent is to satirize conventional piety and at the same time to speak the truth, even if it be from the mouth of devils:

From *Plate 7*
PROVERBS OF HELL
In seed time learn, in harvest teach, in winter enjoy.
Drive your cart and your plow over the bones of the dead.
The road of excess leads to the palace of wisdom.
Prudence is a rich, ugly old maid courted by Incapacity.
He who desires but acts not, breeds pestilence.
The cut worm forgives the plow.
Dip him in the river who loves water.
A fool sees not the same tree that a wise man sees.
He whose face gives no light, shall never become a star.
Eternity is in love with the productions of time.
. . . .
The most sublime act is to set another before you.
If the fool would persist in his folly he would become wise.
Folly is the cloke of knavery.
Shame is Pride's cloke.

(K150-151)

From *Plate* 9

The fox provides for himself, but God provides for the lion.
Think in the morning. Act in the noon. Eat in the evening. Sleep
in the night.
He who has suffer'd you to impose on him, knows you.
As the plow follows words, so God rewards prayers.
The tygers of wrath are wiser than the horses of instruction.
....

As the catterpiller chooses the fairest leaves to lay her eggs on, so
the priest lays his curse on the fairest joys.
To create a little flower is the labour of ages.
Damn braces: Bless relaxes.
The best wine is the oldest, the best water the newest.
Prayers plow not! Praises reap not!
Joys laugh not! Sorrows weep not!

(K152)

Fuseli's own personality, his wit, his highly refined sense of irony, and his
predilection for the aphoristic style was a catalyst which emboldened the
younger artist to join the battle of the philosophers. If, as Erdman supposes,
the impact of Rousseau's thought on Blake coincides with his introduction
to Lavater, Fuseli must be seen as the intermediary not only of ideas, but
also the condensed aphoristic style. The Rousseau pamphlet, which Fuseli
could have brought to Blake even before he introduced him to the
Aphorisms, abounds, as we have seen, with audacious and devilish maxims.
Fuseli's transformation of Lavater's diffuse sayings into pithy aphorisms
should be viewed as a direct influence of the "literary" Fuseli on the
"literary" Blake.

Conclusion

50. Genius may adopt, but never steals.

Coroll.—An adopted idea or figure in the works of
genius will be a foil or a companion; but an idea of
genius borrowed by mediocrity scorns the base alliance
and crushes all its mean associates—it is the Cyclop's
thumb, by which the pigmy measured his own
littleness,—"or hangs like a giant's robe upon a dwarf-
ish thief."

—Henry Fuseli
Aphorism No. 50

All those who have spent time exploring the mind and art of William Blake
would agree that no one single strain of thought or influence can be named
as the begetter of the prodigious intellect that conceived and molded his
great life's work. Since the beginning of modern Blake scholarship, when
T.S. Eliot pronounced that it was "impossible to regard him as naïf, a wild
man, a wild pet for the supercultivated," until the present day, when many
studies have been devoted to placing Blake in this world and in tradition, his
"peculiarity"—in Eliot's words "the peculiarity of all great poetry,"[1]—remains undiminished and unexplained. There is, in the greatness of Blake's
best works, that quality which is perhaps still best described as "Genius," in
the sense that Fuseli and Blake both understood the term. That conception
of genius is, by its very definition, an invidious formulation. One is genius
by virtue of one's differentness, and one's differentness is delineated on
contrast to, not in isolation from, other men's minds. Blake's mind eagerly
sought out the philosophical, aesthetic, theological, and political ideas of
his fellows, living and dead. It is his reaction to and against these confronta-
tions that are of interest in trying to unravel the paths of Blake's self-directed
education, and it is in this process that the intellect and learning of Fuseli
served his younger associate.

An extraordinary set of circumstances and coincidences brought Henry
Fuseli to William Blake. Fuseli's deep erudition, which, as we have seen, was
the result of native intelligence in conjunction with a rigorous formal education, was never to give him the sense of fulfillment he felt in front of one of

his huge canvasses. In like manner, Blake was not content to sheath the arrows of his intellect under the cloak of the respectable craft for which he had been admirably trained. Fuseli's personality and outrageous wit provided Blake with a model of audacity and a determination not to be enslaved by systems, while at the same time studying them well.

The irony of the relationship begins before the time of their actual meeting, with Blake's acquisition of Fuseli's translations of Winckelmann's early essays, the first major publication Fuseli attempted in English. Blake's artistic style, which became increasingly mannered and exaggerated after his association with Fuseli, was nonetheless based on his own perception of neoclassical aesthetic principles. Blake's faith in the divine origin of the gift of genius, his consistent use of the idealized human form, and the difficult degree to which he wove allegory into all his work, may all be described as neoclassical precepts. It is not necessary to say that Blake developed these attitudes solely as a result of his confrontation with Fuseli's translation of Winckelmann, but they most certainly served as primer in attitudes that neither artist would ever abandon. Later, when Blake was personally introduced to Fuseli and came to admire his art and mind, he saw the theory of a neoclassicism interpreted from the perspective of *Sturm und Drang* translated from theory to practice.

Fuseli's fervent admiration for Jean-Jacques Rousseau was responsible for his landing on British soil. His attempt to live up to the ideals of Rousseau was based upon an intellectual respect that was to last his lifetime. Fuseli was deeply moved by the hope held out by the events leading up to the French Revolution in the late 1780s. Although there is no physical evidence to connect Blake with Fuseli's Rousseau pamphlet, the similarity of tone, posture and satirical intent in the *Remarks on the Writings and Conduct of J.J. Rousseau* and in Blake's *The Marriage of Heaven and Hell* strongly suggests that Fuseli might have brought the pamphlet and Rousseau to Blake in the same intensified manner that his early translation presented the ideas of Winckelmann to the young apprentice. Investigation of Fuseli's experiences in Zurich and his profound knowledge of Rousseau's works and troubled life leads to the conclusion that, among Blake's acquaintances, Fuseli was the most knowledgeable about Rousseau. Equally important with the fact that Fuseli provided Blake's first contact with the philosophy of Rousseau is the posture in which the philosopher is placed in the *Remarks* and Fuseli's view of him in general: genius opposed; a voice crying in the wilderness. The scepticism and irony with which Fuseli juxtaposed Rousseau's religious views with the piety and hypocrisy of conventional morality might be seen as the stimulus for Blake's own series *There Is No Natural Religion* and *All Religions Are One* and for his irrevocable turning away from cults, sects, and institutional religions of all description. In the person of Fuseli, spoiled priest, Blake saw, firsthand, that all of the Devil's party had once adhered to the milder school of angels.

The association of Blake with Fuseli's adaptation of Lavater's *Vermischte unphysiognomische Regeln (Aphorisms on Man)* is well known. That Fuseli was responsible for making terse aphorisms out of the rambling and homey sayings of Lavater has not been generally recognized. The impact of the

Lavater work, which was probably concomitant with Fuseli's transmission of Rousseau to Blake, is more stylistic than philosophic. This is seen in the sudden burst of aphorisms that are found in *The Marriage of Heaven and Hell* and in Blake's fondness for the epigram thereafter, especially when he was sizing up human behavior, or attacking the weaknesses of an enemy. Blake was introduced to Lavater by Fuseli, who loved him and was intimate with all his works. He influenced the fondness which Blake felt for the *Aphorisms on Man* and the seriousness with which he annotated the little book exactly as instructed. The possible influence of Lavater's large work, *Essays on Physiognomy*, on Blake is a subject which has yet to be sufficiently pursued. If Blake turned to that problematic and fascinating work of uneven genius, Fuseli must surely be credited with having provided the impetus.

Fuseli's role in transmitting the ideas of two of his early idols, Winckelmann and Rousseau, to Blake and his introduction of his dearest friend, Lavater, to the younger artist may constitute but a fraction of the actual impact that Fuseli the man and artist had upon Blake, the man and artist. It is hoped that this beginning will lead to further investigations of areas where their minds came together, that we might better understand the kinship of the two men to each other and to the age in which they lived, but from which they stood apart.

> 13. It is the lot of genius to be opposed, and to be invigorated by opposition; all extremes touch each other; frigid praise and censure wait upon attainable or common powers; but the successful adventurer in the realms of discovery leaps on an unknown or long-lost shore, ennobles it with his name, and grasps immortality.
>
> —Henry Fuseli
> Aphorism No. 13

Notes

Introduction

1 Alexander Gilchrist, *The Life of William Blake: With Selections from his Poems and other Writings*, 2nd ed. (1880 repr. New York: Phaeton Press, 1969), I, 6. Hereinafter referred to as Gilchrist, with volume and page number.

2 Gilchrist, I, 6.

3 John Knowles, *The Life and Writing of Henry Fuseli* (London, 1831), I, 30.

4 *The Lives of the Most Eminent British Painters, Sculptors, and Architects*, 2nd ed. (London, 1830), p. 264.

5 Gilchrist's statement is clearly meant to show that Fuseli was indebted to Blake, but that Blake was "placed above all need for inclination to borrow from others," Gilchrist, I, 52.

6 Morton D. Paley, *William Blake* (New York: E.P. Dutton, 1978), p. 12.

7 "Switzerland's Contribution to International Appreciation of Dante Alighieri," *Studies in Philology*, XLII (1945), 452.

8 Especially the indispensible work done by G.E. Bentley in *Blake Records* (Oxford: At the Clarendon Press, 1969) and the companion volume, *Blake Books* (Oxford: At the Clarendon Press, 1977).

9 All quotations of Blake's works will be taken from *Blake: Complete Writings*, ed. Geoffrey Keynes (London: Oxford University Press, 1972), and will be noted in the text as "K," with the appropriate page number.

10 Schweizerisches Institut für Kunstwissenschaft (Zürich: Verlag Berichthaus, 1973). Volume I contains biographical, bibliographical, and textual information to accompany Volume II, which is the authoritative catalogue of reproductions of Fuseli's graphic works. All of Fuseli's known works have received a "Schiff" number.

11 Fuseli never approved this biography; in fact, he was angry with Nüscheler, a boyhood acquaintance, for having written it. Only the biography was published, and it contained for the most part details from Fuseli's early days in Switzerland.

12 John Knowles, a physician, met Fuseli after 1805 and was the executor of his works after he died. Volume I of *The Life and Writing of Henry Fuseli* contains the biography, many details of which were supplied Knowles by Fuseli himself; Volume II contains his *Lectures on Painting* and Volume III contains Fuseli's *History of Art in the Schools of Italy* and his *Aphorisms on Art*.

13 John Knowles, *The Life and Writings of Henry Fuseli, the Former Written, and the Latter edited by John Knowles with a New Introduction by David H. Weinglass*, 3 vols. (Milwood, New York: Kraus International Publications, 1982).

14 Henry Fuseli, *Lectures on Painting*. Garland Series on Connoisseurship, Criticism and Art History in the Nineteenth Century. Selected by Sydney J. Freedberg (New York and London: Garland Publishing, 1979).

15 Millwood, New York: Kraus International Publications, 1982.

16 Wirz's dissertation was written for the University of Basel.

17 Zurich and Leipzig: Orell Füssli Verlag, 1927.

18 Klosterberg/Basel: Verlag Benno Schwabe & Co., 1942.

19 London: Routledge & Kegan Paul, 1954.

20 Bern-Olten: Urs Graf Verlag, 1947.

21 London: Routledge & Kegan Paul, 1951.
22 London: Routledge & Kegan Paul, 1956.
23 Columbia University, 1964.
24 London: Thames and Hudson, 1972.
25 Zurich: Orell Füssli Verlag, 1973.
26 "Fuseli Studies: *The Mind of Henry Fuseli* by Eudo C. Mason," *The Burlington Magazine* 96 (August 1954), 261.
27 *German Thought and Culture in England 1700-1770: A Preliminary Survey Including a Chronological Bibliography of German Literature in English Translation* (Chapel Hill: University of North Carolina Press, 1969), p. 73.
28 *The Sister Arts: The Tradition of Literary Pictorialism and English Poetry from Dryden to Grey* (Chicago: University of Chicago Press, 1958), p. 133.
29 In 1982 a facsimile edition of Blake's copy of the *Aphorisms* was published with an informative introduction by R.J. Shroyer: *Aphorisms on Man (1788) by Johann Caspar Lavater. A Facsimile Reproduction of William Blake's Copy of the First English Edition With an Introduction by R.J. Shroyer* (New York: Scholars' Facsimiles & Reprints, 1980).
30 *The Drawings of Henry Fuseli* (London, 1949), p. 176.
31 "Füssli und Blake," *Von Englands geistigen Beständen: Ausgewählte Essays* (Frauenfeld, 1944), p. 120.

Part One:
Fuseli's European Background and his Literary Activities 1749-1787

Fuseli and Lavater in Switzerland 1741-1764

1 A thorough overview of the artistic Füssli family is found in Arnold Federmann, *Johann Heinrich Füssli, Dichter und Maler 1741-1825* (Zürich and Leipzig: Orell Füssli Verlag, 1927), pp. 11-12. In this first book-length treatment of Fuseli as a literary and artistic figure, Federmann appends a "Stammfolge der Füssli," p. 168.
2 Gert Schiff, *Johann Heinrich Füssli, Dichter und Maler: 1741-1825,* Oeuvrekatalog Schweizer Künstler, Bd. 1, Nr. 1, Schweizerisches Institut für Kunstwissenschaft (Zürich: Verlag Berichthaus, 1973), p. 23. Only second hand reports exist concerning Fuseli's childhood. His early (and unauthorized) biographer, Nüscheler, is the only source for details of his very early childhood and family life. John Knowles, the English friend of his old age, wrote the only "official" biography which became volume I of *The Life and Works of Henry Fuseli, R.A.* (London, 1831), Volumes II and III contain the works of the artist as edited by Knowles. References to this biography will be noted as Knowles I, with the page number. Gert Schiff has made the most recent and authoritative compendium of these sources in the first volume of his monumental catalogue. Henceforth all references to the *Ouevrekatalog* will read: "Schiff, I, page number" for the text, and "Schiff, catalogue number" for reference to drawings and paintings.
3 Johann Caspar Füssli recognized Winckelmann's great potential in pioneering the study of antiquity. In 1758 he was instrumental in collecting a sum of money from his friends in Zurich to finance Winckelmann's trip to Naples—a favor which Winckelmann never forgot. In 1762, Johann Caspar published Mengs' *Gedanken über die Schönheit.* Schiff, I, 23-24.
4 Johann Caspar Lavater, *Lavaters Jugend von Ihm Selbst Erzählt,* ed. Oskar Farner (Zurich, Zwingli: Verlag, 1939), p. 12. Information concerning Lavater's childhood is provided in his own memoirs, 1779, "allein meinen Kindern und den nächsten meiner Familie gewidmet." The first biography of Lavater was written by his son-in-law, Georg Gessner—*Lavater's Lebensbeschreibung*, three volumes—in Zurich in 1802/1803. This work was translated in abbreviated form into English by P.J. Heisch: *Memoirs of Lavater* (London, 1842). Gessner had access to the Lavater manuscript of 1779, and had included much of it in his biography. In 1939, the entire manuscript was published in the edition cited above, edited by Farner, hereinafter referred to as "Lavater, *Jugend,* page number."
5 Lavater, *Jugend,* p. 12.
6 G. de Reynold, *Bodmer et l'Ecole Suisse: Histoire Littéraire de la Suisse au XVIIIe Siècle,* Vol. II (Lausanne: G. Bridel & Cie., 1912), 78-79.

7 Heisch, *Memoirs of Lavater*, p. 8.
8 Lavater, *Jugend*, p. 28.
9 Heisch, *Memoirs*, p. 8.
10 Knowles, I, 7.
11 Fuseli was the second of eighteen children, three sons and two daughters among whom lived to maturity. Johann Rudolf, the elder son, was trained as a painter, although he was never
   really able to earn his living by art alone. He held a number of official posts in arts-connected
   departments of the Austro-Hungarian government. Eventually, he became the founder and
   curator of the print collection of the *Wiener kaiserliche Akademie der bildenden Künste*. The
   younger brother, Caspar, and his two sisters, Elisabeth and Anna, became insect and flower
   painters, and all three died young. Schiff, I, 24.
12 Schiff, p. 25.
13 Knowles, I, 7.
14 Knowles, I, 10.
15 Knowles, I, 11.
16 Schiff, I, 23.
17 Joseph Farington, *Farington Diary*, ed. James Grieg (London: Hutchinson, 1923-1938), II, 46.
18 Allan Cunningham, *The Lives of the Most Eminent British Painters, Sculptors, and Architects*, Vol. II (London: John Murray, Albemarle Street, 1830), 261.
19 Cunningham, II, 262.
20 Cunningham, II, 261.
21 *Johann Jakob Bodmer* (1698-1783) born in Greifensee, son of a respected minister. Bodmer
   chose the career of merchant over that of churchman, although he maintained a lifelong interest in Enlightenment theology. Following his desire to travel and his natural inclination
   for other languages and cultures, he left Zurich in 1718 for Lyon and Genf after having
   studied theology at the *Carolinum* for a few years. There he was to become apprenticed in
   the silk trade. From Lyon he traveled to Lugano and northern Italy, less interested in
   business than in the culture and language which he encountered there. He wrote Latin,
   French, and Italian letters back home. When he returned to Zurich after some months, he
   brought with him a copy of Addison's *Spectator* in French translation. From that time on, he
   knew that his life belonged to literature. He founded his first journal after the model of Addison in 1720—*Discourse der Mahlern*. It was during this period that his friendship and collaboration with Breitinger began.
       Johann Jakob Breitinger (1701-1776) born in Zurich, son of a prosperous baker. He studied
   at the *Collegium Humanitatis* and the *Carolinum* in Zurich. There he became remarkably pro-
   ficient in Latin, Greek, and Hebrew. He passed the theological examination at the age of
   nineteen, and was ordained as a Zwinglian minister. After several church positions, he was
   made professor of Hebrew in 1731. In 1735 he was professor of rhetoric and logic, and in 1745
   professor of Greek. Cf. Emil Ermatinger, *Dichtung und Geistesleben in der deutschen
   Schweiz* (Munich: Verlag C.H. Beck, 1933), pp. 317-318.
22 Ermatinger, p. 372.
23 *Johann Jakob Hess* (1741-1828), classmate and close friend of Lavater and Fuseli. As a child
   he heard Klopstock recite from the *Messias*, which was the "greatest experience" of his life.
   The second greatest was his reading of Rousseau. As a youth he wrote poems in the manner
   of Klopstock. Later he wrote a great many theological treatises and much religious poetry.
   His most famous work is *Lebensgeschichte Jesu*. He died a highly respected minister of the
   church, and was one of Lavater's most trusted friends in later life.
24 Johann Heinrich Füssli, *Briefe,* ed. Walter Muschg (Klosterberg/Basel: Verlag Benno
   Schwabe & Co., 1942), p. 45. The letter is dated 1758(?) by Muschg. Hereinafter, all reference
   to this collection of letters will be indicated as *"Briefe,"* with page number.
25 Letter of June 14, 1770, from Rome to Lavater. *Briefe*, p. 154.
26 Hans Schnorf, *Sturm und Drang in der deutschen Schweiz* (Zurich: Schulthess & Co., 1914),
   p. 81. See also Karl S. Guthke, "Im Schatten Klopstocks: J.H. Füsslis Gedichte,"
   Literarisches Leben im achtzehnten Jahrhundert (Bern/Munich: Francke Verlag, 1975),
   pp. 242-260.
27 Guthke, p. 244.
28 Eudo C. Mason, *The Mind of Henry Fuseli* (London: Routledge & Kegan Paul, 1951), p. 16.

29 In a letter to Felix Hess, brother of Johann Jakob. Cited by G. von Schultess-Rechtburg, "Lavater als religiöse Persönlichkeit," *Johann Caspar Lavater 1741-1801: Denkschrift zur hundertsten Wiederkehr seines Todestages* (Zurich: Commissions Verlag von Alb. Müller, 1902), p. 161.

30 Wolfgang Bender, *J.J. Bodmer und J.J. Breitinger*, Sammlung Metzler, 113 (Stuttgart: Metzler, 1973), pp. 44-50.

31 Mason, *Mind*, p. 16.

32 Letter dated by Muschg, "*Sommer*, 1759," *Briefe*, p. 47. The first English quotation is a slightly altered quotation from Shakespeare's *Richard II*, III, 2. The second quote is again from *Richard II*, V, 2. This time Fuseli has arbitrarily altered the last two lines from: "Even so, or with much more contempt, men's eyes/Did scowl on gentle Richard. No man cried 'God save him!'"

462. The "Thompson" of whom he speaks in this letter is James Thompson (1748), poet of the *Seasons*, who was much admired and translated in the Bodmer circle.

33 Allan Cunningham, in his *The Lives of the Most Eminent British Painters, Sculptors, and Architects*, Vol. II (London: John Murray, Albemarle Street, 1830), 291, gives the following account: "It pleased Fuseli to be thought one of those erudite gentlemen whom the poet describes: Far seen in Greek—deep men of letters; and he loved to annoy certain of his companions with the display of his antique lore. He sometimes composed Greek verses in the emergency of the moment, and affected to forget the name of the author. He once repeated half-a-dozen lines to Porson and said, 'With all your learning now you cannot tell me who wrote that.' The professor, 'much renowned for Greek,' confessed his ignorance and said, 'I don't know him. How the devil could you know him?' Chuckled Fuseli, 'I made them this moment.' When thwarted in the Academy, and that was not seldom, his wrath aired itself in a polyglott. 'It is a pleasant thing and an advantageous,' said the painter...'to be learned. I can speak Greek, Latin, French, English, German, Danish, Dutch, Icelandic, and Spanish, and so let my folly or my fury get vent through nine different avenues.'"

34 *Briefe*, p. 51. To Jakob Hess, dated "Horgen, 16, August, 1760."

35 That Fuseli was reading everything that Rousseau wrote, almost immediately after it was published, is clear from the impressive knowledge of the works that he displayed in his English pamphlet on the philosopher in 1767. A warrant was issued for Rousseau's arrest in 1763, and he renounced his Genevan citizenship in the same year.

36 Frederick Antal, *Fuseli Studies* (London: Routledge & Kegan Paul, 1956), p. 7.

37 Among the famous scholars of Zurich who preceded Bodmer and Breitinger were: Conrad Gessner, the famous sixteenth-century scientist, who was the first to classify living things according to genus and species; Josias Simler (1530-1576) who wrote geographical and historical studies, chief of which was *De Alpibus commentarius*, a commentary containing all knowledge about the alps from the earliest times; and the famous Johann Jakob Scheuchzer, physician, explorer, naturalist, and above all, accumulator of facts. Scheuchzer was typical of the scholars who, at the beginning of the eighteenth century, dealt with such scholastic questions as whether or not a two-headed monster had two souls, why Moors were black, and whether the wine transformed from water at Cana was red wine or white wine. Cf. G. de Reynold, "Le Milieu de Bodmer et de Breitinger," *Histoire Litteraire de la Suisse au XVIIIe Siècle*, pp. 90-93.

38 de Reynold, p. 89.

39 Opitz was considered second only to Horace in Bodmer's pantheon of poets. In 1745 he and Breitinger published an edition of the German poet's works: *Martin Opitzens von Boberfeld Gedichte*. This is considered the first attempt at a critical edition of the works of any literary text of a New High German writer. Cf. Wolfgang Bender, *J.J. Bodmer and J.J. Breitinger*, p. 18.

40 Johann Christoph Gottsched (1700-1766), the German literary theorist and critic who introduced French eighteenth-century classical standards to German literature. His *Versuch einer kritischen Dicht-Kunst für die Deutschen* (1730) advocated the standards of beauty and criteria for taste as dictated by Boileau. The literary quarrel that ensued between Gottsched and the Swiss School is famous in the history of German literature. See Jakob Baechtold, *Geschichte der deutschen Literatur in der Schweiz* (Frauenfeld, 1892), pp. 557-578, 581-584, 615-620; Max Wehrli, *Johann Jakob Bodmer und die Geschichte der Literatur* (Frauenfeld: Huber & Co., 1936), p. 89 ff.

41 de Reynold, pp. 150-151.

42 Emil Ermatinger, *Dichtung und Geistesleben in der deutschen Schweiz*, pp. 338-344. Gott-sched's opinion cited in Wolfgang Bender's "Nachwort" to the facsimile edition of Johann Jacob Bodmer, *Critische Abhandlung von dem Wunderbaren in der Poesie*, Deutsche Neudrucke, Reihe: Texte des 18. Jahrhunderts (Zurich, 1740, facsim.: Stuttgart: J.B. Metzlersche Verlagsbuchhandlung, 1966), p. 3.

43 Bender, "Nachwort," p. 9.

44 Bender, "Nachwort," pp. 5-11.

45 Taken from Johann Jacob Bodmer, *Critische Abhandlung*, passim.

46 Fuseli Studies, p. 7.

47 *Johann Jakob Bodmer und die Geschichte der Literatur*, p. 32.

48 *J.J. Bodmer und J.J. Breitinger*, p. 55.

49 Klopstock's personal behavior was a great disappointment to Bodmer. The best description of the "tragikomische Verlauf" of Klopstock's visit to Zurich is given by Baechtold, *Geschichte der deutschen Literatur in der Schweiz*, pp. 592-595.

50 Bodmer wrote to a friend in 1773: "Einer von den grossen Fehlern der Geschichte ist, dass sie die Menschen mehr nach ihren bösen Seiten malet. In den Erzählungen und der Geschichte der Stadt Zürich habe ich lieber das Gute aufsuchen wollen." Cf. Max Wehrli, *Johann Jakob Bodmer und die Geschichte der Literatur*, p. 35.

51 Wehrli, p. 35.

52 Wehrli, p. 35.

53 Wehrli, p. 36.

54 Schiff, I, 47.

55 "Vorwort," *Briefe*, p. 22.

56 Leonhard Usteri (1741-1789) studied theology with Fuseli, and went shortly thereafter to Rome where, through the influence of Fuseli's father, he had contact with Winckelmann. In 1764 he became professor of Hebrew at the *Carolinum* and in 1764 *Chorherr* of the *Grossmünster* in Zurich. Founder of the Zurich *Töchterschule*.
   Heinrich Thomann (1738-1785), an early friend of Fuseli's who, according to Nüscheler, was "ein geistreicher Kopf, der sich aber nie als Schriftsteller gezeigt hat und als Diakon zu Wintherthur gestorben ist." Cf. Muschg, *Briefe*, p. 208.

57 The best account of the Grebel affair is found in Gerold Meyer von Knonau, "Lavater als Bürger Zürichs und der Schweiz," *Johann Caspar Lavater 1741-1801: Denkschrift zur hundertsten Wiederkehr seines Todestages* (Zurich: Commissionsverlag von Alb. Müller, 1902), Knonau had access to all the documents concerning the case, most of which are still found in the Zentralbibliothek in Zurich. Hereinafter references to the centennial essays will be designated *"Denkschrift"* with page number. The pamphlet that Fuseli and Lavater wrote is included in Johann Caspar Lavater, *Johann Caspar Lavaters ausgewählte Werke*, ed. Dr. Ernst Staehelin (Zurich: Zwingli Verlag, 1943), 4 vols. All references to this edition will be designated "Lavater, *Ausgewählte Werke*" with page number.

58 Lavater, *Ausgewählte Werke*, I, 35-40.

59 Knonau, *Denkschrift*, p. 63.

60 Heisch, *Memoirs of Lavater*, pp. 31-32.

61 Lavater, *Ausgewählte Werke*, I, 34.

62 Knonau, *Denkschrift*, p. 65.

63 Lavater, *Ausgewählte Werke*, I, 34.

64 Knowles, I, 26.

65 Lavater, *Ausgewählte Werke*, I, 41.

66 See M.H. Abram's appreciation of Sulzer's contribution to aesthetics in *The Mirror and the Lamp: Romantic Theory and the Critical Tradition* (New York: Oxford University Press, 1953). Here, p. 88.

67 Antal, Fuseli Studies, p. 13. For a good discussion of Spalding's place in Enlightenment theology, see Robert T. Clark, Jr., *Herder: His Life and Thought* (Berkeley: University of California Press, 1955), pp. 58 f.

68 Johann Joachim Spalding, *Johann Joachim Spaldings Lebensbeschreibung von Ihm Selbst Erzählt*, ed. Georg Ludwig Spalding (Halle, 1804), p. 66.

69 Spalding, p. 67.

70 Spalding, p. 64.

71 Spalding, p. 65.
72 Schiff, I, 49.
73 *Briefe*, pp. 63-64. The letter is dated: Berlin, 30 März, 1763.
74 Fuseli lists for Lavater the sections of the lexicon that he wrote. Letter of December 7, 1763, *Briefe*, p. 92.
75 Schiff, I, 49.
76 Schiff, I, 50.
77 *Johann Heinrich Füssli: Dichter und Maler, 1741-1825*, p. 27.
78 November 13, 1763, *Briefe*, pp. 75-76.
79 November 16, 1763, *Briefe*, pp. 70-71.
80 *Briefe*, p. 96.
81 Letter to Bodmer of November 23, 1763, *Briefe*, p. 84.
82 *Briefe*, p. 84.
83 Berlin, December 7, 1763, *Briefe*, pp. 86-87.
84 Knowles, I, 29.

The History and Fortune of the Winckelmann Translation

1 *The Mind of Henry Fuseli*, pp. 16, 354-359.
2 Knowles, I, 30.
3 Fuseli reports in a letter to Bodmer of 23 November 1763 that he has received seven gold louis for this translation: *"Ich habe aber daselbst mit Authorarbeit sieben Louis verdienet, weil ich die Montague übersetzet habe, neun Dukaten sind auf der Hin- und Rückreise und für unumgängliche Ausgaben daselbst aufgegangen, dies ist meine kleine Rechnung."* *Briefe*, p. 84. The translation appeared anonymously and was published by the company of Weidmanns, Erben, and Reich in Leipzig under the title, *Briefe der Lady Marie Wortley Montague, während ihrer Reisen in Europa, Asia und Afrika, und Personen vom Stande, Gelehrte etc.* Lord Montague, who died in 1762, had been a friend of Winckelmann. It is possible that Winckelmann, through Fuseli's father, influenced Fuseli's translations of these letters.
4 Knowles, I, 31.
5 Knowles, I, 32.
6 *Dictionary of National Biography*, ed. Sidney Lee, Vol. XXXVIII (London, 1894), 63-65. Hereinafter referred to as *DNB* with volume, year, and page number.
7 DNB, II (1894), 94.
8 Several American editions of this poem published after 1770 are to be found in the rare book room of the Library of Congress.
9 *Briefe*, p. 125.
10 Reprinted in Mason, *Mind*, p. 112.
11 Muschg, "Anmerkungen," *Briefe*, p. 229.
12 This rare monograph was reprinted with commentary in 1882: *Winckelmanns Briefe an seine Freunde in der Schweiz: Nach den auf der Zürcher Stadtbibliothek aufbewahrten Originalen in vermehrter und verbesserter Gestalt*, ed. Hugo Blümer (Freiburg und Tübingen, Akademische Verlagsbuchhandlung, J.C.B. Mohr, 1882), here, pp. 104-105.
13 *Winckelmanns Briefe*, p. 104.
14 *Winckelmanns Briefe*, pp. 104-105.
15 Eudo C. Mason, "Heinrich Füssli und Winckelmann," *Unterscheidung und Bewahrung: Festschrift für Hermann Kunisch zum 60. Geburtstag* (Berlin: Walter De Gruyter & Co., 1961).
16 Mason, *Unterscheidung*, p. 235.
17 Mason, *Unterscheidung*, p. 236.
18 Anne Kostelanetz Mellor in *Blake's Human Form Divine* (Berkeley: University of California Press, 1974) quotes from Fuseli's translation of this essay as an example of ideas that Blake might have borrowed from Winckelmann through Fuseli, and implies that Blake was familiar with this short translation, although it is not known to have existed except in the 1765 periodical. The *Bibliothek der schönen Wissenschaften und der freyen Künste* in which Winckelmann's essay about the Torso of Belvedere first appeared, was edited by Friedrich Nicolai (1733-1811), a friend of Lessing and Mendelssohn. Lessing was the major collaborator in the publication of the journal.

19 Mason, *Unterscheidung*, p. 245.
20 Federmann, p. 113.
21 *Briefe*, p. 100.
22 Between 30 December 1764 and 31 March 1765 in *Gazette Littéraire de l'Europe*.
23 Mason, *Unterscheidung*, p. 249.
24 These "Specimen Opinions on Fuseli" are recorded by Mason in *Mind*: Walpole, p. 70; Cunningham, p. 71; Hazlitt, p. 72; and Colvin, p. 77.
25 In a letter to Lavater, 6 December 1765: *Briefe*, p. 117.
26 *Lives*, II, 265.
27 Anonymous, "Reflections on the Painting and Sculpture of the Greeks: With Instructions for the Connoisseur, and an Essay on Grace in Works of Art." Translated from the German Original of the Abbe Winckelmann, Librarian of the Vatican, R.R.S. & C. by Henry Füsseli," *The Monthly Review or Literary Journal* by several hands Vol. XXXII (London: May 1765), 456.
28 *Monthly Review*, 457.
29 Anonymous, "Reflections on the Painting and Sculpture of the Greeks: With Instructions for the Connoisseur, and an Essay on Grace in Works of Art. Translated from the German Original of the Abbe Winckelmann, Librarian of the Vatican & C. By Henry Fusseli, A.M.," *The Critical Review, or Annals of Literature*, ed. Millar, 19 (London, June 1765), 443.
30 *The Critical Review*, 448.
31 *The Critical Review*, 450.
32 The anonymous translator of the "letters" of Winckelmann introduces his "Thoughts concerning the imitation of the GRECIAN ARTISTS in PAINTING and SCULPTURE. In a Series of letters," with the following statement:

> The following elegant and ingenious remarks are privately attributed to the celebrated Abbe Winhelman [sic], director of the cabinet of Cardinal Alexander Albani; and were communicated to us by a friend of approved taste and literature, now resident at Rome.

> Reprinted from the *London Chronicle* of 13 December 1764 in *The Scots Magazine* (Edinburgh, January 1765) XXVII, No. MDCCLXV, 17.

Fuseli's Continuing Literary Activities and the Meeting with Rousseau

1 Muschg, *Briefe*, 206.
2 *Briefe*, 103.
3 *Briefe*, 103.
4 Fuseli's letters to Lavater during this period are full of requests for money from home. He seemed unable or unwilling to write his father directly.
5 *Briefe*, 101-102.
6 *Briefe*, 111.
7 Rousseau's *Lettres écrites de la Montagne* caused an immediate scandal as soon as they arrived in Geneva, not only among the pastors, but also among the philosophers. After months of turmoil over the work, the government of Geneva issued a manifesto against the *Lettres* in February of 1759. See Crocker, *Jean-Jacques Rousseau*, Vol. II, 244, 249-260. In 1763, he had been similarly banned, and had renounced his citizenship. *Briefe*, p. 113.
8 *Briefe*, 118.
9 *Briefe*, 104.
10 *Briefe*, 111.
11 *Briefe*, 112.
12 *Briefe*, 112.
13 *Briefe*, 142.
14 *Briefe*, 112. The Greek is from *Iliad*, VI, 236: "A hundred oxen's worth for the value of nine," i.e., "a bad exchange."
15 Gilbert West (1703-1756). In 1747 West published his *Observations on the Resurrection*. It had been translated into German in 1748. Evidently, one of his Zurich friends was urging him to read the work. DNB, 60 (1899), 330.
16 *Briefe*, 114.

17 The fullest account of Fuseli's German poetry and the history of its publication is given in Karl S. Guthke, *"Im Schatten Klopstocks: J.H. Füsslis Gedichte,"* Literarisches Leben im achtzehnten Jahrhundert (Bern und München, Francke Verlag, 1975), pp. 242-262.

18 Guthke, *"Im Schatten Klopstocks,"*p. 254.

19 Johann Heinrich Füssli, *Sämtliche Gedichte,* ed. Martin Bircher and Karl S. Guthke (Zürich: Orell Füssli Verlag, 1973).

20 Knowles, I, 356.

21 Lavater wrote to Herder sometime after Fuseli's trip to Rome: *"Füssli in Rom ist eine der grössten Imaginationen. Er ist in allem Extrem—immer Original; Shakespeares Maler—nichts als Engländer und Zürcher, Poet und Maler."* Later in 1774 he wrote Herder again, extolling the genius of his friend: *"Goethe—und Füssli—vortrefflich zusammenge-paart—und doch so sehr wie möglich verschieden. Goethe—mehr Mensch—dieser mehr Poet."Aus Herders Nachlass,* ed. Heinrich Düntzer und Ferdinand G. von Herder, Vol. II (Frankfurt/M.: Heidinger und Comp., 1857),68, 69.

22 *Briefe,* 114.

23 Eudo C. Mason, *"Der Anlass: Rousseau, Hume und Voltaire,"* Remarks on the Writings and Conduct of J.J. Rousseau: Bemerkungen über J.J. Rousseaus Schriften und Verhalten, ed. and tr. Eudo C. Mason, Schweizerisches Institut für Kunstwissenschaft Zürich, Kleine Schriften Nr. 4 (Zürich: Fretz & Wasmuth Verlag, 1962), p. 12.

24 *Briefe,* 125.

History and Fortune of Fuseli's *Remarks on the Conduct and Writings of J.J. Rousseau*

1 All quotations from Fuseli's pamphlet will be taken from this reprint and will be designated, *Remarks,* with page number. Citations from Mason's *"Vorwort"* or *"Anmerkungen"* to this edition will be designated: "Mason" with the subtitle of the section of his *Anmerkungen* in parentheses, followed by page number.

2 Knowles, I, 44.

3 Mason, *"Vorwort,"* p. 38. This mistake in Cunningham has been repeated by other scholars, including Jacques Voisine in his *J.-J. Rousseau en Angleterre a l'Epoque Romantique,* Etudes de Littérature Etrangère et Comparée (Paris: Didier, 1965), p. 26.

4 *Remarks,* p. 76.

5 *Remarks,* p. 76.

6 Lester G. Crocker, *Jean-Jacques Rousseau: The Prophetic Voice (1758-1778),* Vol. II of *Jean-Jacques Rousseau* (New York: The Macmillan Company, 1973), 277.

7 Mason, *"Entstehung,"* p. 38.

8 Joseph Johnson had come from Liverpool in 1760. He set up a partnership with John Payne and a D. Davenport around that time. At the time of Fuseli's *Remarks,* he was in association with Thomas Cadell, who was to take over the lucrative company of Andrew Millar in 1767. DNB, 60 (1899), 21.

9 Blake's only book aside from the *Poetical Sketches* to appear in printed form. It was never published. The extant copy of Book One is a page proof, not a copy of a published edition. William Blake, *The Poems of William Blake,* ed. W.H. Stevenson (London: Longman, 1971), p. 124. "The 'help' which Gilchrist says Johnson gave Blake presumably refers to Blake's poem called *The French Revolution,* which got no further than the proofs of the first of seven books under Johnson's aegis in 1791...." G.E. Bentley, *Blake Records* (Oxford: At the Clarendon Press, 1969), p. 41.

10 H.R. Plomer, G.H. Bushnell, and E.R. McC. Dix, *A Dictionary of the Printers and Booksellers who were at Work in England, Scotland, and Ireland from 1726 to 1775* (London: Oxford University Press, 1932), p. 141.

11 *Briefe,* 125.

12 Mason, *"Entstehung,"* p. 44.

13 Payne stayed in business with Johnson until 1770, and then turned author. He wrote several multivolume studies in history and geography which were published by Johnson. DNB, 44 (1892), 111.

14 Millar was Hume's publisher until 1767, when he sold to Cadell, the joint publisher of the *Remarks.* See also Knowles, I, 33.

15 Mason, *"Entstehung,"* p. 48.

16 Karl S. Guthke, *"Johann Heinrich Füssli und die Anfänge des Rousseauismus in Deutschland,"* *Wege der Literatur* (Bern and München, 1967), pp. 133-146, has given the only other comprehensive treatment of Fuseli's *Remarks* besides Mason's.

17 Fuseli might have obtained such a manuscript as early as 1763, when, in the company of Sulzer, he visited a French Pastor, Jakob Waegelin, in St. Gall. Waegelin had written a defense of Rousseau, which eventually caused his expulsion from St. Gall. In 1765 Sulzer brought him to Berlin and secured for him a professorship at the *Berliner Ritterakademie*. (See Muschg, *Briefe*, 77.) Another possibility for the source of the manuscript is Jakob Hess, Fuseli's correspondent and a fervent Rousseauist who sent Fuseli news of Rousseau's activities.

18 Mason, *"Entstehung,"* p. 61.

19 Henri Roddier, *J.-J. Rousseau en Angleterre au XVIIIe Siècle: L'Oeuvre et L'Homme* (Paris: Boivin & Cie., 1950) has compiled a list of Rousseau's works and the dates and number of translations of each work. From the time of the *First Discourse* (1751) until the publication of Fuseli's *Remarks*, Rousseau's works appeared in the following number of editions: *First Discourse* (1751): three English translations (1751, 1753, 1760); *Second Discourse* (1755): two editions (1762, 1767); *Lettre à D'Alembert* (1758): two editions (1759, 1767); *La Nouvelle Héloïse* (1761): six editions (1761, 1762, 1762, 1762, 1764, 1766); *Emile* (1762): four editions (1762, 1763, 1763, 1767); *Du Contrat Social* (1762): two editions (1764, 1767); *Lettre à Beaumont* (1763): two editions (1763, 1767); *Extrait du Projet de Paix* (1761): two editions (1761, 1767); *Le Devin du Village* (1753): four editions (1766, 1766, 1766, 1767). In 1767 *The Miscellaneous Works of Rousseau* appeared containing all of the major works and letters. In addition to these English translations, many editions were bought in the original French. *"Mais une large partie du public lisait le français,"* Roddier, p. 66.

20 Roddier, p. 67.

21 Roddier, pp. 67-68. Fuseli might have known Kendrick in the close and fiercely competitive world of publishers in which he traveled.

22 Except *Emile*, which was published separately by Kendrick in 1762. The *Miscellaneous Works of J.J. Rousseau*, tr. William Kendrick, 5 vols. (London: T. Becket and P.A. De Hondt in the Strand, 1767).

23 "Remarks on the Writings and Conduct of Rousseau," *The Gentleman's Magazine, and Historical Chronicle*, Vol. XXXVIII, For the Year MDCCLXVII (London, 1767), 318.

24 Mason, *"Vorwort,"* p. 44.

25 Quoted in Eudo C. Mason, *The Mind of Henry Fuseli* (London: Routledge & Kegan Paul, 1951), p. 83.

26 Knowles, I, 46.

27 Mona Wilson, *The Life of William Blake* (1927 rpt. New York: Cooper Square, 1969), p. 294.

28 Allan Cunningham, *The Lives of the Most Eminent British Painters, Sculptors, and Architects*, Vol. 2 (London: John Murray, Albemarle Street, 1830), 272.

29 Frederick Antal, *Fuseli Studies* (London: Routledge & Kegan Paul, 1956), p. 105.

30 Cunningham, p. 266.

31 Knowles, I, 46.

32 *Briefe*, p. 125.

33 Guthke, p. 139. See also Mason, *"Entstehung, Aufnahme,"* p. 51.

34 "Remarks on the Writings and Conduct of J.J. Rousseau. 8 vo. Price 2s. 6d. Cadell," *The Critical Review: or Annals of Literature by a Society of Gentlemen*, Vol. 23 (London: Printed for A. Hamilton, May 1767), 374-376.

35 "Remarks on the Writings and Conduct of J.J. Rousseau. 12mo. 2s. 6d. Cadell, &c." *The Monthly Review; or Literary Journal by Several Hands*, Vol. XXXVI (London, 1767), 459-463.

36 Mason, *"Entstehung,"* p. 46.

37 David Hume, *The New Letters of David Hume*, ed. Raymond Klibansky and Ernest C. Mossner (Oxford: At the Clarendon Press, 1954), p. 160.

38 Hume, *The New Letters of David Hume*, p. 160, note 3.

39 Mason, *"Entstehung,"* p. 55.

Fuseli's Correspondence with Lavater from Italy and his Interest in Lavater's Work

1 *Briefe*, 148.
2 *Briefe*, 149.
3 *Briefe*, 148.
4 *Briefe*, 150.
5 Fuseli catalogued the extent of his loss to Lavater in a letter of 14 June 1770. *Briefe*, 153.
6 *"Eines Mannes nach deinem Herzen"* was the way that Fuseli referred to Coutts and his generosity in his letter to Lavater from London in August 1769. *Briefe*, 148.
7 *Briefe*, 155.
8 The letter from Lavater to Herder is preserved in *Aus Herders Nachlass*, II, 68 f. It is excerpted in *Briefe*, 168.
9 *Briefe*, 166.
10 *Briefe*, 166.
11 Lavater requested heads of Christ from all his friends, among them Tischbein and Goethe. For an excellent treatment of Goethe's problematic relationship with Lavater, see Friedrich Gundolf, *Goethe*, Berlin, 1930, repr. New York, AMS, 1971, pp. 223-234.
12 *Briefe*, 166.
13 The head of a dying man, *"Kopf eines Sterbenden,"* Schiff 1735, a "paraphrase" of a design in Michelangelo's *Last Judgment*. Cf. Schiff, II, 83.
14 *Briefe*, 177.
15 *Briefe*, 178.

Part Two: Fuseli and Blake: Documentary Evidence of their Friendship

The Meeting of Fuseli and Blake (1781-1787?)

1 G.E. Bentley, *Blake Records* (Oxford: At the Clarendon Press, 1969), p. 15.
2 Schiff, I, 86.
3 Schiff, I, 119.
4 Fuseli writes to Lavater on 9 August 1781: *"Meine Adresse hast du nicht verloren? Nr. 1 Broadstreet, Corner of Poland Street."* *Briefe*, 197.
5 Bentley, *Records*, pp. 552-554.
6 Bentley, *Records*, p. 554.
7 Alexander Gilchrist, *Life of William Blake: With Selections from his Poems and Other Writings*, Vol. I (1880; rpt. New York: Phaeton Press, 1969), 34.
8 Mona Wilson, *The Life of William Blake* (1927; rpt. New York: Cooper Square Publishers, 1969), p. 13.
9 Schiff, I, 123.
10 In May 1768 Fuseli speaks in a letter to Lavater of "my friend Johnson," who is sending that evening a package of books to Rotterdam for the use of Bodmer and Lavater and other Swiss friends. Included in the shipment are Gray's "Poems"; "Sentimental Travels" by Sterne; "Sermons to Asses"; Priestley "On Government," ... "Relicks of Ancient Poetry" ... Armstrong's "Poem on Health" *und dessen* "Sketches" *für Nüscheler. Briefe*, 144-145.
11 Bentley, *Records*, pp. 26-27, 610.
12 For the story of the phenomenal success of the painting, for which Fuseli got very little remuneration, see: Nicholas Powell, *Henry Fuseli: The Nightmare*, Art in Context (London: Allen Lane, 1973).
13 Bentley, *Records*, p. 40; Schiff, I, 160.
14 Erdman, *Prophet*, p. 43.
15 Bentley, *Records*, p. 39.
16 Bentley, *Records*, p. 611.
17 "Two Blake Prints and Two Fuseli Drawings," *Blake Newsletter* 5, 3 (Winter 1971-1972):173-181.

Artistic Collaboration, Mutual Praise, and Documents
of the Relationship of Fuseli and Blake (177?-1810)

1 A more detailed discussion of Blake's copy of Fuseli's Winckelmann translation is included in Part Three, "Blake and Fuseli's Winckelmann."

2 A more detailed discussion of Blake's part in this design is included in Part Five, "Blake's Copy of the Aphorisms."

3 G.E. Bentley, Jr., "A 'New' Blake Engraving in Lavater's *Physiognomy*," *Blake Newsletter* VI, 2, (Fall 1972):48-50.

4 The story of this misbegotten venture is told in G.E. Bentley, *Blake Books*, pp. 36-41, and in the commentary to a facsimile edition: Edward Young, *Night Thoughts or the Complaint and The Consolation, Illustrated by William Blake*, ed. by Robert Essick and Jenijoy LaBelle (New York: Dover Publications, 1975).

5 Gilchrist, I, 135. Essick, *Night Thoughts*, p. v.

6 Gilchrist, I, 135. More recently, Bentley has attributed the "Advertisement" to Edwards himself, and calls it a "strange piece of puffing." *Blake Records*, p. 57.

7 Gilchrist, I, 135.

8 Joseph Farington records a conversation that took place on January 11, 1797, between Farington, Hoppner, Stothard, Rigaud, and Opie: "Blake's eccentric designs were mentioned. Stothard supported his claims to Genius, but allowed He had been misled to extravagance in his art & He knew by whom,—" Vol. I, 151-152. Fuseli is the most likely candidate for this accusation, considering the reputation that he had in the Farington circle.

9 Schiff, I, 178.

10 That this engraving is entirely new and not a reworking of the original one is attested to by both Schiff and Ruthven Todd. Schiff, I, 336, Todd, "Two Blake Prints and Two Fuseli Drawings," *Blake Newsletter*, V, 3 (Winter 1971/72):177.

11 *Blake Records*, p. 615.

12 The portrait is in the *Zentralbibliothek*, Zurich, and is reproduced on the frontispiece of the third volume of *Johann Caspar Lavaters ausgewählte Werke*, ed. Dr. Ernst Staehelin (Zurich: Zwingli Verlag, 1943).

13 Reproduced, but not identified by Todd in *Blake Newsletter*, V, 3, 176.

14 *Blake Newsletter*, V, 3, 176.

15 Russell is quoting from Gilchrist's *Life* (1880 ed.), II, 282. Cf. Russell, 169.

16 Archibald G.B. Russell, *The Letters of William Blake Together with a Life by Frederick Tatham* (London, 1906). Also repeated by Mona Wilson, *The Life of William Blake* (1927 repr. New York: Cooper Square Publishers, Inc., 1969), p. 343.

17 Todd, "Two Fuseli Drawings...." *Blake Newsletter*, 176.

18 Schiff, I, 511.

19 The confusing story of Cromek's "betrayal" of Blake's trust is given in detail by Bentley in *Blake Records*, pp. 166-174.

20 The details of Blake's disappointment and anger at Cromek's choice is recorded in Bentley, *Blake Records*, pp. 179-181.

21 Blake had left London to stay in Felpham in Hayley's cottage in 1800, and thus was parted from Fuseli and his other London associates at this time. "Mr. H," is Hayley, who was his patron at this time. Gilchrist, I,156-164.

22 *The Mind of Henry Fuseli*, p. 45.

23 In his anecdotal but reliable account in *Nollekens and His Times* (London, 1828), p. 486. Reprinted in *Nineteenth Century Accounts of William Blake*, Facsimile Reproductions, ed. Joseph Anthony Wittreich, Jr. (Gainesville, Florida: Scholars' Facsimiles & Reprints, 1970), p. 144.

24 In *The Letters of William Blake Together with a Life by Frederick Tatham*, ed. Archibald G.B. Russell (London, 1906), p. 40.

25 *Catalogue of the Small and Very Select Classical Library of the Late Henry Fuseli, Esq. to which is added a Very Fine Collection of Prints, Sold by Mr. Sotheby at his House, No. 3 Wellington Street, Strand, on Friday, July 22, 1825 and three following days*, Sotheby Catalogues, Par I, 1734-1850, January 6 - October 21, 1825, Reel 38 of 71 (Ann Arbor,

Michigan: University Microfilms), p. 19. This catalogue was reprinted as "Appendix IV" by David H. Weinglass in his edition of Fuseli's English letters in 1982, pp. 584-599.
26 Sotheby, *Catalogue*, p. 25.
27 Bentley, *Blake Books*, p. 187.

Part Three: Blake and Fuseli's Winckelmann

The Apprentice's Primer

1 *Blake Studies*, 2nd ed. (Oxford: At the Clarendon Press, 1971), pp. 29-30.
2 G.E. Bentley, *Blake Records* (Oxford: At the Clarendon Press, 1969), pp. 9-12.
3 "Heinrich Füssli und Winckelmann," *Unterscheidung und Bewahrung*, Festschrift *für Hermann Kunisch zum 60. Geburtstag* (Berlin: W. de Gruyter & Co., 1961), pp. 232-258.
4 Mason, *Unterscheidung*, p. 244.
5 Mason, *Unterscheidung*, p. 237.
6 "The Engraver's Apprentice," p. 30.
7 Cunningham, *Lives*, II, 269.
8 Joseph Farington, *The Farington Diary*, ed. James Greig (London, 1922-1928), Vol. II, 46.
9 Knowles, I, 43.
10 6 May 1768: *Briefe*, 143-144.
11 Gilchrist, 17.
12 Gilchrist, 18.
13 For an extensive discussion of the young Blake's knowledge of English poetry, see Kathleen Lowrey, *Windows of the Morning* (1940 repr. New York: Archon Books, 1970).
14 *Blake Studies*, 2nd ed., p. 29.
15 Benjamin Heath Malkin, *A Father's Memoirs of His Child* (London, 1806), p. xix.
16 *The Art of William Blake* (New York: Columbia University Press, 1959), p. 2.
17 *Winckelmann und seine Zeitgenossen, Vierte Auflage* (Leipzig: Koehler & Amelang, 1943), Vol. I, 307-315, 491.
18 Justi, I, 426.
19 Chapel Hill, N.C.: University of North Carolina Press, 1961), pp. 34-35.
20 *Blake's Human Form Divine*, pp. 102-213.
21 Mellor, p. 122.
22 Harper, p. 34.
23 Knowles, II, 12.
24 Knowles, II, 14.
25 Bollingen Series XXXV, 11 (Princeton, New Jersey: Princeton University Press, 1968), Vol. I, xxx.
26 Raine, I, xxx.

Raphael the Sublime

1 Justi, p. 427.
2 The artist Oeser, who never wrote anything on art, and whose aphorisms were never set down by his students, had a reputation for genius. Fuseli includes the following footnote in his translation of the *Gedanken*:

> Fred Oeser, one of the most extensive geniuses which the present age can boast of, is a German, and now lives at Dresden; where, to the honour of his country and the emolument of the art, he gets his livelihood by teaching young blockheads, of the Saxon race, the elements of drawing; and by etching after the Flemish painters. N. of Transl.

Fuseli, *Reflections*, p. 247.
3 Unless otherwise indicated, all quotations from Winckelmann's writings wil be taken from: *Winckelmann's kleinere Schriften zur Geschichte der Kunst des Altertums*, ed. Hermann Uhde-Bernays (Leipzig: Im Insel Verlag, 1913), and will be indicated in the text by "W" with page number.
4 Quotations from Fuseli's translation will be indicated in the text by "FW" with page number.
5 Winckelmann speaks of this plaster copy in a letter of 3 June 1755 cited by Justi, I, 491.

6 Lavater wrote to Fuseli in 1766, asking him to review Lessing's *Laocoön*. Fuseli wrote back on 25 June 1776: *"Lessings 'Grenzen' kenne ich nicht und Thomas nicht, und wenn ich ihn kennte, so würde ich doch nicht rezensieren"* (*Briefe*, 135). The reference to "Thomas" is unclear. Fuseli does not appear to have read Lessing's famous essay until the early nineties. Mason, *Mind*, p. 203.

7 Knowles, II, 72.

8 Three of Winckelmann's articles appeared in this journal, edited by Nicolai and Lessing: *Bibliothek der schönen Wissenschaften und der freyen Künste* (Leipzig: Verlag Johann Gottfried Dyck, 1759), Vol. V. *"Erinnerungen über die Betrachtung der Werke der Kunst,"* 1-3; "Von der Gratie im Werke der Kunst," 13-23; *"Die Beschreibung des Torso im Belvedere zu Rom,"* 33-41.

9 The best discussion of Bodmer's adherence to the theories of Longinus is found in: Marilyn Torbrugge, *"Johann Heinrich Füssli und 'Bodmer-Longinus': Das Wunderbare und das Erhabene,"* *Deutsche Vierteljahrschrift für Literaturwissenschaft*, 46. Jahrgang, Heft 1 (January 1972), 161-185.

10 Winckelmann stresses here that the incomparable qualities of Raphael's Madonnas do not rest on perfection of feature alone but on his *"Empfindung"* of beauty that transcends the beauty that occurs in nature.

11 *A Concordance to the Writings of William Blake*, ed. David V. Erdman (Ithaca, New York: Cornell University Press, 1967).

12 Antal, *Fuseli Studies*, p. 57.

13 *A Father's Memoirs of His Child*, p. xix.

14 Mona Wilson, *The Life of William Blake* (1927 repr. New York: Cooper Square Publishers, Inc., 1969), p. 3.

15 Later in Lecture IX of his *Lectures on Art written in 1810*, Fuseli repeats this judgment of Rubens: *"His male forms, generally the brawny pulp of slaughtermen; his females, hillocks of roses in overwhelmed muscles, grotesque attitudes, and distorted joints, are swept along in a gulph tossed and absorbed by inundation."* Knowles, *II, 369*.

16 *Nollekens and His Times* (London, 1828) reprinted by Bentley in *Blake Records*, p. 468.

Naked Beauty Displayed

1 *Blake Dictionary* (Providence, Rhode Island: Brown University Press, 1965), p. 303.

2 *The Art of William Blake*; these figures are reproduced there as Plates 6a and 6b. See also Blunt's article, "Blake's 'Glad Day'," *Journal of the Warburg and Courtauld Institutes*, II (1938), 65-68.

3 *The Neoplatonism of William Blake*, p. 124.

4 Harper, pp. 203-204.

Allegory

1 *Blake Dictionary*, p. 18.

2 *The Stubborn Structure* (Ithaca, New York: Cornell University Press, 1970), p. 169.

3 *Stubborn Structure*, p. 172.

4 *Angel of Apocalypse: Blake's Idea of Milton* (Madison, Wisconsin: University of Wisconsin Press, 1975), pp. 175-176.

5 *Angel of Apocalypse*, p. 175.

6 Justi, I, 446.

7 *The Analytical Review*, Vol. 1 (June 1788), 216.

8 "William Blake and The Eighteenth-Century Mythologists," *Tracks in the Snow* (London: The Grey Walls Press, 1946), pp. 29-60.

9 *Blake Studies*, 2nd ed., pp. 25-27.

10 Raine, I, 93.

11 David V. Erdman, *Blake: Prophet Against Empire: A Poet's Interpretation of the History of his Own Times*, 3rd ed. (Princeton, New Jersey: Princeton University Press, 1977), p. 33.

12 Harper, 116.

13 "Opening the Seals: Blake's Epics and the Miltonic Tradition," *Blake's Sublime Allegory*, ed. Stuart Curran and Joseph Anthony Wittreich, Jr. (Madison, Wisconsin: University of Wisconsin Press, 1973), p. 26.

14 Raine, I, 34.

Part Four: Blake and Fuseli's Rousseau

The Negative Evidence in the Very Early Works: 1770-1784

1 Fuseli paraphrases from the *First Discourse*: "'The origin of human knowledge does not answer our favourite idea of it. Astronomy sprang from superstition; eloquence from ambition, hate, flattery, lies; geometry from avarice; natural history from vain curiosity—all, even the doctrine of morals, from our pride.—We should less dispute on their advantages, were they owing to our virtues.'—Dis. 2 partie, T. i, 30." *Remarks*, p. 71.

2 Erdman points out the "revamping of material" from "Then She Bore Pale Desire" in the Prelude to the *Book of Los* where Blake presents a more complex mythology of the fall some eighteen years later. *Prophet*, p. 259, n. 34. It is interesting to note also that a theme which will become central to Blake's mature works—the hampering effects of self-love—appears at the end of the manuscript fragment of 1777. But Rousseau's ambivalent attitude towards the dominance of self-interest in human behavior need not be considered the source of this problem in Blake. John Howard describes the currency of the controversy in Blake's time in his chapter "The Fall into Selfhood," *Blake's Milton* (London: Associated University Presses, 1976), pp. 56-62.

3 Erdman finds echoes of Voltaire's *Le Philosophe Ignorant* (1766) in the first chapter of *Island in the Moon*. Blake could have been acquainted with this work from the edition *The Works of the late M. de Voltaire*, which appeared in England between 1779 and 1781. See Mary-Margaret H. Barr, *Voltaire in America 1744-1800* (Baltimore: The Johns Hopkins University Press, 1941), p. 12.

4 Erdman has identified most of the characters in *An Island* in his chapter "English Genius and the Main Chance," *Prophet*, pp. 89-114. See also Nancy Bogen, "Blake's Island in the Moon Revisited," *Satire Newsletter*, Vol. V, 2 (Spring 1968), 110-116.

Fuseli, Blake, and the "Two Rousseaus"

1 S. Foster Damon, *A Blake Dictionary: The Ideas and Symbols of William Blake* (Providence, Rhode Island: Brown University Press, 1965), pp. 351-352.

2 Jean H. Hagstrum, *William Blake: Poet and Painter* (Chicago and London: University of Chicago Press, 1964), p. 29.

3 William Blake, *The Illuminated Blake: All of Wiliam Blake's Illuminated Works with a Plate-by-Plate Commentary*, annotated by David V. Erdman (New York: Anchor Press/Doubleday, 1974), p. 177.

4 For a good discussion of the renewed emphasis on Christ in Blake's poetry after 1800, see Jean H. Hagstrum, "The Wrath of the Lamb: A study of William Blake's Conversions," *From Sensibility to Romanticism: Essays Presented to Frederick A. Pottle*, ed. Frederick W. Hilles and Harold Bloom (London: Oxford University Press, 1965), pp. 311-330.

5 *William Blake: The Politics of Vision* (New York: Henry Holt and Company, 1946), p. xi.

6 David V. Erdman, *William Blake: Prophet Against Empire: A Poet's Interpretation of the History of His Own Times*, 3rd ed. (Princeton, N.J.: Princeton University Press, 1977), pp. 172, 258, 298-299, 416-420 et passim; Kathleen Raine, *Blake and Tradition*, The Bollingen Series XXXV, 11 (Princeton, N.J.: Princeton University Press, 1968), I, 15, 168; II, 129; Jacob Bronowski, *William Blake: A Man Without a Mask* (1944; rpt. New York: Haskell House, 1967), pp. 80, 102, 105, 115, 125-126.

7 *Prophet*, pp. 243-279.

8 *Prophet*, p. 249.

9 *Prophet*, p. 141.

10 Paris, 1950, p. 352.

11 Paris, 1956, pp. 25-26.

12 *Blake and Tradition*, II, 129.

13 "...a true daughter of Rousseau," the phrase is Raine's, *Blake and Tradition*, I, 15.

14 Bentley, *Blake Records*, pp. 40, 612. Raine, *Blake and Tradition*, I, 166-168 suggests that "Blake knew and perhaps loved Mary Wollstonecraft," and that Blake's poem "Mary" describes her life—"an attempt to put into practice the philosophy of Eloisa." This interpretation of "Mary" is controversial and by no means accepted by most Blake scholars. See

Erdman, *Prophet*, pp. 156-157, 157 n. 23. If Mary behaved in the mode of Eloisa, it is more likely that she did so in suggesting to Mrs. Fuseli that she live with the married Fuselis in a *ménage à trois*. This story is related by Knowles, I, 167-170; Cunningham, *Lives*, II, 281-283; and by Godwin himself, *Memoirs of Mary Wollstonecraft* (1798 repr. New York, 1972), pp. 57-62.

15 *Memoirs of Mary Wollstonecraft* (1798 repr. 1927 and 1972, Gordon Press), ed. W. Clark Durant, p. 58.

16 Godwin, *Memoirs*, p. 59.

17 Godwin, *Memoirs*, p. 60.

18 See note 14. After Mary's death, the story of Mary and Fuseli became something of a legend. Robert Browning wrote a poem about her unrequited love in 1883, "Mary Wollstonecraft and Fuseli."

19 Aphorism 45 in *Aphorisms on Art*, Knowles III, 77. See also a review of Uvedale Price's *Essay on the Picturesque* in the *Analytical Review*, November 1794, quoted in Mason, *Mind*, pp. 174-175.

20 John Howard has noted aspects of agreement in Blake and Rousseau's vicar, but finds more points of disagreement in his analysis of Blake's religious attitude in *Milton*. I believe that the negative judgment of Rousseau in *Milton* is based on a change of attitude from the positive light in which Blake saw Rousseau during the time of his close association with Fuseli. Cf. *Blake's Milton*, London, 1976.

21 *Prophet*, pp. 129, n. 35, 130, n. 36, 178, n. 7, 428, n. 10.

Fuseli, Blake, and the Savoyard Vicar

1 *Remarks*, p. 79.

2 *Remarks*, pp. 79-80. The reference to "the authentic key" comes from Revelations 3:7: "And to the angel of the church in Philadelphia write: These things saith he that is holy, he that is true, he that hath the key of David, he that openeth, and no man shutteth, and no man openeth"; KJV. The "Babylonian Whore" comes likewise from Revelation 19:2: "For the true and righteous *are* his judgments: for he hath judged the great whore, which did corrupt the earth with her fornication, and hath avenged the blood of his servants at her hand." Eudo Mason suggests that Fuseli is alluding ironically to the craze current in his day of explicating the miraculous and obscure in the Bible in terms of contemporary events. "*Anmerkungen*," *Remarks*, p. 164. The reference to the "Merchants of Tyrus" comes from Ezekiel 27.

3 Joseph Anthony Wittreich has suggested that Fuseli's conception of "sublime allegory" understood in a theological sense influenced Blake's idea of epic. *Angel of Apocalypse* (Madison, Wisconsin: University of Wisconsin Press, 1945), p. 175.

4 *Remarks*, p. 79, note c.

5 *Remarks*, p. 69.

6 Roddier, *J.-J. Rousseau en Angleterre*, p. 401.

7 It is not known whether or not Blake could read French. He quotes Voltaire in French about 1808 in his marginalia to Reynolds' *Discourses*, but Henry Crabb Robinson quotes him as having said in the 1850s that he had had in visions "much intercourse with Voltaire," but when asked which language Voltaire used to address him, Blake replied: "It was like the touch of a musical Key—he touched it probably French, but to my ear it was English." Hayley taught Blake Latin, Greek, Hebrew, according to his own account in a letter of January 30, 1803, "although he had a smattering of Hebrew before." Bentley, *Blake Records*, pp. 526, 547. Blake was interested in languages, but no reliable evidence exists of his proficiency in any language other than English.

8 J.-J. Rousseau, *Emilius and Sophia: or, A New System of Education*. Translated from the French of Mr. J.J. Rousseau By the Translator of Eloisa [Kendrick] vol. III (London: T. Becket and P.A. de Hondt, 1767), 22. "The Profession of Faith of a Savoyard Curate" comprises pp. 16-154 of this volume.

9 *Emilius, p. 29.*

10 *Emilius*, p. 52.

11 *Emilius*, p. 57.

12 *Emilius*, p. 57.

13 *William Blake: The Politics of Vision* (New York: Henry Holt and Company, 1949), p. 129 and passim.

14 *Emilius*, p. 102.

15 *Emilius*, p. 103.

16 *Emilius*, p. 106.

17 *Remarks*, p. 67. This rambling digression is typical of Fuseli's packing of varied and sometimes obscure references to illustrate his point of view. Professor Mason furnishes the following explications in *Anmerkungen*, p. 159: "*Leon*" refers to the Medici Pope Leo X (1513-1521) and his great age of art patronage. "*Smithfield*" is the place where many protestants were burned in London during the reign of Queen Mary (1553-1558). "*Merindol* and *Cabrieres*" were the scenes of executions of many Waldensians in 1545; "*Thoulouse*": many Huguenots were slain in Toulouse in 1562 and 1572. Fuseli refers in this paragraph also to the horrible *Lisbon Earthquake*, the cause of much theological speculation and the subject of a poem by Voltaire, which elicited a rejoinder from Rousseau. *Michael Servetus* was burned by Calvin as a heretic in 1553. The reference to the *Moravians* adoring their ass in the dark refers to the fact that Moravians were persecuted and forced to wear placards on their backs inscribed with the words, "*fauler Esel*." "*Fear and damnation*": a parody of the biblical passage from which the Quakers got their name, Corinthians 2:2. The joke at the end of the passage refers to *Boccaccio (Decameron*, V, 2): One of the false relics that Fra Cipolla has is one of the ribs of the word made flesh. The reference to the "*host of black, white and grey*" refers to Dominicans, Carmelites, and Franciscans: Fuseli is thinking of the lines in *Paradise Lost* in which "Eremits and Friers/White Black, and Grey, with all their trumperies" appear (Book III). It is interesting to note that Blake employs a "Grey Monk" in the later works, as the righteous victim of Gibbon, Voltaire, and "the schools." *Jerusalem*, the *Note-Book*, and the *Pickerling Manuscript*. By this time, Blake is fanatically dedicated to fighting deism.

18 *Briefe*, p. 158.

19 Knowles, I, 392.

20 *Remarks*, p. 84.

21 *Remarks*, p. 84, note a.

22 *Emilius*, p. 40.

23 *Blake Dictionary*, p. 330.

24 *Remarks*, p. 80. Fuseli adds his own footnote to explain the reference to Aretino (1492-1557), who wrote obscene works and then "repented." The "course of natural history" to which he refers here are the early *Sonetti lussuriosi*. Fuseli's note reads: "*Aretin*, when he had finished his course of natural history, and demonstrated upwards of forty *Schemata Amoris*—repented, dissolved his name into that of *Parthenio Etyro*, and fell to writing psalms, lives of J. and the saints, prayers and meditations."

25 *Remarks*, p. 72.

Pernicious Maxims and Truth-Bringing Devils

1 Harold Bloom, *Blake's Apocalypse: A Study in Poetic Argument* (Garden City, New York: Doubleday and Company, 1963), pp. 69-70. John Gordon Davies, *The Theology of William Blake* (Oxford: At the Clarendon Press, 1948), p. 51; Erdman, *Prophet*, pp. 176-182, have also commented upon the satirical aspect of M.H.H.

2 "An Audience for *The Marriage of Heaven and Hell*," *Blake Studies* 3, 1 (Fall 1970), 20.

3 Howard, "An Audience for *The Marriage of Heaven and Hell*," p. 20.

4 Howard, p. 33.

5 *Fearful Symmetry: A Study of William Blake* (Princeton, New Jersey: Princeton University Press, 1947), p. 201.

6 *Prophet*, p. 178.

7 Roddier, pp. 320-321.

8 *Briefe*, 113.

9 *Briefe*, 124.

10 The best discussion of Fuseli's Milton undertaking is contained in Gert Schiff's commentary in his edition of the extant pictures from the "Milton Gallery": Gert Schiff, *Johann Heinrich Füsslis Milton-Galerie* (Zürich/Stuttgart, 1963).

11 *Remarks*, p. 67.

12 Erdman, *Prophet*, p. 175.
13 *Remarks*, p. 69.
14 *Remarks*, p. 98.
15 *Remarks*, p. 74.
16 *Remarks*, p. 74, note b.
17 *Remarks*, p. 75.
18 *Remarks*, p. 75.
19 "This idea is not peculiar to Blake, nor to his master Boehme; it is to be found in Aristotle, in Brahmanism, in Traherne, and Berdyaev; God or Brahma or Tao is the union of these opposites...." *The Religion of William Blake*, p. 134.
20 *Emilius*, p. 53.
21 *Emilius*, p. 53.
22 *Emilius*, p. 54.
23 *Emilius*, p. 149.
24 *Remarks*, p. 70.
25 *Remarks*, p. 73. The quote from Milton comes from *Paradise Lost*, II, 948-950.
26 Knowles, II, 65.

Part Five: Blake and Fuseli's Lavater

Blake's Copy of the *Aphorisms on Man*

1 By Ruthven Todd in London in 1970. Todd recounts his discovery and his speculation based on the finding of "Two Blake Prints and Two Fuseli Drawings," *Blake Newsletter*, Vol. V, *3* (Winter 1971-1972):173-181.
2 Todd, p. 174.
3 Schiff catalogues the engraving as No. 789, *Oeuvrekatalog*, II, 201.
4 Todd, p. 179.
5 This is particularly noticeable on pages 179, 180, and 181, where Blake makes lengthy notations: Aphorisms 532 and 533 (K81, K82). Blake had the book bound in sheepskin. This was replaced by another owner in the late nineteenth century, who had it bound in morocco. *Blake Books*, p. 691.
6 In his textual notes to his edition of *The Poetry and Prose of William Blake*, commentary by Harold Bloom (New York: Doubleday & Company, rev. ed., 1966), p. 799. See also *Blake Books*, p. 690.
7 The description of Blake's copy of the *Aphorisms* is based on examination of a microfilm of the book made available to me by the Huntington Library in California. There are four American editions of the *Aphorisms on Man* in the collection of the Rare Book Room in the Library of Congress: (Boston, 1790) from Johnson's fourth edition listing 633 aphorisms; (Newburyport, Mass., 1793), fifth edition listing 633 aphorisms; (Catskill, New York, 1795), fifth edition listing 133 aphorisms; (Lancaster, Penn., 1830), calling itself the first (!) American edition and likewise listing 633 aphorisms.
8 Erdman hypothesizes that of four notes written in pencil after the time of Blake's original annotations in ink two are by Blake: Nos. 287 and 384, and that Nos. 20 and 503 were written by two different hands, "probably friends to whom Blake showed his marked copy as instructed in No. 643." Erdman, "Textual Notes," *The Poetry and Prose of William Blake*, p. 799.
9 Gilchrist, 62.
10 Gilchrist, 61.
11 S. Foster Damon, *William Blake: His Philosophy and Symbols*, p. 92.
12 "Nor could the book's complete lack of mysticism and poetry have been soothing," i.e., to Blake. Damon, *Philosophy and Symbols*, p. 92.
13 For a survey of Lavater's popularity in England, especially relating to his physiognomical works and theories, see John Graham, "Lavater's *Physiognomy* in England," *Journal of the History of Ideas* XXII (1961), and John Graham, "Lavater's *Physiognomy*: A Checklist," *Bibliographical Society of America*, pp. 297-301.
14 Gilchrist, 62.
15 *Blake Records*, p. 288.
16 The book also contains Samuel Palmer's signature. Palmer was a painter and friend of Blake, and one of Gilchrist's informants.

The Epigrammatic Style

1 Gilchrist, I, 61-67.

2 Gilchrist, I, 67. Gilchrist, ever eager to preserve the complete originality of every notion of Blake's, admits that Lavater, "the Swiss enthusiast," had an international reputation at the time Blake was reading him, but seems not to have known much about Lavater himself. For example, he states of one of the *Aphorisms*: "Surely golddust may be described in these notes; and when we remember it is a painter, not a metaphysician, who is writing, we can afford to judge them less critically" (p. 66). It is puzzling that Gilchrist should refer to Lavater as a painter, when his reputation was, in fact, based on his qualities as a minister to the soul of man and as a religious philosopher. Or, was he attributing the *Aphorisms* to Fuseli?

3 Bronowski, *William Blake: A Man Without a Mask* (1944, repr. New York: Haskell House Publishers Ltd., 1967): Bronowski sees the Lavater *Aphorisms* as the companion piece to Swedenborg in Blake's formation of his own form of dissent, and says that in *The French Revolution*, "He is writing in the very language of the two aphorisms of Lavater [No. 1 and No. 2] which were to him 'true Christian philosophy'" (pp. 40,849, 136). Mark Schorer, *William Blake: Politics of Vision* (New York: Henry Holt and Company, 1946) uses the annotations to explicate various attitudes, especially toward Christianity, throughout the work of Blake (pp. 67, 104, 168, 225, 226, 238, 345). Erdman sees the impact of Lavater's Christian humanism as an important influence on the development of Blake's thought, and has given more attention to Fuseli's role in "furnishing" the mind of Blake than any other critic besides Mason. He has seen traces of the *Aphorisms* throughout the works of Blake and has called the marginalia "the nearest thing we have to a commentary on the Songs themselves" (pp. 127-129, 43, 139-141, 90, 116, 117, 143, 145, 177). Paley, *Energy and Imagination: A Study of the Development of Blake's Thought* (Oxford: Clarendon Press, 1970) traces the first tentative formation of Blake's concept of energy in the Lavater annotations, and finds the beginnings of some of the most complex of Blake's statements in these early notes (pp. 10-11, 15, 105, 183).

4 *William Blake: His Philosophy and Symbols* (1924, repr. London: Dawsons of Pall Mall, 1969), p. 92.

5 *Vermischte unphysiognomische Regeln zur Selbst- und Menschenkenntniss von* ("Johann Caspar Lavater" handwritten in ink), (Zurich, no publisher given, 1787). On the last page of this volume, after *Regel 500*, is the notation: "Zürich Freytags den 30. Nov. 1787," p. 224. *Vermischte unphysiognomische Regelns zur Menschen- und Selbstkenntniss von* (again, the name autographed by hand), (Zürich, no publisher given, 1788). On the last page, the date is given: 'Samstags den 17 May."

6 The name "Johann Caspar Lavater" appears to have been written in Lavater's hand in the 1787 volume that I examined in the Special Collections Rare Book room at the Milton S. Eisenhower Library at Johns Hopkins University. In the 1788 volume in the same collection, however, the name of the author was clearly written in by the owner of the book, a "Frau Gassmann."

7 Johann Caspar Lavater, *Aphorisms on Man*, translated FROM THE ORIGINAL MANUSCRIPT of THE REV. JOHN CASPAR LAVATER, CITIZEN OF ZURIC (London: Printed for J. Johnson, St. Paul's Churchyard, MDCCLXXXVIII), pp. iii-iv. Hereinafter, the references to "Lavater, *Aphorisms*" refer to Blake's copy.

8 In the introduction to his facsimile edition of Blake's copy of *Aphorisms on Man* (New York: Scholars' Facsimiles & Reprints, 1980), pp. xi-xii.

9 Lavater, *Aphorisms*, pp. v-vi.

10 Knowles, I, 160.

11 61-152.

12 The page numbers in parentheses here refer to the respective page numbers in Lavater's *Regeln* ... (1787) and Fuseli's translation.

13 The marginalia that are now considered to belong to the prose writings of William Blake are:
    Annotations to Lavater's Aphorisms on Man
    Annotations to Swedenborg's Heaven and Hell
    Annotations to Swedenborg's Divine Love and Divine Wisdom
    Annotations to Swedenborg's Divine Providence

Annotations to An Apology for the Bible by R. Watson
Annotations to Bacon's Essays Moral, Economical and Political
Annotations to Boyd's Historical Notes on Dante
Annotations to The Works of Sir Joshua Reynolds
Annotations to Spurzheim's Observations on Insanity
Annotations to Berkeley's Siris
Annotations to Wordsworth's Poems
Annotations to Wordsworth's preface to The Excursion
Annotations to Thornton's The Lord's Prayer, Newly Translated
Annotation to Cellini (?)

The best commentary and most inclusive printing of the marginalia is found in *The Poetry and Prose of William Blake*, ed. David V. Erdman, commentary by Harold Bloom (Garden City, New York: Doubleday & Company, Inc., 1970), pp. 572-659, rev. ed.

14 Henry Fuseli, "Aphorisms," *The Life and Writings of Henry Fuseli, Esq, M.A. R.A.*, Vol. III. The page numbers after each aphorism refer to the page numbers in this volume, edited by Knowles and published in 1831.

15 Farington, III, 60.

Bibliography

Primary Sources

"Abstract of a letter concerning Herculaneum, and the other adjacent subterraneous towns; from the abbe Winckelmann, librarian of the Vatican, and antiquary to the Pope, the count Bruhl, chamberlain to his Polish majesty." *The Annual Register, or a View of the History, Politics, and Literature for the Year 1765.* 2nd ed. Vol. 8. London: Dodsley in Pall Mall, 1788, pp. 182-189. [Unsigned, falsely attributed to Fuseli.]

[Armstrong, John.] "Remarks on the Writings and Conduct of Rousseau," *The Gentleman's Magazine, and Historical Chronicle,* Vol. XXXVIII, For the Year MDCCLXII (London, 1767):318.

Armstrong, John, M.D. *The Art of Preserving Health; in Four Books.* 2nd ed. London: Printed for A. Millar, 1745.

Bibliothek der schönen Wissenschaften und der freyen Künste. Edited by Friedrich Nicolai. Vol. V. Leipzig: Verlegts Johann Gottfried Dyck, 1759.

Blake, William. *Letters of William Blake.* Edited by Geoffrey Keynes. 2nd rev. ed. London: Hart-Davis, 1968.

_____. *Poetry and Prose of William Blake,* rev. ed. Edited by David V. Erdman with commentary by Harold Bloom. Garden City, New York: Doubleday, 1970.

_____. *The Complete Graphic Works of William Blake.* Edited by David Bindman, assisted by Deirdre Toomey. New York: G.P. Putnam's Sons, 1978.

_____. *The Complete Works of William Blake, with Variant Readings,* new ed. Edited by Geoffrey Keynes. London: Oxford University Press, 1966, rev. ed., 1972.

_____. *The Engravings of William Blake.* Edited by Archibald G.B. Russell. London: Grant Richards Ltd., 1712.

_____. *The Illuminated Blake: All of William Blake's Illuminated Works with Plate-by-Plate Commentary.* Annotated by David V. Erdman. New York: Anchor Press/Doubleday, 1974.

_____. *The Letters of William Blake Together with a Life by Frederick Tatham.* Edited by Archibald G.B. Russell. London, 1906.

_____. *The Poems of William Blake.* Edited by W.H. Stevenson with text by David V. Erdman. London: Longman, 1971.

_____. *The Prophetic Writings of William Blake.* Edited by D.J. Schloss and J.P.R. Wallis. Oxford: Oxford University Press, 1964.

Bodmer, Johann Jacob. *Critische Abhandlung von dem Wunderbaren in der Poesie.* Zürich, 1740. Deutsche Neudrucke, Reihe: Texte des 18. Jahrhunderts. Facsimile. Stuttgart: J.B. Metzlersche Verlagsbuchhandlung, 1966.

Boydell, John. *A Catalogue of the Pictures in the Shakespeare Gallery.* London: J. and J. Boydell, 1789.

Catalogue of the Small and Very Select Classical Library of the Late Henry Fuseli, Esq. to which is added a Very Fine Collection of Prints, Sold by Mr. Sotheby at his House, No. 3 Wellington Street, Strand, on Friday, July 22, 1825 and three following days. Sotheby Catalogues, Part I,

162

1734-1850, January 6-October 21, 1825. Reel 38 of 71. Ann Arbor, Michigan: University Microfilms.

Cunningham, Allan C. *The Lives of the Most Eminent British Painters, Sculptors and Architects.* 2nd ed. London: Heaton, 1830.

Dragonetti, Giacinto. *A Treatise on Virtues and Rewards.* Translated by Henry Fuseli. London: J. Johnson, 1769.

Farington, Joseph. *The Farington Diary. 1793-1821.* 8 vols. Edited by James Grieg. London: Hutchinson, 1922-1938.

Füssli, Johann Caspar, and Füssli, Johann Heinrich. *Geschichte der besten Künstler in der Schweiz nebst ihren Bildnissen.* 5 vols. Zürich: Füsslin und Compagnie, 1769-1774.

Füssli, Johann Heinrich. "Aphorismen von H. Füssli." Translated by Marie Kurella. *Zeitschrift für bildende Kunst,* 56. Jg. New Series, Vol. 32, No. 1 (January 1962).

——————. *Bemerkungen über J.J. Rousseaus Schriften und Verhalten/Remarks of the Writings and Conduct of J.J. Rousseau.* Introduction, German translation, commentary and editing by Eudo C. Mason. Kleine Schriften No. 4. Schweizerisches Institut für Kunstwissenschaft, Zürich. Zürich, 1962.

——————. *Briefe.* Edited by Walter Muschg. Klosterberg/Basel: Verlag Benno Schwabe & Co., 1942.

——————. *Johann Heinrich Füssli: Abbildungen.* Vol. II of *Johann Heinrich Füssli: 1741-1825.* Edited by Gert Schiff. Oeuvrekatalog Schweizer Künstler. Zürich: Verlag Berichtshaus, 1973.

——————. *Sämtliche Gedichte.* Edited by Karl S. Guthke and Martin Bircher. Zürich: Orell Füssli Verlag, 1973.

——————. "Unveröffentlichte Gedichte von Johann Heinrich Füssli." Edited by Eudo C. Mason. *Zürcher Kunstgesellschaft Neujahrsblatt.* Zürich: Zürcher Kunstgesellschaft, 1951.

——————. *Zeichnungen von Johann Heinrich Füssli: 1741-1825.* Edited and catalogued by Gert Schiff. Zürich: Fretz & Wasmuth Verlag, 1959.

Fuseli, Henry [Henry Fussle]. "A Description of the famous marble trunk of Hercules, dug up at Rome, commonly called the Torso of Belvedere; wrought by Apollonius, the son of Nestor, and universally allowed to have been made for a statue of Hercules Spinning." Translated from the German of the abbe Winckelmann, librarian of the Vatican, and the antiquary to the Pope &c. by Henry Fussle. *The Annual Register, or a View of the History, Politics, and Literature for the Year 1765.* 2nd ed. Vol. 8. London: J. Dodsley in Pall Mall, 1778, pp. 180-182.

Fuseli, Henry. *Lectures on Painting Delivered at the Royal Academy, March 1801.* London: T. Cadell and W. David, 1820.

[Fuseli, Henry.] *Remarks on the Writings and Conduct of J.J. Rousseau.* London: T. Cadell, Payne, and J. Johnson, 1767.

Fuseli, Henry. *Remarks on the Writings and Conduct of J.J. Rousseau.* Edited and with an introduction by Karl S. Guthke. Augustan Reprint Society, No. 82. Los Angeles: William Andrews Clark Memorial Library, University of California, 1960. [Reprint of Fuseli's pamphlet, Chapter I only.]

——————. *The Life and Writings of Henry Fuseli, Esq. M.A. R.A.: Keeper, and Professor of Painting to the Royal Academy in London: Member of the First Class of the Academy of St. Luke at Rome. 3 vols.* Edited by John Knowles, F.R.S. London: Henry Colburn and Richard Bentley, New Burlington Street, 1831.

Gessner, Georg. *Johann Kaspar Lavaters Lebensbeschreibung von seinem Tochtermann Georg Gessner.* Winterthur, 1802.

Gilchrist, Alexander. *Life of William Blake: With Selections from his Poems and Other Writings.* 2 vols. 1880; reprint, New York: Phaeton Press, 1969.

Godwin, William. *The Memoirs of the Author of the Vindication of the Rights of Women.* 2nd ed. London: Printed for J. Johnson, 1798.

Goethe, J.W. *Briefe von Goethe an Lavater aus den Jahren 1774 bis 1783.* Edited by Heinrich Hirzel. Leipzig: S. Hirzel, 1833.

Haydon, Benjamin Robert. *Diary of Benjamin Robert Haydon*. Edited by William Bissell Pope. 5 vols. Cambridge, Mass.: Harvard University Press, 1960-1963.

Heisch, P. *Memoirs of John Caspar Lavater*. London: Samuel Bagster & Sons, 1842.

Herder, Johann Gottfried. *Aus Herders Nachlass*. Vol. II. Edited by Heinrich Düntzer and Ferdinand G. von Herder. Vol. II. Frankfurt/M.: Heidinger and Comp., 1857.

Hume, David. *The New Letters of David Hume*. Vol. II. Edited by Raymond Klibansky and Ernest C. Mossner. Oxford: At the Clarendon Press, 1954.

Lavater, Johann Caspar. *Aphorisms on Man*. Translated by Henry Fuseli. London: J. Johnson, 1788.

_____. *Essays on Physiognomy: Designed to Promote the Knowledge and Love of Mankind. Illustrated by engravings, accurately copied; and some duplicates added from originals. Executed by or under the supervision of Thomas Holloway*. Translated from the French by Henry Hunter. 5 vols. in 3. London: Murray, Hunter et al., 1787-1798.

_____. *Johann Caspar Lavaters Ausgewählte Werke*. 4 vols. Edited by Dr. Ernst Staehelin. Zürich: Zwingli Verlag, 1943.

_____. *Lavaters Jugend von ihm selbst erzählt*. Edited by Oskar Farner. Zürich: Zwingli Verlag, 1939.

_____. *Vermischte unphysiognomische Regeln zur Selbst- und Menschenkenntniss*. Zürich, no publisher, den Freytags 30. Nov. 1787. [Lavater's autographed signature on the title page.]

_____. *Vermischte unphysiognomische Regeln zur Menschen- und Selbstkenntniss*. Zürich, no publisher, Samstags den 17. Mai, 1788.

Malkin, Benjamin Heath. *A Father's Memoirs of his Child*. London, 1806.

Mengs, Anton Raphael. *Gedanken über die Schönheit*. Translated and edited by Johann Caspar Füssli and Johann Heinrich Füssli. Zürich: Füsslin und Compagnie, 1774.

Montagu[e], Lady Marie Wortley. *Briefe der Lady Marie Wortley Montagu*. Translated by Heinrich Füssli. 3 vols. Leipzig: M.G. Weidmanns Erben und Reich, 1763.

"Observations on the Influence of the different climates upon the polite arts; taken from a history of the fine arts by the abbe Winckelman, librarian of the Vatican, and antiquary to the Pope." *The Annual Register, or a View of the History, Politics and Literature for the year 1765*. 2nd ed. Vol. 8. London: Dodsley in Pall Mall, 1778, pp. 250-253. [Unsigned, falsely attributed to Fuseli.]

Pilkington, A.M. *A Dictionary of Painters from the Revivals to the Present Period: A New Edition with Considerable Additions, an Appendix and an Index by Henry Fuseli, R.A.* London: J. Walker, J. Johnson, et al., 1810.

"Remarks on the Writings and Conduct of J.J. Rousseau. 8 vols. Price 2s. 6d. Cadell," *The Critical Review: or Annals of Literature by a Society of Gentlemen*. Vol. 23. London: Printed for A. Hamilton, May 1767, pp. 374-376.

"Remarks on the Writings and Conduct of J.J. Rousseau. 12 mo. 2s. 6d. Cadell, &c." *The Monthly Review; or Literary Journal by Several Hands*. Vol. XXXVI. London, 1767, pp. 459-463.

Reynolds, Sir Joshua. *Discourses on Art*. Edited by Robert W. Wark. Published for the Paul Mellon Centre for British Art, New Haven, Conn., Yale University Press, 1975.

Robinson, Henry Crabb. *Blake, Coleridge, Wordsworth, Lamb, etc.: Being Selections from the Remains of Henry Crabb Robinson*. Edited by Edith Julia Morley. London: Longmans, Green & Co., 1922.

Rousseau, Jean-Jacques. *Corréspondence avec Léonard Usteri*. Zürich: Orell Füssli Verlag, 1910.

_____. *Emilius and Sophia: or, A New System of Education*. Translated from the French of Mr. J.J. Rousseau by the translator of Eloisa [William Kendrick]. 3 vols. London: T. Becket and P.A. De Hondt, 1767.

_____. *The Miscellaneous Works of Mr. J.J. Rousseau*. 5 vols. Translated by William Kendrick. London: T. Becket and P.A. De Hondt in the Strand, 1767. Reprint ed., New York: Burt Franklin, 1972.

Smith, John Thomas. *Nollekens and His Times: Comprehending a life of that celebrated sculptor; and memoirs of several contemporary artists from the time of Roubiliac, Hogarth, and Reynolds, to that of Fuseli, Flaxman, and Blake.* 2 vols. London: H. Coburn, 1829.

Spalding, Johann Joachim. *Johann Joachim Spaldings Lebensbeschreibung von Ihm Selbst Erzählt.* Edited by Georg Ludewig Spalding. In der Buchhandlung des Waisenhauses Halle, 1804.

Sulzer, J.G. *Allgemeine Theorie der schönen Künste.* Leipzig, 1764. Reprint ed., Leipzig: Erben und Reich, 1773. Fuseli was responsible for the following articles: "Allegorie," "Ausarbeitung," "Anordnung," "Gruppen," "Anatomie des Homers," "das Erhabene," and "Schönheit."

"Thoughts concerning the imitation of the GRECIAN ARTISTS in PAINTING and SCULPTURE. In a Series of letters." *The Scots Magazine,* Edinburgh, January 1765, Vol. XXVII, No. MDCCLXV, 17. [Spurious "translation" of Winckelmann.]

Winckelmann, Johann Joachim. *Kleinere Schriften zur Geschichte der Kunst des Altertums mit Goethes Schilderung Winckelmanns.* Edited by Hermann Uhde-Bernays. Leipzig: Im Insel Verlag, 1913.

——————. *Kunsttheoretische Schriften: Gedanken über die Nachahmung der griechischen Werke in der Malerei und Bildhauerkunst. Mit Sendschreibung und Erläuterung.* Dresden, 1756. Facsimile edition. Baden-Baden/Strasbourg: Verlag Heitz GMBH/Editions P.H. Heitz, 1962.

——————. *Kunsttheoretische Schriften: Nachricht von einer Mumie im Königlichen Kabinett der Altertümer in Dresden; Erinnerung über die Betrachtung der Werke der Kunst; Von der Grazie in Werken der Kunst; Nachrichten von dem Berühmten Stossischen Museo in Florenz; Beschreibung des Torso im Belvedere zu Rom; Anmerkungen über die Baukunst der alten Tempel zu Gircenti.* Leipzig, 1759. Facsimile edition; Baden-Baden: Verlag Valentin Koerner, 1971.

——————. *Reflections on the Painting and Sculpture of the Ancient Greeks: With Instructions for the Connoisseur, and An Essay on Grace in Works of Art.* Translated from the German original of the Abbe Winckelmann, Librarian of the Vatican, F.R.S. &c. by Henry Fusseli. A.M. London: A. Millar, 1767.

——————. *Winckelmanns Briefe an seine* Zürcher Freunde: Nach den auf der Zürcher Stadtbibliothek aufbewahrten Originalen in vermehrter und verbesserter Gestalt. Edited by Hugo Blümer. Freiburg and Tübingen, Akademische Verlagsbuchhandlung von J.C.B. Mohr, 1882.

Wittreich, Joseph Anthony. *Nineteenth Century Accounts of William Blake.* Facsimile Reproductions, Gainsville, Florida: Scholars' Facsimiles & Reprints, 1970.

Young, Edward. *Night Thoughts or the Complaint, Illustrated by William Blake.* Edited by Robert Essick and Jenijoy LaBelle. New York: Dover Publications, 1975.

Secondary Literature

Books

Abrams, M.H. *The Mirror and the Lamp: Romantic Theory and the Critical Tradition.* London and New York: Oxford University Press, 1953.

Allentuck, Marcia. "Fuseli's Translations of Winckelmann: A Phase in the Rise of British Hellenism with an aside on William Blake." *Studies in Voltaire and the Eighteenth Century,* Vol. II. Papers presented at the Second David Nichol Smith Memorial Seminar, Canberra, Australia, 1970. Edited by R.F. Brissenden. Canberra: Australian National University Press, 1973, pp. 162-185.

Antal, Frederick. *Fuseli Studies.* London: Routledge and Kegan Paul, 1956.

Baechtold, Jakob. *Geschichte der deutschen Literatur in der Schweiz.* Frauenfeld: T. Huber, 1892.

Bagdasarianz, Waldemar. *William Blake: Versuch einer Entwicklungsgeschichte des Mystikers.* Zurich and Leipzig: M. Niehaus, 1935.

Ballantyne, Archibald. *Voltaire's Visit to England.* London: John Murray, Albemarle Street, 1919.

Balmano, Mary. "Reminiscences of Henry Fuseli, Esq., R.A." *Pen and Pencil.* New York: D. Appleton & Co., 1858.

Barr, Mary Margaret H. *Voltaire in America 1744-1800*. Baltimore: The Johns Hopkins University Press, 1941.

Bender, Wolfgang. *J.J. Bodmer and J.J. Breitinger*. Sammlung Metzler No. 113, Stuttgart: J.B. Metzler Verlag, 1973.

Bentley, G.E. *Blake Books: Annotated Catalogues of William Blake's Writings in Illuminated Printing, in Conventional Typography and in Manuscript and Reprints thereof; Reproductions of his Designs; Books with His Engravings; Catalogues; Books he Owned; and Scholarly Works about Him*. Oxford: At the Clarendon Press, 1977.

_____. *Blake Records*. Oxford: At the Clarendon Press, 1969.

Besterman, Theodore. *Voltaire*. New York: Harcourt, Brace & World, Inc., 1969.

Bircher, Martin; Hafner, Franz; and Zürcher, Richard. *Geist und Schönheit im Zürich des* 18. Jahrhunderts: Literarische Text- und Bilddokumente. Zürich: Orell Füssli Verlag, 1968.

Bishop, Evelyn Morchard. *Blake's Hayley: The Life, Works and Friendships of William Hayley*. London, Gollancz, 1951.

Bloom, Harold. *Blake's Apocalypse: A Study in Poetic Argument*. Garden City, New York: Doubleday & Co., 1963.

Blunt, Anthony. *The Art of William Blake*. New York: Columbia University Press, 1959.

Boase, T.S.R. *English Art: 1800-1870*. Oxford: At the Clarendon Press, 1959.

Bodemann, Eduard. *Julie von Bondeli und ihr Freundschaftskreis: Wieland, Lavater, Leuchsenring, Usteri, Sophie Laroche, Frau v. Sandoz u.a.* Hannover, Hahn'sche Hofbuchhandlung, 1874.

Boulton, James. "Editor's Introduction." Edmund Burke, *A Philosophical Inquiry into the Origin of our Ideas of the Sublime and Beautiful*. New York: Columbia University Press, 1958, pp. xv-cxx.

Bronowski, Jacob. *William Blake: A Man Without a Mask*. 1944; reprint ed., New York: Haskell House Publishers, 1967.

_____. *William Blake and the Age of Revolution*. London: Routledge & Kegan Paul Ltd., 1972.

Chavannes [Mlle. Hermine]. *Essai sur la Vie de Jean-Gaspard Lavater*. Lausanne: G. Bridel, 1858.

Clark, Kenneth. *The Nude: A Study in Ideal Form*. Bollingen Series XXXV2. Princeton, New Jersey: Princeton University Press, 1956.

Clark, Kenneth. *Blake and Visionary Art*. Glasgow: University of Glasgow Press, 1973.

Cohen, Ralph. "On the Interrelations of Eighteenth-Century Literary Forms." *New Approaches to Eighteenth-Century Literature*. New York and London: Oxford University Press, 1974, pp. 33-78.

Cranston, Maurice. "Rousseau's Visit to England: 1776-7." *Essays by Diverse Hands: Transactions of the Royal Society of Literature*. London: Oxford University Press, 1962.

Crocker, Lester G. *The Prophetic Voice* (1758-1778). Vol. II of *Jean-Jacques Rousseau*. New York: The Macmillan Company, 1973.

Damon, S. Foster. *A Blake Dictionary: Ideas and Symbols of William Blake*. Providence, Rhode Island: Brown University Press, 1965.

_____. *William Blake: His Philosophy and Symbols*. London, 1924; reprint ed., London: Dawsons of Pall Mall, 1969.

Davis, Garold N. *German Thought and Culture in England 1700-1770: A Preliminary Survey, Including a Chronological Bibliography of German Literature in English Translation*. Chapel Hill, N.C.: University of North Carolina Press, 1969.

Davies, J.G. *The Theology of William Blake*. Oxford 1948; reprint ed., Oxford: At the Clarendon Press, 1966.

Draper, John W. *Eighteenth Century Aesthetics*. Heidelberg: C. Winter, 1931.

Eliot, T.S. "Blake." *The Sacred Wood: Essays on Poetry and Criticism*. 2nd ed. London: Methuen & Company Ltd., 1928, p. 152.

Erdman, David. *A Concordance to the Writings of William Blake.* 2 vols. Ithaca, New York: Cornell University Press, 1967.

Erdman, David V. *Blake: Prophet Against Empire: A Poet's Interpretation of his own Times.* 3rd rev. ed. Princeton, New Jersey: Princeton University Press, 1977.

Ermatinger Emil. *Dichtung und Geistesleben in der deutschen Schweiz.* Munich: C.H. Beck, 1923.

Federmann, Arnold. *Johann Heinrich Füssli: Dichter und Maler 1741-1825.* Zürich and Leipzig: Orell Füssli Verlag, 1927.

Fehr, Bernard. "Fussli und Blake." *Von Englands geistigen Beständen: Ausgewählte Essays.* Frauenfeld: Huber & Co., 1944, pp. 119-123.

Fiorillio, J.D. *Geschichte der zeichnenden Künste in Deutschland und den vereinigten Niederlanden.* 5 vols. Göttingen/Hannover: Brüder Hahn, 1815-1820.

Frye, Northrop. *Fearful Symmetry: A Study of William Blake.* Princeton, N.J.: Princeton University Press, 1977.

_____. *The Anatomy of Criticism: Four Essays.* Princeton, N.J.: Princeton University Press, 1957.

_____. *The Stubborn Structure: Essays on Criticism and Society.* Ithaca, New York: Cornell University Press, 1970.

Fülleborn, Georg Gustav. *Beyträge zur Geschichte der Philosophie.* Züllichau and Freystadt, 1794; reprint ed., Brussels: Culture et Civilisation, 1968.

Funck, Heinrich. *Goethe und Lavater: Briefe und* Tagebücher. Schriften der Goethegesellschaft, 16. Band, Weimar, Goethe Gesellschaft, 1901.

Ganz, Paul. *Die Zeichnungen Hans Heinrich Füsslis.* Bern-Olten: Urs Graf Verlag, 1947.

Geller, Hans. *Deutsche Künstler in Rom: Von Raphael Mengs bis Hans von Marées.* Rome: Herder, 1961.

Gerard, Frances A. *Angelica Kauffmann: A Biography.* London: Ward and Downey, 1893.

Gessner, Solomon. *New Idylls with a Letter to M. Fuslin on Landscape Painting and, The two Friends of Bourbon, a Moral Tale by M. Diderot.* Translated by W. Hooper, M.D. London, 1776.

Grimsley, Ronald. *Rousseau and the Religious Quest.* Oxford: At the Clarendon Press, 1968.

Guillemin, Henri. *Cette Affaire Infernale: L'Affaire J.J. Rousseau - David Hume.* Paris: Librairie Plon, 1942.

Gundolf, Friedrich. *Goethe.* Berlin, 1930; reprint ed., New York: AMS, 1971.

_____. *Shakespeare und der deutsche Geist.* Berlin: G. Bondi, 1922.

Guthke, Karl S. "Im Schatten Klopstocks." *Literarisches Leben im achtzehnten Jahrhundert.* Bern and Munich: Francke Verlag, 1975, pp. 242-265.

_____. "J.H. Füssli und die Anfänge des Rousseauismus in Deutschland." *Wege der Literatur.* Bern and Munich: Francke Verlag, 1966, pp. 133-146.

Hagstrum, Jean H. *The Sister Arts: The Tradition of Literary Pictorialism and English Poetry from Dryden to Grey.* Chicago: University of Chicago Press, 1958.

_____. "The Wrath of the Lamb: A Study of William Blake's Conversions." *From Sensibility to Romanticism: Essays Presented to Frederic A. Pottle.* Edited by Frederick W. Hilles and Harold Bloom. London: Oxford University Press, 1965, pp. 311-330.

_____. *William Blake: Poet and Painter.* Chicago and London: University of Chicago Press, 1964.

Harper, George Mills. *The Neoplatonism of William Blake.* Chapel Hill, North Carolina: University of North Carolina Press, 1961.

Hilles, Frederick Whiley. *The Literary Career of Sir Joshua Reynolds.* New York: The Macmillan Company, 1936.

Howard, John. *Blake's Milton.* London: Associated University Presses, 1976.

Johann Caspar Lavater 1741-1780: Denkschrift zur hundertsten Wiederkehr seines Todestages. Edited by Oskar Farner. Zurich: Commissionsverlag von Alb. Müller, 1902.

Jones, Ernest. *On the Nightmare.* New York: Grove Press, 1959.

Jost, Francois. *Jean-Jacques Rousseau Suisse: Etude sur sa* Personalité et sa Pensée. 2 vols. Fribourg, Suisse: Editions Universitaires, 1973.

Justi, Carl. *Winckelmann in Rom. Vol. II of Winckelmann und seine Zeitgenossen.* 5th ed. Köln: Phaidon Verlag, 1956.

Keynes, Geoffrey Langdon. *Blake Studies: Notes on His Life and Works in Seventeen Chapters.* London, 1949; reprint ed., New York: Oxford University Press, 1971.

_____. *The Complete Portraiture of William and Catherine Blake.* The Blake Trust: Trianon Press, 1977.

Korff, H.A. *Voltaire im Deutschland des XVIII Jahrhunderts: Ein Beitrag zur Geschichte des deutschen Geistes von Gottsched bis Goethe.* Heidelberg: Carl Winter Verlag, 1917.

Lankheit, Klaus. *Das Freundschaftsbild der Romantik.* Heidelberger kunstgeschichtliche Abhandlungen. Neue Folge, Vol. I. Heidelberg, 1952.

Leduc-Fayetter. *Jean-Jacques Rousseau et le mythe de l'antiquité.* Paris: Librairie Philosophique: J. Vrin, 1974.

Lemaitre, Jules. *Jean-Jacques Rousseau.* Translated by Jeanne Mairet. New York, 1907; reprint ed., Kenikat Press, 1968.

Leslie, Charles Robert. *The Life and Times of Sir Joshua Reynolds.* 2 vols. London: J. Murray, 1865.

Lipking, Lawrence. *The Ordering of the Arts in Eighteenth-Century England.* Princeton, N.J.: Princeton University Press, 1968.

Manners, Lady Victoria, and Williamson, Dr. G.C. *Angelica Kaufmann, R.A. and Her Works.* London, 1924; reprint ed., New York: Hacker Books, 1976.

Margoliouth, H.M. "Blake's Drawings for Young's *Night Thoughts." The Divine Vision: Studies in the Poetry and Art of William Blake.* Edited by Vivian De Sola Pinto. London: Victor Gollancz, 1957.

Mason, Eudo C. *Deutsche und englische Romantik.* Göttingen: Vandenhoeck & Ruprecht, 1959.

_____. "Heinrich Füssli und Winckelmann." *Unterscheidung und Bewahrung: Festschrift für Hermann Kunisch zum 60. Geburtstag. 27. Oktober 1961.* Berlin: W. de Gruyter, 1961, pp. 232-258.

_____. *The Mind of Henry Fuseli.* London: Routledge & Kegan Paul, 1951.

Mellor, Anne Kostelanetz. *Blake's Human Form Divine.* Los Angeles and London: University of California Press at Berkeley, 1974.

Miles, Josephine. "The Sublimity of William Blake." *Eras and Modes in English Poetry.* Berkeley and Los Angeles: University of California Press, 1957, pp. 78-99.

Morris, Herbert Newall. *Flaxman, Blake, Coleridge and Other Men Influenced by Swedenborg.* London: New Church Press, 1915.

Nurmi, Martin K. "Blake's Ancient of Days and Motte's Frontispiece to Newton's *Principia." The Divine Vision: Studies in the Poetry and Art of William Blake.* Edited by Vivian De Sola Pinto. London: Victor Gollancz Ltd., 1957.

Orel, Harold. "Blake's Hostility to the Enlightenment." *English Romantic Poets and the Enlightenment: nine essays on a literary relationship.* Studies in Voltaire and the Eighteenth Century, Vol. CIII. Edited by Theodore Besterman. London: Oxford University Press, 1973.

Paley, Morton. *William Blake.* New York: E.P. Dutton, 1978.

Plomer, H.R.; Bushnell, G.H.; and Dix, Mc C. *Dictionary of the Printers and Booksellers Who were at Work in England, Scotland, and Ireland from 1726 to 1775.* London: Oxford University Press, 1932.

Powell, Nicholas. *The Drawings of Henry Fuseli.* London: Faber and Faber, 1951.

Praz, Mario. "Fuseli." *La casa della fama.* Milan/Naples: R. Ricciardi, 1952, pp. 212-216.

_____. *On Neoclassicism.* Translated by Angus Davidson. London: Thames and Hudson, 1969.

Price, L[awrence] M[arsden]. *English-German Literary Influences: Bibliography and Survey.* Berkeley, California: University of California Press, 1919.

_____. *English Literature in Germany.* Berkeley and Los Angeles: University of California Press, 1953.

168

Price, Martin. *To the Palace of Wisdom: Studies in Order and Energy from Dryden to Blake.* Garden City, New York: Doubleday & Co., 1964.

Raine, Kathleen. *Blake and Tradition.* 2 vols. Bollingen Series XXXV-11. Princeton, N.J.: Princeton University Press, 1968.

Renwick, W.L. *English Literature 1789-1815.* Oxford: At the Clarendon Press, 1963.

Reynold, Georges de. *Bodmer et l'Ecole Suisse: Histoire Littéraire de la Suisse au XVIIIᵉ Siècle.* Vol. II. Lausanne: G. Ridel & Cie., 1912.

Ridgway, R.S. *Voltaire and Sensibility.* Montreal and London: McGill-Queen's University Press, 1973.

Roddler, Henri. *J.-J. Rousseau en Angleterre au XVIIIᵉ Siècle; L'Oeuvre et l'Homme. Etudes de Littérature Etrangère et Comparée.* Paris: Bolvin & Cie., Editeurs, 1950.

Saurat, Denis. *Blake and Milton.* Bordeaux: Y. Cadoret, 1920.

Schiff, Gert. "Fuseli, Lucifer and the Medea." *Henry Fuseli 1741-1825.* Catalogue of the Tate Gallery. London: 1975.

_____. *Johann Heinrich Füssli: Text und Oeuvrekatalog.* Vol. I of *Johann Heinrich Füssli: 1741-1825.* Schweizerisches Institut für Kunstwissenschaft. Zürich: Verlag Berichtshaus, 1973.

_____. *Johann Heinrich Füsslis: Milton-Gallerie.* Zurich/Stuttgart: Fretz & Wasmuth, 1959.

_____. *Zeichnungen von Johann Heinrich Füssli.* Zurich: Fretz und Wasmuth, 1959.

Schollmeier, Joseph. *Johann Joachim Spalding: Ein Beitrag zur Theologie der Aufklärung.* Gütersloh: Gütersloher Verlagshaus, 1967.

Schorer, Mark. *William Blake: The Politics of Vision.* New York: H. Holt and Co., 1949.

Schweizer, Rudolf. *The Ut Pictura poesis Controversy in Eighteenth-Century England and Germany.* Series XVIII, Comparative Literature, Vol. II. Frankfurt/Main: Herbert Lang and Peter Lang, 1972.

Stephen, Sir Leslie. *History of English Thought.* 2 vols. London: Smith, Elder & Co., 1902.

Steinbrucker, Charlotte. *Lavaters physiognomische Fragmente im Verhältnis zur bildenden Kunst.* Berlin: Friedrich-Wilhelms Universität. Verlag von Wilhelm Borngräber, 1915.

Stern, Bernard. *The Rise of Romantic Hellenisms in English Literature 1732-1786.* Menasha, Wisconsin: George Banta Press, 1940.

Stockley, V.M.A. *German Literature as Known in England 1750-1830.* London: G. Routledge and Sons, Ltd., 1929.

Süssenberger, Claus. *Rousseau im Urteil der deutschen Publizistik bis zum Ende der französischen Revolution: Ein Beitrag zur Rezeptionsgeschichte.* Frankfurt/M.: Peter Lang, 1974.

Tayler, Irene. *Blake's Illustrations to the Poems of Grey.* Princeton, N.J.: Princeton University Press, 1971.

Texte, Joseph. *Jean-Jacques Rousseau and the Cosmopolitan Spirit in Literature: A Study of the Literary Relations between France and England during the Eighteenth Century.* Translated by J.W. Matthews. 1899; reprint ed., New York: Burt Franklin, 1970.

Todd, Ruthven. *Tracks in the Snow.* London: The Grey Wall Press, 1946.

Tomory, Peter. *The Life and Art of Henry Fuseli.* London: Thames and Hudson, 1972.

Trousson, Raymond. *Rousseau et sa fortune littéraire.* Paris: A.G. Nizet, 1977.

Van Tieghem, Paul. *Le Préromanticisime: Etudes d'histoire littéraire européene. La découverte de Shakespeare sur le continent.* Paris: F. Rieder & Cie., 1924.

Venturi, Lionello. *History of Art Criticism.* Translated by Charles Marriott. New York: E.P. Dutton & Co., Inc., 1938.

Viatte, Auguste. *Les Sources Occultes du Romanticisme, Illuminisme-Théosophie 1770-1820.* 2 vols. Paris, 1928; reprint ed., Paris: Champion, 1965.

Voisine, Jacques. *J.-J. Rousseau en Angleterre à l'Epoque Romantique: Les Ecrits Autobiographiques et la Légende.* Etudes de Littérature Etrangère et Comparée. Paris: Didier, 1956.

Wardle, Ralph M. *Mary Wollstonecraft: A Critical Biography.* Lincoln, Nebraska: University of Nebraska Press, 1966.

Wehrli, Max. *Johann Jakob Bodmer und die Geschichte der Literatur.* Leipzig: Frauenfeld, Huber & Co. Aktiengesellschaft, 1936.

Wilson, Mona. *The Life of Wiliam Blake.* 1927; reprint ed., New York: Cooper Square Publishers, 1969.

Wittreich, Joseph Anthony. *Angel of Apocalypse: Blake's Idea of Milton.* Madison, Wisconsin: University of Wisconsin Press, 1975.

_____. "Opening the Seals: Blake's Epics and the Milton Tradition." *Blake's Sublime Allegory.* Edited by Stuart Curran and Joseph Anthony Wittreich, Jr. Madison, Wisconsin: University of Wisconsin Press, 1973.

_____. *The Romantics on Milton.* Cleveland and London: Case Western Reserve Press, 1970.

Periodicals

Allentuck, Marcia. "A Note on Eighteenth-Century Disinterestedness." *Journal of Aesthetics and Art Criticism* 21 (Fall 1962):89-90.

_____. "Eudo Mason's 'The Mind of Henry Fuseli'." *College Art Journal* 11 (Summer 1952): 300-301.

_____. "Fuseli and Lavater: Physiognomical Theory and the Enlightenment." *Studies in Voltaire and the Eighteenth Century* 55 (1967):88-112.

_____. "Fuseli as Illustrator of Milton." *Studies in English Literature* 2 (Winter 1962): 151-153.

_____. "Morgan and Hohlfeld's *Bibliography* and the Füsslis." *Notes and Queries* 105 (March 1960):99.

Antal, Frederick. "Fuseli Studies: *The Drawings of Henry Fuseli* by Nicholas Powel." *The Burlington Magazine* 96 (August 1954):260.

Atkins, Stuart Pratt. "J.C. Lavater and Goethe: Problems of Psychology and Theology in *Die Leiden des jungen Werthers.*" *PMLA* 63 (1948):520-576.

Bentley, G.E., Jr. "A 'New' Blake Engraving in Lavater's *Physiognomy.*" *Blake Newsletter* 6, 2 (Fall 1972):48-50.

Benz, Ernst. "Swedenborg und Lavater: Über die religiösen Grundlagen der Physiognomik." *Zeitschrift für Kirchengeschichte* 57 (Stuttgart, 1938):153-216.

Bircher, Martin. "Johann Heinrich Füsslis Freundschaft mit Johann Kaspar Lavater." *Zürcher Taschenbuch* N.F., 49. Jg. (Zürich, 1973):69-86.

Blunt, Anthony. "Blake's Pictorial Imagination." *Journal of the Warburg and Courtauld Institutes* 6 (1943):190-212.

Boase, T.S.R. "Illustrations of Shakespeare's Plays in the Seventeenth and Eighteenth Centuries." *Journal of the Warburg and Courtauld Institutes* 10 (1947):83-108.

Bogen, Nancy. "Blake's *Island in the Moon* Revisited." *Satire Newsletter* 5, 2 (Spring 1968):110-116.

Clough, Wilson O. "Reason and Genius: An Eighteenth Century Dilemma." *Philological Quarterly* 23, 4 (October 1944):33-35.

Copley-Sargent, John. "Formidable Fuseli." *Art News* (April 1950):51-57.

Denk, Ferdinand. "Goethe und die Bildkunst des Sturms und Drangs." *Deutsche Vierteljahrsschrift für Literaturwissenschaft und Geistesgeschichte* 8, Jg. 8 (1930):109-135.

Evans, Elizabeth. "Physiognomics in the Ancient World." Transactions of the American Philosophical Society. New Series, Vol. 59, Part 5, Philadelphia, August 1969.

Friedrich, Werner Paul. "Switzerland's Contribution to International Appreciation of Dante Alighieri." *Studies in Philology* 42 (1945):452-464.

Graham, John. "Lavater's *Physiognomy:* A Checklist." *Papers of the Bibliographical Society of America* 55 (First Quarter 1961):297-308.

_____. "Lavater's *Physiognomy* in England." *Journal of the History of Ideas* 22 (October-December 1961):561-572.

Grigson, Geoffrey. "Fuseli—Painter to the Devil." *Picture Post* 44 (February 1950):135-137.

_____. "Painters of the Abyss." *Architectural Review* 108 (October 1950):215-220.

Guthke, Karl S. "A Note on Herder and Rousseau." *Modern Language Quarterly* 19 (1958):303-306.

_____. "Füssli und Shakespeare." *Neuphilologische Mitteilungen* 58 (1957):206-215.

Hagstrum, Jean. "Kathleen Raine's Blake." *Modern Philology* 68 (1970):75-82.

Hammelmann, H.A. "Eighteenth-Century English Illustrators: Henry Fuseli, R.A." *The Book Collector* 6 (Winter 1957):350-360.

Hoffman, Edith. "Johann Heinrich Füssli." *The Burlington Magazine* 82 (March 1943):77-78.

Hofmann, Werner. "Zu Füsslis geschichtlicher Stellung." *Zeitschrift für Kunstgeschichte* 15, 2 (Munich, 1952):163-178.

Howard, John. *"An Audience for The Marriage of Heaven and Hell."* Blake Studies 3, 1 (Fall 1970):19-20.

_____. "Swedenborg's Heaven and Hell and Blake's *Songs of Innocence." Papers on Languages and Literature* 4, 1 (Winter 1968):390-399.

Irwin, David. "Fuseli's Milton Gallery: Unpublished Letters." *The Burlington Magazine* 101 (December 1959):436-440.

Jaloux, Edmund. "Un grand Artiste Suisse: Johann Heinrich Füssli." *Le Mois Suisse* 4 (1942):1-2.

Keetz, Hans. "Füssli: Leben, Briefe, Kunst." *Das innere Reich* 8 (May 1941):71-80.

Lankheit, Klaus. "Zur Füssli-Forschung. Gedanken im Anschluss an Paul Ganz." *Zeitschrift für Kunstgeschichte* 14 (1951):107-119.

Leopold, Werner. "Die religiöse Wurzel von Carlyles literarischer Wirksamkeit: Dargestellt in seinem Aufsatz 'State of German Literature' *I°: Studien zur englischen Philologie* 62 (Halle, 1922):11-15.

MacAndrew, Hugh. "Henry Fuseli and William Roscoe." *The Liverpool Bulletin* (The Liverpool Art Gallery, 1959-60):60-63.

Macphail, J.H. "Blake and Switzerland." *Modern Language Review* 2 (April 1943):81-87.

Nordmann, Hans. "Spalding und seine Zeitgenossen." *Jahrbuch für Brandenburgische Kirchengeschichte* 26 Jg. (Berlin, 1931):100-120.

Pestalozzi, F.O. "Johann Kaspar Lavaters Kunstsammlung." *Neujahrsblatt auf das Jahr 1916: Zum Besten des Waisenhauses in Zürich* 138 (Zürich, 1916).

Pollnow, Hans. "Historisch-kritische Beiträge zur Physiognomik." *Jahrbuch der Charakterologie* 5.Jg. (Berlin, 1928):159-206.

Powell, Nicholas. "Recent Fuseli Studies." *The Burlington Magazine* 116 (June 1974):335-336.

Praz, Mario. "Painter Ordinary to the Devil." *Art News* 51 (January 1953):33-35, 61-62.

Richter, Helene. "Blake und Hamann: Zu Hamanns 200. Geburtstag." *Archiv für das Studium der neueren Sprachen*, 85. Jg. Vols. 158 and 159. New Series (Berlin and Hamburg, December 1930):36-45, 195-210.

Schiff, Gert. "Einige Bemerkungen über die künstlerischen Beziehungen zwischen Füssli und Blake." *Kunstchronik* 15. Jg., Heft 10 (October 1962):296-297.

Stange, Alfred. "Die Bedeutung des subjektivistischen Individualismus für die europäische Kunst von 1750-1850." *Deutsche Vierteljahrsschrift für Literaturwissenschaft und Geistesgeschichte*, 9. Jg., Heft 1 (1931):89-124.

Todd, Ruthven. "Fuseli and Blake: Companions in Mystery." *Art News* 52 (February 1954):26, 57-58.

_____. "Two Blake Prints and Two Fuseli Drawings." *Blake Newsletter* 5, 3 (Winter 1971/72):173-181.

Torbruegge, Marilyn K. "Johann Heinrich Füssli und 'Bodmer-Longinus': Das Wunderbare und das Erhabene." *Deutsche Vierteljahrsschrift für Literaturwissenschaft und Geistesgeschichte* 46 Jg. Heft 1 (January 1972):161-185.

Wittreich, Joseph Anthony. "A Note on Fuseli and Blake." *Blake Newsletter* 3, 1 (June 15, 1969):3-4.

_____. "Sublime Allegory: Blake's Epic Manifesto and the Milton Tradition." *Blake Studies* 4, 2 (Spring 1972).

Unpublished Dissertations

Allentuck, Marcia. "Henry Fuseli: The Artist as a Man of Letters and Critic." Ph.D. dissertation, Columbia University, New York, 1964.

Barnick, Hildegard. "Die Stellung der englischen Romantik zur italienischen Renaissance." Ph.D. dissertation, University of Freiburg, 1927.

de Bussy, Carvel. "A Study of William Kendrick's English Translation of Rousseau's *Julie, ou la Nouvelle Héloïse*." Ph.D. dissertation, The Catholic University of America, Washington, D.C., 1971.

Dichtborn-Bosch, Ursula. "Johann Heinrich Füsslis Kunstlehre und ihre Auswirkung auf seine Shakespeare-Interpretation." Ph.D. dissertation, University of Zürich, 1960.

Hartmann, Wolfgang. "Die Wiederentdeckung Dantes in der deutschen Kunst." Ph.D. dissertation, Rheinische Friedrich-Wilhelms Universität zu Bonn, Bonn, 1969.

Sutter, Monika. "Die kunsttheoretischen Begriffe des Malerphilosophen Anton Raphael Mengs." Ph.D. dissertation, Ludwig-Maximilians-Universität zu München, Munich, 1968.

Torbrügge, Marilyn Klein. "Bodmer and Füssli, 'Das Wunderbare' and the Sublime." Ph.D. dissertation, University of Wisconsin, 1968.

Wirz, Ernst. "Die literarische Tätigkeit des Malers Johann Heinrich Füssli." Ph.D. dissertation, University of Basel, 1922.